HANDBOOK of TESTS and MEASUREMENT in EDUCATION and the SOCIAL SCIENCES

PAULA E. LESTER, Ph.D.
Long Island University, C. W. Post Campus

LLOYD K. BISHOP, Ph.D.
University of Nevada at Las Vegas

TECHNOMIC
PUBLISHING CO., INC.
LANCASTER · BASEL

Contents

Handbook of Tests and Measurement in Education and the Social Sciences
a **TECHNOMIC**®publication

Published in the Western Hemisphere by
Technomic Publishing Company, Inc.
851 New Holland Avenue, Box 3535
Lancaster, Pennsylvania 17604 U.S.A.

Distributed in the Rest of the World by
Technomic Publishing AG
Missionsstrasse 44
CH-4055 Basel, Switzerland

Printed in the United States of America
10 9 8 7 6 5 4 3 2 1

Main entry under title:
    Handbook of Tests and Measurement in Education and the Social Sciences

A Technomic Publishing Company book
Bibliography: p.
Includes index p. 233

Library of Congress Catalog Card No. 96-60521
ISBN No. 1-56676-434-3

INTRODUCTION

In 1993, Bishop and Lester compiled an anthology of instruments in education and the social sciences for Garland Publishing, Inc. Bibliographic references were provided for over 700 instruments developed over the last 40 years in over 30 related areas. This anthology was based on more than a dozen major reference books that were written in the 1960s and 1970s. Many of these books are presently out-of-print and no longer available. These reference books varied in the amount of information provided. Some sources included the actual instruments, while others provided only a summary of the psychometric characteristics. Still other sources presented critiques of instruments and general bibliographic information. Consequently, there was a need to include in one book not only the specific psychometric information about the instruments and bibliographic references related to the instrument, but the actual instrument (published and/or unpublished). This handbook was written for that purpose. In several cases, only sample items were provided with the approval of the publisher of the instrument.

STRUCTURE OF THE HANDBOOK

Instruments Included:

The handbook contains over 80 instruments which are arranged under the following 32 topics:

alienation	mentoring
anxiety	morale
change/innovation	motivation
climate	needs/need deficiency
communication	organizational assessment
conflict/conflict management	organizational structure
culture	power/authority/control
decision making/problem solving	professional performance/autonomy
dogmatism	role/role conflict/ambiguity
gender (sex role) identification	self-actualization
interpersonal relations	self-concept
job commitment	self-efficacy
job involvement	self-esteem
job satisfaction	supervisory/managerial behavior
leadership/leader style/behavior	stress/burnout
locus of control	teacher attitudes/beliefs

Two types of indices are included: author and title. Consequently, if the researcher knows the name of the author, he/she can use the author index. Similarly, if the researcher knows the name of the instrument, he/she can use the title index.

In addition, there is a section on measurement and measurement theory that includes information on measurement problems and scaling; instrumentation construction and evaluation; basic measurement procedures; validity; reliability; relation of validity to reliability; reliability of difference, change, or growth scores; and selected references.

This work was supported by the Dean of the School of Education and the C. W. Post Research Committee.

Instruments Not Included

This handbook does not include instruments which focus exclusively on personality or psychology.

Reference Sources

Three major databases were searched to locate instruments and/or references to existing instruments. The first was ERIC (Educational Resources Information Center) which contains published and unpublished documents. In addition, it also contains papers from national and local conferences that were written by researchers from numerous institutions. Another was Dissertation Abstracts International which provides references to dissertations that focus on developing instruments and also provide references to existing instruments. Finally, Psychological Abstracts was used to discover information about new or existing instruments.

In addition, a concise annotated bibliography for each of the reference sources follows:

Bishop, L. and P. E. Lester. 1993. *Instrumentation in Education: An Anthology*. New York: Garland Publishing, Inc.
Identify approximately 700 instruments in the areas of organizational administration and school effectiveness. At least one-three instruments are described in detail and included sample items in each of the 31 main categories.

Bonjean, C. et al. 1968. *Sociological Measurement*. San Francisco: Chandler Publishing Company.
Refer to over 2,000 questionnaires, although only 50 questionnaires are described in detail.

Conoley, J.C. and J.C. Impara, eds. 1995. *The twelfth mental measurements yearbook*. Lincoln, Nebraska: Buros Institute of Mental Measurements, University of Nebraska, Lincoln.
Provide a complete bibliography and review of tests. Entries include a test title, purpose, description of the groups for which the test is intended, date of publication, special comments, part scores, forms, cost, author, publisher, and cross references.

ETS Test Collection. 1990. *Annotated Bibliography of Tests*. Princeton, NJ: Educational Testing Service.
Provides annotated bibliographies for many areas related to education. Each reference contains some of the following information: name of the instrument, personal or institutional author, year test was published or copyrighted, test publisher or distributor, components within the overall test which assess particular skills or factors, target audience, and a description of the test and its purposes.

Keyser, D.J. and R.C. Sweetland, eds. 1993. *Test Critiques*. Austin, TX: Pro-Ed.
Report psychometric information in three sections: introduction (development of the test and its historical significance), practical applications/uses (information about the sample, administration, scoring, and interpretation), and technical aspects (information about reliability and validity studies). An overall critique is provided at the end of each review.

Lake, D.G. et al. eds. 1973. *Measuring Human Behavior*. New York: Teachers College Press, Teachers College, Columbia University.

Review 84 instruments related to personal variables (cognitive-perceptual, affective-motivational, and overt behavior), interpersonal variables, group variables, and organizational variables.

Miller, D.C. 1970. *Handbook of Research Design and Social Measurement.* New York: David McKay Company, Inc.
Provides scales and indexes that focus on: social status, group structure and dynamics, morale and job satisfaction, community, social participation, leadership in the work organization, scales of attitudes, values, and norms, family and marriage, and personality measures.

------1991. *Handbook of Research Design and Social Measurement.* Newbury Park: Sage Publications.
Includes scales and indexes that focus on social indicators and measures of organizational structure.

Price, J.L. 1972. *Handbook of Organizational Measurement.* Massachusetts: D.C. Heath and Company.
Identifies measures of: absenteeism, administrative staff, alienation, autonomy, centralization, communication, complexity, consensus, coordination, dispersion, distributive justice, effectiveness, formalization, innovation, mechanization, motivation, bases of power, routinization, satisfaction, size, span of control, and succession.

Robinson, J.P. et al. 1969. *Measures of Occupational Attitudes and Occupational Characteristics.* Ann Arbor, MI: Institute for Social Research, University of Michigan.
Includes instruments assessing: general job satisfaction, job satisfaction with specific job features, concepts related to job satisfaction, occupational values, leadership styles, other work-relevant attitudes, vocational interest measures, and occupational status measures.

Robinson, J.P. and P.R. Shaver. 1978. *Measures of Social Psychological Attitudes.* Ann Arbor, MI: Institute for Social Research, University of Michigan.
Provide instruments assessing self-esteem and related constructs, internal-external locus of control, alienation and anomia, authoritarianism, dogmatism, and related measures, other socio-political attitudes, values, general attitudes toward people, religious attitudes, and methodological scales.

------1972. *Measures of Political Attitudes.* Ann Arbor, MI: Institute for Social Research, University of Michigan.
Include instruments assessing: liberalism-conservatism, democratic principles, domestic government policies, racial and ethnic attitudes, international affairs, hostility-related national attitudes, community-based political attitudes, political information, political participation, and attitudes toward the political process.

Shaw, M. E. and J.M. Wright. 1967. *Scales for the Measurement of Attitudes.* New York: McGraw-Hill Book Company.
Discuss methods of scale construction as well as scales that focus on: social practices, social issues and problems, international issues, abstract concepts, political and religious attitudes, ethnic and national groups, significant others, and social institutions.

Sweetland, R.C. and D.J. Keyser, eds. 1986. *Tests.* Kansas City: Test Corporation of America.

Provide concise descriptions of thousands of instruments. Entries contain the following information: test title and author, purpose, major features, scoring method, cost, availability, and primary publisher.

Criteria For Inclusion

This handbook includes instruments for each of the major constructs identified by the authors. In general, an instrument is included because it provides adequate support for its reliability and validity. In other words, the instrument is psychometrically sound. In some cases, an instrument is included because it is most representative of the construct under study. In addition, some instruments are included because they are the most frequently cited. Occasionally, an instrument is included because it was recently developed and the potential exists for additional research. Some instruments were not included because the authors were either unable to receive permission from the test publisher or because the organization/journal that holds the copyright wanted substantial fees in order to grant permission. Researchers and school administrators should obtain permission from the author(s) of the instrument(s) and/or original publisher(s) prior to their research.

Format of Entries

The authors sought to provide each entry with the following information. Where the information is not readily available or is inapplicable, the category is omitted.

Title: Identifies instrument in bold print.

Source: Provides a primary reference. Tells where the instrument is available.

Comments: Describes what the instrument measures as well as the number of items in the instrument. Includes comments and/or suggestions by the original author(s). Points out strengths and/or weaknesses. Provides general information.

Scale Construction: Describes how the instrument was developed including the theoretical basis for the instrument.

Sample: Describes the original sample who participated in developing the instrument as well as additional normative data.

Reliability: Discusses internal consistency coefficients, equivalent forms, and other data analysis techniques.

Validity: Describes the types of validity addressed: concurrent, construct, content, discriminant, and predictive.

Factor Analysis: Reports the results of factor analytic procedures. Contains information about the subscales and the number of items for each scale (item numbers are included in parentheses).

References: Provides references to articles, books, dissertations, and ERIC documents that describe the development of the instrument or its use. Provides no more than five representative references.

Scoring: Describes how to score the instrument.

MEASUREMENT IN EDUCATION
AND THE SOCIAL SCIENCES

Introduction

This section emphasizes the importance of measurement in educational research. A basic understanding of measurement concepts, of measurement theory, and of correct psychometric procedures provides the foundation for educational research. It is axiomatic that if one's research variables cannot be appropriately measured, then one cannot conduct empirical research. The development of new, and the refinement of existing instruments, are basic research activities. *A researcher should not assume that an existing measure, or a measure published or reported in the literature, is a psychometrically sound tool*. Basic procedures of acceptable test construction are frequently violated in the reported research literature in the Social Sciences. For this reason, competent researchers must understand and develop the skills required for correct test construction in order to either develop their own tools, or critically evaluate those which are available. The purpose of this section is to provide a review of the basic information concerning the development of tests and measures in education and the social sciences. This information can be used also to evaluate the efficacy of many of the instruments found in this book.

Measurement and Measurement Theory

Measurement is the assigning of numbers (quantification) to individuals in a systematic way as a means of representing properties of the individuals. These numbers must be assigned according to a carefully prescribed, repeatable procedure. The particular test generates scores by using the same instructions, questions, and scoring procedure for each subject. Numbers can be assigned based on the properties to be measured utilizing various forms depending upon the type of scale to be generated. That is, numbers can be assigned to subjects in categories forming nominal scales, in ranks forming ordinal scales, or as continuous scores forming either interval or ratio scales.

Measurement theory is a branch of applied statistics that attempts to describe, categorize, and evaluate the quality of measurements (tests, instruments, scales, etc.). It attempts to improve the usefulness, accuracy, and meaningfulness of instruments. It proposes methods for developing new and better measurement tools. Several disciplines in the Social and Behavioral Sciences have adopted, or created, their own unique measurement approaches with an accompanying label. For example, in psychology and education, these measurement approaches are referred to as **psychometrics**, in economics as **econometrics** and in sociology as **sociometrics**. Although most of the foundation for present-day measurement theory was completed by the 1950's, research and development into newer approaches to psychological measurement (or psychometrics) continues. As stated, psychometrics tends to dominate measurement approaches in the behavioral sciences and education, as opposed to econometrics which are used in business and economics.

Overview to Measurement Problems and Scaling

Measurement in the social sciences is by no means an exact science. A number of techniques are used to obtain measures (observations) from human subjects. Such techniques are "**paper and pencil**" tests (questionnaires, instruments, inventories, scales), **interviews, observations, ratings**, and

tests. Because paper and pencil tests (questionnaires or instruments) are so frequently used in education to obtain information from respondents, these tests will be emphasized primarily in this section.

In order to obtain an objective quantitative indication from each respondent to the items, or statements, in a questionnaire or instrument, some method of scoring these statements is required. This is referred to as **scaling**. That is, scales, or **anchors,** are devices employed by test developers to quantify the responses of a subject on a particular item, or statement, of a test. Several of the more commonly used scales are:

Forced Choice	(True-False)
Likert	(Summated-rating)
Thurstone	(Equal-appearing interval)
Guttman	(Cumulative scale)
Semantic Differential	(Bipolar adjectives)

Forced-Choice Scale

The forced-choice scale accomplishes what the name implies. It forces the respondent generally to one of two (or three) possible choices. The **true-false** response is typical of this type scale. Numerical values of either one (true response) or zero (false response) are assigned. This type scale, or some slight modification, is often used with personality tests. Responses such as "like -- dislike", "agree -- disagree" might be used. A third neutral response may be used also -- "like - undecided - dislike." The scale could be numerically coded either 1 = dislike, 2 = undecided, 3 = like; or -1 = dislike, 0 = undecided, +1 = like.

Likert Scale

The Likert scale, or **summated-rating scale**, is perhaps the most frequently used in the social sciences. Any measure obtained by adding together the response scores of a number of items is referred to as a Likert or summated scale. Alternately, the terms **linear composite, homogeneous scale, composite scale,** or **additive scale** may be used to characterize the Likert scale. Typically, this scale contains a set of items, or statements, which are considered approximately equal in attitude or value. The number of items may be as few as five or six, or as many as 30 to 40. The subject responds with varying degrees of intensity on a five-point scale ranging between extremes. For example, statements such as **Strongly Agree - Agree - Undecided - Disagree - Strongly Disagree** may be used. The scale can be expanded to seven or more positions, or used as a modified forced-choice scale, by eliminating the middle (undecided) position.

Briefly, a Likert scale can be described as follows. A set of items composed of approximately an equal number of favorable and unfavorable responses concerning the attitude, event, phenomenon, or object to be measured is given to a group of subjects. They respond to each statement in terms of their degree of agreement or disagreement by generally selecting one of five responses (anchors) from Strongly Agree to Strongly Disagree. Each subject's responses to the set of items are combined (summated, yielding a composite score) so that the most favorable attitude will have the highest score while the least favorable will have the lowest score. A major assumption of this scale is the ability to **linearly combine** the items in the scale producing a **homogeneous** measure. All items to be linearly combined must be related to a single common factor. The sum of these items is expected to contain all the important information contained in the individual items. This suggests three important and interrelated tasks necessary for constructing Likert measures: 1) item construction, 2) item selection, and 3) item scoring. Likert suggested two methods of **item analysis** in order to evaluate the ability of the individual items to measure the attitude, or object, measured by the total scale: correlation analysis, and analysis based on the criterion of internal consistency. Each of these procedures will be discussed later in this section.

Thurstone Scale

The Thurstone scale is referred to as an **equal-appearing interval** scale. In the case of the Likert scale, each item within a set of items is considered to be approximately equal in attitude or value to be assessed. With the Thurstone Scale, items are scaled along the attitude to be measured. Each item is assigned a scale value indicating the strength of attitude for an agreement response to the item. The items in the scale are assumed to be **differentially ordered, rather than equal**. It is more difficult to construct a Thurstone Scale than the Likert, summated scale, and both scales yield similar results. Table 1 below illustrates a Thurstone Scale.

Table 1

ATTITUDE TOWARD DIVORCE
(Thurstone Scale)

The following statements express opinions about divorce. Please indicate your agreement, or disagreement, with each of the statements by marking them as follows:

(✓) Mark with a check if you agree with the statement.
(X) Mark with an X if you disagree with the statement.

Scale
Value

Scale Value	Statement
0.5	1. Divorce is disgraceful.
0.8	2. Divorce is legalized adultery.
1.2	3. Lenient divorce is equivalent to polygamy.
1.6	4. Divorce lowers the standard of morality.
3.3	5. Divorce should be discouraged in order to stabilize society.
3.7	6. Divorce is justifiable only after all efforts to mend the union have failed.
4.2	7. Divorce should be discouraged but not forbidden.
5.8	8. The evils of divorce should not prevent us from seeing its benefits.
6.2	9. A divorce is justifiable or not, depending on the desires of the persons involved.
7.1	10. Divorce should be permitted so long as the rights of all parties are insured.
8.1	11. Permanence in marriage is unnecessary for social stability.
8.4	12. Divorce is desirable for adjusting errors in marriage.
8.8	13. Easy divorce leads to a more intelligent understanding of marriage.
9.4	14. The marriage contract should be as easily broken as made.
9.8	15. Divorce should be granted for the asking.
10.1	16. A person should have the right to marry and divorce as often as he or she chooses.

The scale was taken from Shaw and Wright (1967). The original scale contained 22 statements. For the sake of brevity some items were omitted.

The respondent checks the items with which he agrees. The points (scale value) corresponding to each item are totaled and then divided by the number of answered items to yield an average score for each respondent. A high score indicates a favorable attitude toward divorce.

The construction of a Thurstone Scale and the assignment of scale values is accomplished through the use of **judges**. After the collection of a series of short, concise statements reflecting various degrees of the attitude to be measured, these are subjected to a group of judges working independently. They sort the statements into eleven piles according to their relative degree of favorableness to unfavorableness. The scale above was created using 26 judges. Shaw and Wright (1967) indicate that it has been shown that as few as 20 judges can be used to compute reliable scale values.

Guttman Scale

The Guttman Scale is referred to as a **cumulative scale**. This scale consists of a relatively small set of homogeneous items that are considered to be **unidimensional**, measuring one, and only one, attitude, event, or phenomenon. Items are ordered in difficulty or complexity, so that to answer correctly or approve the last implies success, or approval, on all the preceding items. Table 2 below is an example of a Guttman-type scale.

Table 2

HOMOSEXUALITY ATTITUDE SCALE
(Guttman Scale)

Homosexual relations between two consenting adult males should be dealt with in which of the following ways? Respond to each statement using the following key:

1 - Strongly Disagree   4 - Agree
2 - Disagree   5 - Strongly Agree
3 - Not Sure

_____ 1. They should be punished by execution.
_____ 2. They should serve at least five years in prison.
_____ 3. They should be given a short prison sentence.
_____ 4. They should be required to accept treatment or go to jail.
_____ 5. They should be offered treatment if they want it but not punished in any way, but warned not to recruit others.
_____ 6. They should not be made to feel deviant or warned about recruiting others.
_____ 7. They should be praised for choosing their own form of sexual satisfaction as long as it does not interfere with others.
_____ 8. They should be praised and encouraged to recruit others into homosexuality.

The scale was taken from Gorden (1977).

Semantic Differential Scale

The Semantic Differential is an attitude-type scale developed by Osgood, Suci, and Tannenbaum in 1957. It is a method for measuring the meanings of concepts, and it has two applications: 1) to measure the semantic properties of words and concepts, and 2) as an attitude scale restricting its focus to the affective domain and the evaluative dimension. In applying the method, the respondent is asked to rate an object, for example school, teacher, supervisor, etc., on a series of bipolar adjectives anchored by a seven-point scale. The respondent is instructed to put a check in the position indicating both the direction and intensity of his feelings toward the object.

Osgood and Suci, using factor analysis, established three general factors of meaning measured by the semantic differential: an **evaluative factor** -- bipolar adjectives such as good-bad, wise-foolish, kind-cruel; a **potency factor** -- hard-soft, strong-weak; and an **activity factor** -- hot-cold, fast-slow. Pairs of these bipolar adjectives are selected according to the purpose of the research, and the emphasis upon either evaluative, potency, or activity dimensions. Approximately fifteen to twenty adjective pairs should be selected with the concept to be rated placed at the top of the combined scale (see Table 3).

The semantic differential yields a large amount of data with a relatively short questionnaire, and with minimum effort. In variance terms, it produces three main sources of variance: **concepts, scales,** and **subjects.** Thus, scores can be produced and analyzed for differences between **concepts** (school, teacher, and supervisor); **scales** (evaluative, potency, and activity dimensions); and among **subjects,** or analyses may be conducted in any combination of the three.

Table 3

SUPERVISOR
(Semantic Differential Scale)

Good	:	:	:	:	:	:	Bad
Slow	:	:	:	:	:	:	Fast
Large	:	:	:	:	:	:	Small
Ugly	:	:	:	:	:	:	Beautiful
Clean	:	:	:	:	:	:	Dirty
Weak	:	:	:	:	:	:	Strong
Dark	:	:	:	:	:	:	Bright

In this example, the respondent is instructed to rate the concept "supervisor" according to how he or she perceives, or feels, toward the supervisor at the moment by placing an "X" someplace along the seven-point scale.

Instrumentation Construction and Evaluation

As suggested earlier, the measurement of research variables is perhaps one of the greatest weaknesses in conducting meaningful and useful research in the social and behavioral sciences. Much research in education, when evaluated against appropriate psychometric and measurement procedures, must be discounted, if not totally rejected. Thus, the development of new measures, and the refinement of existing instruments are fundamental research activities. Again, one should not assume that a measure that is published, or reported, in the research literature is necessarily a psychometrically sound tool, including many of the instruments included here. Basic procedures of acceptable test construction are frequently violated or totally ignored. This was aptly reported by Mitchell (April, 1985) in a recent survey of the research literature. Some 21% of studies did not report reliability, and only 26% provided information on construct validity. Both measures of reliability, and procedures for obtaining validity are essential, and required, types of information that should be reported in all quantitative research studies.

The purpose of this section is to provide information on several specific procedures which are useful in instrumentation development. It should be noted that these techniques can be used whether one is interested in developing their own instrument, or in the process of critiquing and evaluating an existing tool. First, an outline will be provided listing in order the major steps one should following in instrumentation construction. Second, several of these procedures will be discussed in greater detail providing, where appropriate, specific statistical procedures which can be employed. Six steps are listed below which should be considered in good scale construction.

Steps in Instrumentation Construction and Evaluation

1. A **theory and accompanying concepts** (or a taxonomy) should be selected first. Many instruments developed in the social sciences and education have no conceptual or theoretical basis to serve as a guide in the selection of items, and the construction of scales. The concepts to be measured should be defined as carefully and precisely as possible, and considered in relation to the specific population (selection of subjects) to be studied. An example of an instrument developed without a conceptual foundation is the *Organizational Climate Description Index* (Halpin, 1963). On the other hand, examples of instruments employing a theoretical base are the Stern climate indices which used the Murray Need-Press Model.

2. Next, an **item pool** should be written. This will be accomplished based on the theoretical and conceptual framework provided in step one. Statements, or items, will be created to which subjects may respond, and will serve as **stimuli** to the content or subject matter to be measured. One may obtain items from a variety of sources: review of the theoretical and research literature, other instruments, documents, through observation of the phenomena, behavior, trait, or attitude to be studied. In writing items, one should be sensitive to the following: 1) frame of reference and item formats; 2) content and population specificity; 3) descriptive vs. evaluative items; 4) items which are clear, concise, and as unambiguous as possible; and 5) simple, as opposed to compound statements.

Frame of Reference--Smith, et al. (1969) provided the research evidence that indicates that **perceptual selectivity** in human judgments is dramatic. When two individuals with different frames of reference are exposed to the same object or stimulus, they will select different aspects and provide different summary evaluations of the situation. Van de Ven and Ferry (1980) have suggested that frames of reference are the cognitive filters (perceptual screens) a person uses in describing or evaluating a situation. They indicate that for the purpose of instrumentation construction and evaluation that there are three issues to be examined relative to a respondent's frame of reference: 1) the characteristics of the stimulus a person is exposed to; 2) the systematic; and 3) the unsystematic individual differences and biases that respondents bring to a stimulus as a result of their prior experiences, predilections, expectations, and personalities.

The first issue deals with the interaction between a respondent's frame of reference and the **composition of the instrument** (item format). Specifically, such features as test length, complexity of items, time perspective, and anchor points on an answer scale have been found to significantly influence a respondent's frame of reference at the point of measurement (Smith et al., 1969).

There are also effects due to composition and item selection of an instrument on the frame of reference of respondents due to position, past experiences, and predilections of the individual. For example in studies of job satisfaction, climate or morale perceptions have been found to differ systematically among respondents of different age, sex, education, social background, and job tenure (Smith et al., 1969). Unsystematic biases of respondents on frame of references are expected to be randomly and normally distributed among a sample, and therefore, they will cancel out statistically when judgments are averaged together (Van de Ven and Ferry, 1980). This suggests that more accurate responses may be made by respondents if one is careful in constructing unambiguous statements which are sensitive to the following:

Content and population specificity suggests that the item wording should be specific to a particular population, or selection of subjects. Measurement created in one test situation may not be appropriate for another. Items should be rewritten to be **situationally specific**.

Descriptive and evaluative items should be distinguished during test construction. Van de Ven (1980) suggested that descriptive items are positive and value-free focusing on the factual characteristics and behaviors that actually exist. Evaluative items are normative and value-laden which ask a respondent to provide an opinion about the strengths or weaknesses, likes or dislikes of events or behaviors. They indicate that evaluative statements are more susceptible to variation in frames of reference, and perceptions of respondents than descriptive items.

Number of scale points (anchors) on the answer sheet may also influence response bias. If too few scale points are used, the answer scale is a coarse one and much information may be lost because the scale does not discriminate sufficiently among respondents. However, if too many scale points are used, the scale points may be graded so finely that it is beyond the ability of respondents to discriminate among response cues. The effect of the number of scale points on the reliability of measures has received much attention and considerable empirical investigation. To summarize these findings, Van de Ven (1980) indicates for homogeneous, Likert-type measures, there is very little increase in scale reliability beyond five scale points for a single (unipolar) scale, and nine points for a bipolar scale.

Simple vs. compound statements should be analyzed. Compound items are generally more ambiguous statements, and lead to greater response bias. A compound item is one in which two or more, somewhat mutually exclusive, pieces of information are addressed in one statement. The following is an example of a compound item with inherent ambiguity due to its complexity: "The goals of education should be dictated by children's interests and needs, as well as by the larger demands of society." A respondent could have varying attitudes on three different aspects of the item: 1) goals of education dictated by children's *interests*, 2) goals dictated by children's *needs*, and 3) goals dictated by the *larger demands of society*. Such compound statements appear frequently in many attitude questionnaires. These statements should be rewritten into simple statements with only one idea (stimulus or cue) for each item.

It has been recommended that one should create approximately twice as many statements in the initial item pool, as the number to be retained in the final test (Thorndike, 1982). However, twice as many items is probably a low estimate. To assure high quality selection in the refinement of items and scales, it would be better if the initial item pool contained three or four times the number required in the final instrument.

3. **Content validation** should be used with the item pool. (Even though this procedure is only mentioned once, it is not uncommon for one to repeat this step several times in the process of refining the item pool.) Determining content validity, sometimes referred to as **subject matter** validity, is primarily a judgmental process. Generally, a panel of five to seven experts (judges) will be selected who are experts in the area of study and with the concepts to be measured. At this stage the researcher is attempting to accomplish at least two objectives: 1) to determine which items from the item pool are most representative of the total universe of items that could be selected dealing with the subject matter to be measured -- to determine if voids in statements exist (new items should be included), and if items should be discarded or rewritten; 2) if the theory to be measured is multiconceptual (most social sci-

11

ence theories are), then to determine which items logically cluster or deal with which subconcepts. To accomplish this, each judge should work independently rating each statement in the item pool, and categorizing it under the appropriate concept or subconcept. Usually, a criterion of at least 80% agreement among judges is established for the inclusion of an item in the final or revised pool.

4. **A pilot study** should be conducted with the statements retained from step three for the purpose of performing some initial item analyses. The items can be appropriately "packaged" and administered to a small sample of subjects similar to those to be used in the final study (subjects for whom the instrument was designed). Generally, 25-40 subjects should be sufficient for a pilot study. Reliability estimates can be obtained, and several item analyses can be performed with the data (to be discussed in a following section in more detail).

Note: The steps listed above may be repeated several times in the process of developing and refining a reasonably sound tool. It may be necessary to use a new panel of judges, or to administer the test to additional subjects for further pilot study.

5. The **final study** will be conducted. In the case of most dissertation research, the instrument developed from steps one through four will be administered to the final study sample. Depending on the concepts to be measured, 40 to 50 items may survive the initial screening. One need not be too critical in rejecting statements during steps three and four because much of this work will be repeated with the final study sample. This provides for a refinement of the instrument repeating statistical procedures with a much larger selection of subjects. Also, some statistical procedures, such as factor analysis, can be used with a larger study sample which is not possible with the smaller pilot group. It is important to recognize that no instrument should be considered the "final" or "completed" version; additional and continued refinement to any instrument is generally always useful and necessary.

6. With the larger study sample, a number of additional statistical techniques can be used for further instrument refinement. These are only listed briefly in as much as each procedure is discussed at length in the following sections. These techniques include: 1) the establishing of **criterion-related validity** both in terms of concurrent and predictive validity; 2) establishing **construct validity** both convergent and discriminant validity; 3) obtaining final **reliability estimates** for total scale and all subscales, and the reliability of raters if appropriate; and 4) conduct additional item analysis procedures in particular tests of item-to-scale homogeneity.

Basic Measurement Procedures

Item Analysis

Each item analysis procedure discussed provides a way of using item data from a number of respondents to evaluate the quality and usefulness of test items. These techniques provide a means of choosing the "best" items for inclusion in the refined version of the measure. Sometimes, item analysis can offer information also about ways that poor items may be made better. Because of the overwhelming occurrence of Likert-type scales in education measurement, techniques useful in creating Likert scales will be emphasized. Texts are listed at the end of this section which deal with procedures for developing other scale types, i.e., Guttman, Thurstone, or Semantic Differential scales.

The **Item-Difficulty Index** (P) is used to determine the proportion of respondents (examinees) who get the item correct compared to those who missed the item. This technique is most useful in developing classroom tests and has little utility in creating other types of instrumentation. The best range is a ratio of 0.3 to 0.7.

Several **Item Discrimination Indices** are available, and are useful, in evaluating items individually or collectively. Generally, these procedures are used to assess the difference between the proportion of **high-scoring** respondents, those who score high on the attitude, to **low-scoring** respondents. Several techniques are discussed below.

Critical Ratio (t-test) compares the upper 25% of respondents with the lower 25% of the respondents on the means of the two groups on each item. If the low scoring group has a low mean on an item, when compared to a high mean of the high scoring group, which is statistically significant, one then concludes that the individual item is discriminating properly between high and low scoring subjects. With this procedure, each item can be analyzed in three ways: 1) low scoring 25% with a low mean - high scoring 25% with a high mean, the difference between the two means is statistically significant at the .05 level; 2) the difference between means in the low 25% and high 25% is not statistically significant; and 3) there is statistical significance between the means, but the low scoring group has the high mean and the high scoring group has the low mean, indicating a reverse in the intended response pattern.

The first example above indicates that the item is discriminating correctly between low and high scoring respondents. The second case indicates that the item does not discriminate between low and high respondents. The little difference in means between the two groups could have occurred by chance. The third example suggests that the item is stimulating a reversed response pattern from each subject. Both examples two and three indicate that either the item should be discarded from the test, or rewritten in an attempt to correct the problem of proper discrimination among subjects.

Corrected Item-Total Correlations compare each individual item in the scale with the total composite score for the scale. This technique correlates each individual item in the test with the composite score of all of the remaining items. A low item-to-total score correlation indicates that the individual item fails to measure that which the other items measure. Again, the item should be either discarded or rewritten. This procedure is regarded also as a test of item-to-scale **homogeneity**. Likert regarded this procedure as being essential in developing Likert-type scales. The method evaluates the ability of the individual items to measure the attribute measured by the total scale. It should be noted that this test is found in many statistical programs.

Item Means and Variances (standard deviations) may be used also to obtain an initial indication of the item's ability to discriminate along the Likert scale (anchor). For example, if a five-point (1-5) scale is used, one would like an item mean of about 3.0, and a standard deviation of at least 1.0, in order to assure a reasonable degree of dispersion of responses along the scale. In contrast, a high mean of 4.5 and standard deviation of less than 1.0 (i.e., .5), or a low mean of 1.5, would suggest a skewed response pattern (either high or low) to the item.

Item Frequency Distributions may be computed for each item in the scale. One hopes to obtain a fairly normal distribution of responses across the five-point Likert scale. Responses to scale anchors two, three, and four would be greater than to anchors one and five.

Reliability Estimates are extremely useful for evaluating the internal consistency of items within a scale. Likert stressed the importance of using the criterion of internal consistency in developing homogeneous scales. Two statistical procedures are available to satisfy this test--the **ALPHA COEFFICIENT**, and either the **KR-20** or **KR-21** formulas. The **split-halves** method, also known as the **Spearman-Brown Prophecy Formula**, is also available as a test of internal consistency. However, ALPHA is preferred as an estimate of scale reliability. ALPHA is the generalized form of the estimate based on the **interitem correlation matrix**, and it is used with Likert-type scales. The KR-20 and KR-21 formulas are special cases of reliability estimates used with forced-choice scales.

For example, the SPSS RELIABILITY procedure provides an individual item analysis technique referred to as "**If Item Deleted**." This evaluates the reliability contribution of the individual item against the total overall reliability estimate of the scale. If the item (if item deleted) reliability estimate is several points greater than the total scale reliability, this suggests that the item **is not** contributing to the internal consistency of the other scale items as a whole. Potentially, the item should be discarded or rewritten based on this test.

Finally, **Factor Analysis** can also be a useful procedure for conducting item analysis in determining the individual contribution of items to total scale consistency and homogeneity. Items with large factor loadings would contribute more to the measurement of the particular scale, than items with small factor loadings (less than .30). Also, items that load somewhat equally on two or more factors show tendencies toward ambiguity, and might be discarded. Again, factor analysis is useful for developing homogeneous scales where measures have inherent **multidimensionality**.

Validity

The general definition of validity refers to whether an instrument accurately measures what it is intended to measure. Three types of validity are discussed in the literature and will be reviewed briefly. These are **content validity, construct validity** and **criterion-related validity**. Criterion-related validity includes two types: **concurrent validity and predictive validity**. Of the three general types of validity, construct validity is by far the most important to establish for most instruments in the social sciences and education. This is sometimes the most difficult to accomplish while content validity, which provides the least information concerning the validity of the scale, is generally the easiest to operationalize.

Nunnally (1978) indicates that scientific generalization is at the heart of understanding and applying validity to measurement methods. Each type of validity constitutes different issues concerning scientific generalization. That is, each type addresses a different aspect of validating a scale, and each should not be used interchangeably. Nunnally continues that of the three types, the logical issues of relating construct validity to scientific generalization are considerably more complex than those in criterion or content validity.

Content Validity

Content validity is concerned with the extent to which an instrument reflects a specific domain of content. That is, the extent to which items appear to be logical and understandable indicators of the constructs or concepts under consideration. Test items should be a *sample of all possible items taken from a universe of content* dealing with the concepts to be measured. It is sometimes referred to as **subject matter** validity. The operationalization of content validity of any instrument ultimately rests with the degree of **consensus** that can be obtained from a heterogeneous group of judges--experts in the field. Thus, content validity is established by individual, subjective judgments of expert reviewers. A minimum of five to seven individuals should be used; each working independently with an 80% criterion level of agreement being reached on the appropriateness of each item in the measure.

Criterion-related Validity

This deals with the degree of correspondence, or correlation, between the instrument and some other measure of the same concepts or attributes. This may be obtained by correlating the instrument with other measures of similar characteristics or attributes, or in some cases using what is referred to as a **known-group** procedure. Individuals are used who are known to possess varying degrees of the attribute or behavior to be measured by the test. Thorndike (1982) suggested that if we are dealing with two extreme groups, then the ability of the measure to discriminate between the two groups can be expressed as a point-biserial correlation. Nevertheless, this type of criterion-related validity is referred to as **concurrent validity**. **Predictive validity** is obtained in those instances when the test must be used to predict to some future behavior, or the future acquisition of some skill. An example would be the predictive validity of the SAT test battery to predict successful completion of the freshman year of college.

Construct Validity

Construct validity focuses on the extent that a measure (scale or subscales within a larger instrument) perform in accordance with **theoretical expectations**. Construct validity has limited application unless the instrument has been developed from some theoretical base--a theoretical system (conceptual or taxonomic system) underlies the scales development. **Factor analysis** is an often used statistical procedure for establishing construct validity (sometimes called factorial validity). When using factor analysis, the questions addressed are: How well do items designed to measure a construct (concept) **converge** by loading together as a single factor? This may also be referred to as **convergent validity**. Next, How well do items designed to measure other constructs **discriminate** by breaking out as different factors? This is sometimes referred to as **discriminate validity** (Carmines and Zeller, 1979, 54).

Thorndike (1982) indicated that there are at least four methods of obtaining evidence for the construct validity of a measure. One is judgmental--using judgmental comparisons of behavior or attributes to be measured and the test items. Next is correlational--obtaining correlations between the test and other measures. One's test should show substantially higher correlations with other measures designed to assess the same attribute than with measures designed to assess other attributes. This can be accomplished through factor analysis. The third is group difference data--comparing subgroups that might be expected to differ on the attribute. And finally, the use of treatments, or experimental interventions, that might be expected to influence expression of the attribute.

Reliability

Reliability is concerned with the consistency, stability, and dependability (accuracy) with which an instrument measures a set of dimensions, characteristics, behaviors, etc. of research subjects. Reliability coefficients are **estimates** of the degree to which a scale score for each respondent represents either **true measurement**, or some degree of **measurement error**. For the purposes of instrumentation development, there are three types of reliability estimates discussed in the literature. These are the **coefficients of stability**, **equivalence**, and **internal consistency**. Each reliability estimate serves a distinct research purpose, and *one procedure should not be used in place of the other*.

Coefficient of Stability

This procedure determines the reliability--the stability--of a test **over time**. The technique for establishing this type of reliability is referred to generally as the **test-retest method**. A correlation coefficient is computed between the first test administration with a second test administration with the same subjects, and with an approximately four to six week separation in time. The extent to which subjects second test scores are similar to their first test scores determines the degree to which a large correlation coefficient is obtained between the two test administrations, and the extent to which the test is considered to be **stable**. This reliability procedure is most useful with pretest-posttest experimental research, where one should establish the stability of the pretest and posttest scores (over time). However, the procedure also suffers from a number of inherent weaknesses due to the necessity of establishing the reliability coefficient with human subjects over a prescribed time period. Internal validity factors such as history, maturation, and testing effect, to mention a few, often distort the reliability estimate obtained from the test-retest procedure.

Nunnally (1978) indicates that except for certain special instances, there are serious defects in using the retest method. The major problem is that experience in the first testing usually influences responses in the second testing. He recommends that this method generally not be used to estimate reliability.

Coefficient of Equivalence

This technique is referred to as **alternate forms**, and it is used to provide a reliability estimate between two parallel forms of the same test. A correlation coefficient is computed between Form A of a test with the alternate, or parallel, Form B of the same test across the same group of subjects. This reliability estimate is used primarily with the development of standardized tests, such as the GRE and SAT test batteries, where more than one form of the test is used. The **split-half** estimate corrected with the **Spearman-Brown Prophecy Formula** is a special case of the coefficient of equivalence. However, Nunnally (1978) suggested that the difficulty with the split-half method is that the correlation between halves will vary depending on how the items are divided, which raises questions regarding what the reliability is.

Coefficient of Internal Consistency

This reliability procedure provides an estimate of item to total scale homogeneity. Thorndike (1982) states that the analysis is built on the assumption that all items are measures of the same underlying attribute. That is, it is a test of the homogeneity of items in a scale. If the coefficient is low for a particular scale, the items in the scale are probably not measuring the same construct, behavior, or attribute. The internal consistency of items within a scale are evaluated from the **average correlation** among all items in the scale with **Coefficient Alpha** (Cronbach Alpha). Most measurement texts agree that this procedure provides the best method for determining estimates of internal consistency of tests. And, the internal consistency method of reporting reliability in most research situations is probably the more useful method. Nunnally (1978) states that even if other estimates of reliability are made for a particular measure, coefficient alpha should be obtained first. If it proves to be low, then there is no need to make other estimates of reliability because they will prove to be even lower (coefficient alpha sets an upper limit to the reliability of a test).

Although coefficient alpha is commonly used, there is considerable disagreement on what magnitudes of the coefficient are adequate for various types of measurement scales. Nunnally (1978) indicates that a satisfactory level of reliability depends greatly on how a measure is to be used. Exploratory, or preliminary, research may require less demanding levels of reliability estimates than basic research, or hypotheses testing. The magnitude of the coefficient is *directly related to the number of items* in a test. All things being equal, a short test (four or five items) should yield a lower alpha coefficient than a longer test (20 or 25 items). It is generally desirable that longer tests have alpha coefficients of at least 0.80, while shorter tests may be acceptable with coefficients in the high 0.60s or low 0.70s

Cronbach alpha is the generalized form of this test, and it is used with multiple choice, or Likert-type scales. The KR-20 and KR-21 formulas are special cases to be used with forced-choice (T-F) type scales.

Reliability of Raters

This reliability procedure (referred to also as **interrater reliability**) should be used in those cases where one's data gathering method employs raters, or judges, rather than some type of "paper and pencil test." There are two basic methods for estimating the reliability of ratings from a number of judges. The first is a method developed by Guilford (1954), and the second is an analysis of variance approach described by Ebel (1951). The Guilford formula requires that the k raters rank the N persons from high to low, and then the following formula may be used:

$$r = 1 - \frac{k(4N + 2)}{(k-1)(N-1)} + \frac{12S^2}{k(k-1)N(N^2-1)}$$

r = the average intercorrelation among individual judges and, more importantly, **the reliability of one judge**.

k = the number of judges (raters)

N = the number of individuals (persons being rated)

S = the sum of ranks for any individual

It is important to note that this formula, when applied to a set of ratings, provides the reliability estimate for **one rater**. To determine the reliability estimate of an entire set of ratings (more than one judge), it is necessary to employ the Spearman-Brown Prophecy Formula with **n** in that formula equal to the **number of raters or judges**. The Spearman-Brown Formula is:

$$r = \frac{nr}{1+(n-1)r}$$

The data in Table 4 below demonstrate this reliability procedure using the rank-order ratings of four raters for nine individuals.

Table 4

DATA TABLE OF RANKINGS OF NINE INDIVIDUALS (N)
BY FOUR JUDGES (k)

JUDGES

Individual	S 1	2	S^2 3	4	Total Rating	$(Rating)^2$
1	7	9	6	8	30	900
2	3	1	1	2	7	49
3	2	2	5	1	10	100
4	8	8	9	7	32	1024
5	5	4	3	4	16	256
6	9	7	8	6	30	900
7	1	5	2	3	11	121
8	6	3	4	7	20	400
9	4	6	7	5	22	484

$$S^2 = 4234$$

By inserting data from the table above into the formula, we would obtain the following results:

$$r = 1 - \frac{(4)(38)}{(3)(8)} + \frac{(12)(4234)}{(4)(3)(9)(80)}$$

$$r = 1 - \frac{152}{24} + \frac{50{,}808}{8{,}640} = 1 - 6.333 + 5.881$$

$$r = .548$$

Note, that the result, r = .548, is the reliability estimate for one rater. The Spearman-Brown formula must be used to determine the reliability estimate for the four judges in the example above. By inserting the data into the formula, we obtain the following:

$$r = \frac{(4)(.548)}{1+(3)(.548)} = \frac{2.192}{1 + 1.644} = \frac{2.192}{2.644} = .829$$

It has been shown that gains in interrater reliability may be made by adding raters when the initial reliability estimate is low. However, when the number of judges is greater than five or six, the increase in reliability is usually not justified by the addition of more raters. For example, one might perform a pilot study by having three judges rate student performance on a certain task. If the reliability estimate for the three judges is not sufficiently large, one could keep incrementing the value of n (number of raters) in the Spearman-Brown formula to determine the number of raters required until the desired reliability estimate is obtained.

Relation of Validity To Reliability

Both validity and reliability are highly interdependent, mathematically. From a practical standpoint, Campbell (1976) has indicated that the concept of reliability becomes indistinguishable from that of validity. *The precision of the estimate of criterion validity is reduced as reliability is reduced.* Criterion validity of a test is affected by the reliability of a test. Thus, a test or measure may be reliable but not valid. **A test can not be valid if it is not reliable**. An index of this relationship between reliability and validity is the **index of reliability**.

Index of Reliability

The validity of a test cannot exceed the square root of the reliability of the test. If test, X, is used to predict a criterion, Y, then P_{xy} is the validity coefficient. P_{xy} cannot be larger than the square root of P_{xx}--the reliability coefficient of test X.

The square root of the reliability of a measure provides an **upper bound** for its correlation with any other measure. For example, a measure with a reliability estimate of only .65 can never correlate greater with another test or variable than .81. This is referred to as the **index of reliability**.

That is: $r_{xy} = r_{xx} = \text{Index of Reliability}$

This demonstrates the close relationship between reliability and criterion validity, as well as the importance of establishing the highest possible reliability estimates for all measures employed in a study when those measures will be correlated with other variables.

Attenuation

If scores obtained from two measures, a predictor X and a criterion Y, are unreliable, or found to have low reliability estimates, the correlation coefficient between the two measures will be reduced in value, or **attenuated**. When this occurs a correction for attenuation can be made. To correct for errors of measurement in both variables, the following formula may be used:

$$r_c = \frac{r_{xy}}{r_{xx}r_{yy}}$$

Where:

r_c = the corrected correlation coefficient

r_{xx} and r_{yy} = the reliability coefficients of the two measures

r_{xy} = the correlation coefficient between the two measures

With this correction formula for attenuation, one might obtain the following results: If measure X has a reliability of .52 and measure Y has a reliability of .61, with a correlation coefficient of .43 between X and Y, the corrected correlation coefficient will be:

$$r_c = \frac{.43}{(.52)(.61)} = \frac{.43}{(.721)(.70)} = \frac{.43}{.505} = .85$$

The correlation coefficient is increased from .43 to .85 after being corrected for attenuation due to the low reliability of the two measures. Often test developers can only increase the reliability of an instrument by a small amount, and therefore, it is of interest to know the correlation between two measures if both were perfectly reliable.

Restriction of Range

If one uses a selected (homogeneous) subgroup of subjects with a limited range of scores on any measure, this will affect the outcome of correlation coefficients generally, and the computation of reliability and validity estimates specifically. When a range of scores is **restricted**, the **variance is also restricted**. The scores of a selected group of respondents between 95 and 100 on a test will have a lower correlation with a criterion (Y variable) than will those of the entire, more heterogeneous, group receiving scores across the entire range, i.e., 1 to 100. In the case with restricted scores, too little variation is present in the rawscore data.

Table 5 provides an example of the differences encountered when a total group is used, and when a group is restricted to one portion of the score range

Table 5

RESTRICTED RANGE OF SCORES

	Total Group	Total	Selected Group	Total
Test X	1 4 8 11 16 26 25	91	16 26 25	67
Test Y	5 6 7 8 9 10 11	56	9 10 11	30

Test X	*Test Y*	*Test X*	*Test Y*
$N = 7$	$N = 7$	$N = 3$	$N = 3$
$X = 13$	$X = 8$	$X = 22.3$	$X = 10$
$sd^2 = 82.3$	$sd^2 = 4$	$sd^2 = 20.2$	$sd^2 = .667$
$sd = 9.1$	$sd = 2$	$sd = 4.5$	$sd = .82$
$r_{xy} =$		$r_{xy} =$	

Test developers may encounter this problem, particularly in a pilot study, when one or more measures are used with a small and selected group of subjects. Both reliability and validity estimates may be lower than with a larger selection of subjects obtained from the final study.

Reliability of Difference, Change, or Growth Scores

In some studies dealing with students and classroom research, it is not uncommon that one may wish to compute scores on subjects from a pretest measure to posttest of the same measure. The purpose is to determine the amount of change, difference, or growth that may occur from pretest to posttest condition. Serious problems arise as to the reliability of difference, or change, scores between such measurement. Generally, *the difference between two scores is less reliable than the reliability of the individual scores*, even though the individual scores are quite reliable. Because these two scores measure essentially the same thing, they are, therefore, highly correlated. The high correlation between the two scores (pretest to posttest) tends to **reduce** the reliability of the difference, or change scores.

Although the computation of change scores is questionable and frequently difficult to properly interpret, Cronbach has provided a formula for estimating the reliability of a difference, or change, score between two standard scores:

$$r_{diff} = \frac{r_{aa} + r_{bb} - 2r_{ab}}{- 2r_{ab}}$$

It should be noted that r_{aa} and r_{bb} are the reliabilities of the subtests and r_{ab} is the correlation between the scores on the two test.

Selected References

These references were used, in part, in developing this section.

Allen, M.J. & W.M. Yen. 1979. *Introduction to Measurement Theory*. Monterey, Cal.: Brooks-Cole.

Blood, D.F. & W.C. Budd. 1972. *Educational Measurement and Evaluation*. New York: Harper & Row.

Campbell, J.P. 1976. Psychometric theory. In Dunnette (ed.). *Handbook of Industrial and Organizational Psychology*. Chicago: Rand-McNally.

Dick, W. & N. Hagerty. 1971. *Topics in Measurement: Reliability and Validity*. New York: McGraw-Hill.

Ebel, R.L. 1951. Estimation of the reliability of ratings. *Psychometrika*, 16, 407-424.

Gorden, R.L. 1977. *Unidimensional Scaling of Social Variables*. New York: The Free Press.

Guilford, J.P. 1954. *Psychometric Methods* (2nd. ed.). New York: McGraw- Hill.

Isaac, S. 1976. *Handbook in Research and Evaluation*. San Diego: Edits.

McIver, J.P. & E.G. Carmines. 1981. *Unidimensional Scaling* (#24). Beverly Hills: Sage.

Mitchell, T.R. 1985. An evaluation of the validity of correlational research conducted in organizations. *The Academy of Management Review*, 10, 192-205.

Nunnally, J.P. 1978. *Psychometric Theory* (2nd. ed.). New York: McGraw- Hill.

Osgood, C.E., G.J. Suci, & P.H. Tannenbaum. 1957. *The Measurement of Meaning*. Urbana, Ill.: University of Illinois Press.

Shaw, M.E. & J.M. Wright. 1967. *Scales for the Measurement of Attitudes*. New York: McGraw-Hill.

Smith, P.C., L.M. Kendall. & C.L. Hulin. 1969. *The Measurement of Satisfaction in Work and Retirement: A Strategy for the Study of Attitudes*. Chicago: Rand-McNally.

Snider, J.G. & C.E. Osgood (eds.). 1969. *Semantic Differential Technique*. Chicago: Aldine.

Sullivan, J.L. & S. Feldman. 1979. *Multiple Indicators: An Introduction* (#15). Beverly Hills: Sage.

Thorndike, R.L. 1982. *Applied Psychometrics*. Boston: Houghton Mifflin.

Van de Ven, A.H. & D.L. Ferry. 1980. *Measuring and Assessing Organizations*. New York: Wiley.

Alienation

Alienation Scale

Dean, D.G. 1961. Alienation: Its meaning and measurement. *American Sociological Review* 26:753-758.

Comments: The 24-item AS assesses three aspects of alienation: powerlessness, normlessness, and social isolation. In addition, the AS has served as a model for the development of more recent instruments.

Scale Construction: This scale is based on the five meanings described by Seeman (powerlessness, normlessness, meaninglessness, isolation, and self-estrangement).

Sample: The original stratified sample consisted of 384 men from Columbus, Ohio in 1955. Additional samples consisted of 135 women from a Protestant liberal arts college in 1960; 121 women from a Catholic women's college in 1960; 75 women from a Protestant liberal arts college in 1955; and 65 women from a Catholic women's college.

Reliability: Corrected split-half correlation coefficients for the three scales were: 0.73 normlessness, 0.79 powerlessness, and 0.84 social isolation. The total reliability was 0.78.

Validity: Content validation was performed through a panel of seven judges. The Adorno F Scale was correlated with the Alienation Scale producing correlation coefficients ranging from 0.26 (alienation and authoritarianism) to 0.37 (powerlessness and authoritarianism).

Scales: There are three subscales. The powerlessness scale contains nine items: 2, 6, 9, 13, 15, 18, 20, 21, and 23; the normlessness scale contains six items: 4, 7, 10, 12, 16, 19; and the social isolation scale contains nine items: 1, 3, 5, 8, 11, 14, 17, 22, and 24.

References:
Calabrese, R.L. and J.E. Fisher. 1988. The effects of teaching experience on levels of alienation. *Journal of Psychology* 122:147-153.

Dean, D. 1956. Alienation and political apathy. Ph.D. dissertation, Ohio State University.

de Man, A.F. 1990. Repression-sensitization and measures of adjustment. *Social Behavior and Personality* 18:13-16.

Alienation Scale

1. Sometimes I feel all alone in the world.
2. I worry about the future facing today's children.
3. I don't get invited out by friends as often as I'd really like.
4. The end often justifies the means.
5. Most people today seldom feel lonely.
6. Sometimes I have the feeling that other people are using me.
7. People's ideas change so much that I wonder if we'll ever have anything to depend on.
8. Real friends are as easy as ever to find.
9. It is frightening to be responsible for the development of a little child.
10. Everything is relative, and there just aren't any rules to live by.
11. One can always find friends if he shows himself friendly.
12. I often wonder what the meaning of life really is.
13. There is little or nothing I can do towards preventing a major "shooting" war.
14. The world in which we live is basically a friendly place.
15. There are so many decisions that have to be made today that sometimes I could just "blow up."
16. The only thing one can be sure of today is that he can be sure of nothing.
17. There are few dependable ties between people any more.
18. There is little chance for promotion on the job unless a man gets a break.
19. With so many religions abroad, one doesn't really know which to believe.
20. We're so regimented today that there's not much room for choice even in personal matters.
21. We are just so many cogs in the machinery of life.
22. People are just naturally friendly and helpful.
23. The future looks very dismal.
24. I don't get to visit friends as often as I'd really like.

Scaling: Strongly Agree = 4; Agree = 3; Uncertain = 2; Disagree = 1; and Strongly Disagree = 0. The scoring is reversed for items: 5, 8, 11, 14, and 22. Scores range from a low of 0 to a high of 96.

Reprinted with permission of the American Sociological Association.

Pupil Attitude Questionnaire

Kolesar, H. 1967. An empirical study of client alienation in the bureaucratic organization. Ph.D. dissertation, University of Alberta, Edmonton, Canada.

Comments: The 60-item PAQ is based on Seeman's (1959) five alienation subscales: powerlessness, self-estrangement, normlessness, meaninglessness, and isolation.

Sample: As part of the pilot study, 163 high school students from Alberta, Canada responded to the PAQ. The original 164 items were reduced to 60 items based on three types of analysis. The revised PAQ was administered to 92 students over a one-week interval. Approximately 1,764 students in twenty high schools in Alberta, Canada completed the revised PAQ.

Reliability: Test-retest reliability for the entire PAQ with 92 students over a one-week period was 0.79.

Validity: Four kinds of validity were established: content, face, construct, and factorial validity. Content validity was established by using a large number of items representing various relationships between the student and the school. Face validity was established by using a panel of 14 judges who determined that the questionnaire measures what it purports to measure. Construct validity was established by correlating student scores on the PAQ with teacher ratings (significant at the 0.001 level). Factorial validity was established by performing several factor analyses.

Factor Analysis: A five-factor solution was accepted. The five factors are: 12 items on powerlessness (5, 7, 8, 13, 28, 29, 30, 34, 41, 51, 53, and 59); 12 on self-estrangement (10, 12, 16, 21, 26, 31, 32, 36, 40, 43, 44, and 54); 14 on normlessness (1, 2, 3, 11, 15, 18, 24, 27, 35, 42, 52, 56, 57, and 58); 12 on meaninglessness (6, 14, 17, 19, 33, 37, 38, 39, 45, 46, 47, and 60); and 10 on isolation (4, 9, 20, 22, 23, 25, 48, 49, 50, and 55).

Definition of Factors: Student *powerlessness* pertains to the student's sense of a lack of personal control over his/her state of affairs in school. *Meaninglessness* pertains to a sense of inability to predict outcomes. Student *normlessness* pertains to the belief that socially unapproved behaviors are required to achieve school goals. The *isolated student* is one who does not accept the goals of the school as his/her own. The *self-estranged student* is one who is unable to find school activities which are self-rewarding.

Data Analysis: Scores on each of the five scales were correlated with the scores on the other scales as well as with the total score. The results of all these correlations were all positive and significant, except the correlation between the meaninglessness and isolation scales.

Reference: Rafalides, M. and W.K. Hoy. 1971. Student sense of alienation and pupil control orientation of high schools. *High School Journal* 55:101-111.

Pupil Attitude Questionnaire

1. White lies are justified when they help to avoid punishment.
2. It is a good policy to tell teachers only what they want to hear.
3. In this school success is to be aimed for by any means that pupils can devise.
4. It is most important that right always be achieved even if it requires tremendous effort.
5. Schools are run by others and there is little that pupils can do about it.
6. I think that I can now predict what I can achieve in an occupation after graduation.
7. The school experiences of pupils are controlled by plans devised by others.
8. There really isn't much use complaining to the teachers about the school because it is impossible to influence them anyway.
9. The reason I endure some unpleasant things now is because I feel that it will benefit me later on.
10. Pupils should have most of their time free from study.
11. Sometimes it is necessary to make promises to school authorities which you don't intend to keep.
12. In order to get ahead in this school pupils are almost forced to do some things which are not right.
13. Pupils often are given the opportunity to express their ideas about how the school ought to be run.
14. It is possible on the basis of the level of my present school achievement, to predict with a high degree of accuracy, the level of achievement I can expect in adulthood.
15. It is very desirable that pupils learn to be good citizens
16. I think my teachers would have given me the same marks on the last report card no matter how well I really had done.
17. My school experiences will help me to become a good citizen.
18. It doesn't matter too much if what I am doing is right or wrong as long as it works.
19. At school we learn habits and attitudes which will guide us in the achievement of a good life.
20. I know that I will complete my high school education.
21. These days a pupil doesn't really know who he can count on.
22. I often worry about what my teachers think of me.
23. Pupils must try to develop an interest in their school subjects even when the content is dull.
24. It is more important to achieve enjoyment and personal satisfaction than to sacrifice yourself for others.
25. I study hard in school mainly because I want to get good grades.
26. I often read and study in my courses beyond what is required by my teachers.
27. Really, a pupil has done wrong only if he gets caught.
28. The school principal is really interested in all pupils in this school.
29. In discipline cases the pupil's explanation of the circumstances is carefully weighed by the school authorities before punishment is decided upon.
30. The teachers will not listen to pupil complaints about unfair school rules.
31. Usually, I would rather play hooky than come to school.
32. I would rather go to work now than go to school, but more education now will help me to get a better job later.
33. What I am doing at school will assist me to do what I want when I graduate.
34. Pupils have adequate opportunities to protect themselves when their interests conflict with the interests of those who run the school.
35. Copying parts of essays from books is justified if this results in good marks on the essays.
36. I get more satisfaction from doing an assignment well than from the marks which I receive on the assignment.
37. What we do at school will help us to affect the world in which we live.
38. Participation in student government activities will help me in anything I try to do in the future.
39. As a result of my school experiences I know what I will do when I graduate.
40. No matter how I try I don't seem to understand the content of my courses very well.
41. In this school the teachers are the rulers and the pupils are the slaves.

42. It is unlikely that in this school the pupils will achieve the goals in which they believe.
43. If homework assignments were not required, I would seldom do homework.
44. I like to do extra problems in mathematics for fun.
45. I understand how decisions are made regarding what we are to study in this school.
46. My school studies will help me to make predictions about the kind of world in which I will live in the future.
47. My present school studies will help me to understand others.
48. Pupils must be very careful to make the best possible impression with their teachers.
49. If I had my way, I'd close all schools.
50. Having lots of friends is more important than is getting ahead in school.
51. In this school pupils can complain to the principal and be given a fair hearing.
52. Copying another pupil's homework is justified if he agrees to let you do it.
53. Pupil's ideas about how the school should be run are often adopted in this school.
54. I find it easy to please my teachers.
55. I want to finish high school.
56. It is necessary to misbehave at school if you're going to have any fun.
57. Giving an answer to someone else during an examination is not really cheating.
58. Pupils must take advantage of every opportunity, fair or unfair, because good opportunities occur very infrequently at this school.
59. Pupils in this school are given considerable freedom in planning their own programs to meet their future needs.
60. Participation in student government activities will assist me to become a good citizen.

Scaling: Strongly Agree = 5; Agree = 4; Undecided = 3; Disagree = 2; Strongly Disagree = 1. The scoring is reversed for the following items: 4, 6, 13, 15, 20, 23, 26, 28, 29, 34, 36, 44, 45, 46, 51, 53, 54, 55, and 59. For the following items on the meaninglessness scale 14, 17, 19, 33, 37, 38, 39, 47, and 60 the scoring is as follows: SA = 1, A = 3, U = 5, D = 3, SD = 1.

Reprinted with permission of the author.

Alienation Scale

Pearlin, L.I. 1962. Alienation from work: A study of nursing personnel. *American Sociological Review* 4:466-479.

Comments: Although the original study was conducted in a mental hospital, the four-item questionnaire has recently been used in educational settings (urban and suburban school districts and universities). The instrument was designed to examine alienation in a bureaucratic setting. Alienation is defined as "a feeling of powerlessness over one's own affairs-a sense that the things that importantly affect one's activities and work are outside his control." Therefore, the relationships between responsibility, authority, and alienation were explored.

Sample: The original sample consisted of 1,138 nursing assistants, charge attendants, and registered nurses in a large mental hospital near Washington, D.C.

Reliability: A coefficient of reproducibility of 0.91 is reported for the four-item Guttman scale.

Data Analysis: Alienation is studied in terms of positional distance and status obeisance. A four-item Guttman scale assessing obeisance is included.

References:

Benson, N. and P. Malone. 1987. Teachers' beliefs about shared decision making and work alienation. *Education* 107:244-251.

Knoop, R. 1986. Causes of alienation among university professors. *Perceptual and Motor Skills* 63:677-678.

Pearlin, L.I. and M.L. Kohn. 1966. Social class, occupation and parental values: A cross-national study. *American Sociological Review* 4:466-479.

Alienation Scale

1. How often do you do things in your work that you wouldn't do if it were up to you? Never; Once in a while; Fairly often; *Very often.*
2. Around here it's not important how much you know; it's who you know that really counts. *Agree;* Disagree.
3. How much say or influence do people like you have on the way the hospital is run? A lot; Some; *Very little; None.*
4. How often do you tell (your superior) your own ideas about things you might do in your work? *Never; Once in a while;* Fairly often; Very often.

Scaling: The alienative answers are italicized.

Anxiety

Teaching Anxiety Scale

Parsons, J.S. 1973. Assessment of anxiety about teaching using the Teaching Anxiety Scale: Manual and research. Paper presented at American Educational Research Association. ERIC ED 079 330.

Comments: The 25-item TCHAS examines the relationship between teaching anxiety and acquiring teaching skills. In addition, the scale helps preservice teachers identify their strengths and weaknesses.

Scale Construction: The TCHAS was originally developed at Stanford University (two equivalent forms) to assess anxiety specifically related to the job of teaching. The scale was geared to preservice teachers. Revised forms are available with 24, 28, and 29 items for use with inservice teachers. About one-half of the items were written negatively.

Sample: Overall, six groups participated in the study. The four groups of preservice teachers consisted of: 55 graduate preservice intern teachers (secondary); 79 undergraduate preservice teachers (secondary); 30 undergraduate preservice student teachers (elementary); and 36 undergraduate and graduate preservice elementary and secondary teachers. The two groups of inservice teachers consisted of: 384 newly hired elementary and secondary teachers; and 23 elementary and junior high school teachers. A description of the samples is provided.

Reliability: Alpha coefficients for preservice teachers were 0.90 (undergraduate and graduate elementary and secondary preservice teachers); 0.92 (undergraduate preservice elementary student teachers; 0.92 (graduate preservice secondary intern teachers; and 0.88 (undergraduate secondary preservice teachers). Alpha coefficients for inservice teachers were: 0.87 (elementary and secondary teachers); and 0.93 (elementary and junior high school teachers). Test-retest correlations for four groups ranged from 0.60 to 0.95, indicating that the TCHAS is stable over short time periods. Detailed test-retest information is provided.

Validity: Component analysis, group differences, internal structure, and change over time are discussed as they establish the construct validity of the TCHAS. The TCHAS was positively correlated with the Taylor Manifest Anxiety Scale. In addition, most anxious and least anxious groups were used based on the opinion of 25 teaching supervisors. The most anxious group scored significantly higher on the TCHAS than the least anxious group. The high alpha coefficients present evidence that teaching anxiety is a single concept. Two factor analyses confirmed the single factor structure. The results of various studies show that teaching anxiety decreases over time for preservice teachers. Tables are presented to support construct validity.

Factor Analysis: The results of two factor analyses using the 25-item TCHAS confirmed a single factor solution with 22 of 25 items loading on one factor. The three items that failed to load on a single factor were 3, 17, and 22. Therefore, a new 22-item TCHAS was validated. On the 29-item TCHAS, items 26-29 failed to load on a single factor as well as three items from the 25-item TCHAS.

Data Analysis: Distribution statistics are provided for preservice and inservice teachers.

Reference:
Pigge, F.L and R.N. Marso. 1994. Relationships of prospective teachers' personality type and locus of control orientation with changes in their attitude and anxiety about teaching. *Midwestern Educational Researcher* 7:2-7.

Teaching Anxiety Scale

1.   I feel calm and collected when I think about holding parent-teacher conferences.
2.   If I have trouble answering a student's question I (will find) find it difficult to concentrate on questions that follow.
3.   I feel uncomfortable when I speak before a group.
4.   I (would feel) feel calm (if I were) when I am preparing lessons.
5.   I'm worried whether I can be a good teacher.
6.   I feel sure I will find teaching a satisfying profession.
7.   I would feel calm and collected if a student's parent observed in my classroom.
8.   I feel inferior to other preservice teachers in my teacher preparation program.
9.   I feel that students will follow my instructions.
10. I feel secure with regard to my ability to keep a class under control.
11. I'm less happy teaching than I thought I'd be.
12. I feel nervous when I am being observed by my college supervisor.
13. I feel confident about my ability to improvise in the classroom.
14. I feel other teachers (will think) think I'm very competent.
15. I (would feel) feel panicky when a student asks me a question I (couldn't) can't answer.
16. I feel anxious because I don't know yet whether I really want to be a teacher.
17. I feel better prepared for teaching than other preservice teachers in my teacher preparation program.
18. Lack of rapport with my students (will be) is one of my biggest worries.
19. I would feel anxious if the principal informed me he was coming to my class to observe.
20. I (would find) find it easy to speak up in the staff room.
21. I worry about being able to keep the students interested in what I (will teach) teach them.
22. I (would find) find it easy to admit to the class that I don't know the answer to a question a student asks.
23. Deciding how to present information in the classroom (would make) makes me feel uncertain.
24. I feel I will have good recall of the things I know when I am in front of the class.
25. I feel I (will be) am as competent in the classroom as other preservice teachers in my teacher preparation program.
26. I'm concerned about how to use my testing of students as a useful indication of how effectively I'm teaching them.
27. I'm worried that differences in background between my students and me (will prevent) prevent me from teaching effectively.
28. I am certain that my own personal "hang-ups" (will not) do not hinder my teaching effectiveness.
29. I'm uncertain whether I (will be able to) can tell the difference between really seriously disturbed students and those who are merely "goofing off" in class.

Scaling: Never = 1; Infrequently = 2; Occasionally = 3; Frequently = 4; and Always = 5. Scoring is reversed for the following items: 1, 4, 6, 7, 9, 10, 13, 14, 17, 20, 22, 24, 25, and 28.

Change

Leadership Actions Survey

Goldstein, M.T. 1982. Using administrative tactics to introduce curriculum innovation. Paper presented at American Educational Research Association. ERIC ED 214 310.

Comments: The 24-item LAS identifies the tactics used by administrators in an attempt to influence the introduction of special education curriculum innovations. The survey was adapted from the work of Hull and others based on their theoretical framework of tactic types.

Sample: Surveys and interviews were obtained from administrators in 39 sites. These were administrators identified as advocates of a particular innovation.

Reliability: Although it was indicated that reliability estimates were obtained, actually reliability values were not provided.

Validity: The categorizing of the initial item pool into tactic types was accomplished by a panel of six administrators serving as a panel of judges. Additional preliminary analyses were conducted to determine the content validity of the instrument.

Factor Analysis: A principal components, varimax rotation factor analysis was conducted which yielded three factors which were named following Chin and Benne's conceptualization of strategies of changing.

Definition of Factors: The three factors are: *empirical-rational* which involves the communication of information; *power coercive* which involves the use of mandates or orders; and the *normative-reeducative* which involves the creation of conditions within which teachers may innovate.

References:
Hull, W.L. et al. 1973. A conceptual framework for the diffusion of innovations in vocational and technical education. Columbus: Center for Vocational and Technical Education, Ohio State University.

Widmer, J.L. 1977. Innovation and bureaucracies: A reexamination of diffusion strategies for state and local systems. Paper presented at American Educational Research Association.

Leadership Actions Survey

1. Provided teachers with printed materials about the innovation.
2. Asked persons respected by the teachers to present the innovation to them.
3. Provided information about how the innovation has been used in other places.
4. Presented the innovation as unfinished to allow teachers to make it their own.
5. Emphasized aspects of the innovation that are consistent with what the teacher expects.
6. Answered questions about the innovation at meetings.
7. Gave recognition to teachers for trying the innovation.
8. Set a deadline for teachers to incorporate the innovation into their classroom activities.
9. Asked teachers to give their reasons for accepting or rejecting the innovation.
10. Observed the effectiveness of the innovation in classrooms.
11. Warned teachers of the consequences of resisting using the innovation.
12. Endorsed the innovation through persons perceived as highly credible by the teachers.
13. Provided explicit instructions by the developer on how to use the innovation.
14. Allowed the teachers to adapt the innovation to local conditions.
15. Explained the innovation through conferences with professional staff.
16. Visited a site which has installed the innovation.
17. Compelled teachers to use the innovation.
18. Conducted a pilot test of the innovation.
19. Gave pay to teachers for using the innovation.
20. Observed the innovation in operation.
21. Established program policies to insure the use of the innovation.
22. Informed teachers about the innovation at meetings.
23. Required teachers to use the innovation in their classrooms.
24. Tried the innovation on a small scale.

Scoring: A five-point Likert-type response set is labeled: All; Most; Half; Few; or None

Reprinted with permission of the author.

Climate

School Level Environment Questionnaire

Fisher, D.L. and B.J. Fraser. 1990. Validity and use of the School-Level Environment Questionnaire. Paper presented at American Educational Research Association. ERIC ED 318 757.

Comments: The 56-item SLEQ measures teachers' perceptions of the psychological environment of a school. The instrument has two answer forms--one measures the actual environment as seen by teachers, the other the preferred, or ideal, form.

Scale Construction: The scale development for this instrument was based on the Work Environment Scale (WES) designed by Moos. This WES has 10 scales. These scales fall into three basic dimensions: relationship dimension, personal development dimension, and system maintenance and system change dimension. The three board dimensions were used for the SLEQ and include seven subscales

Sample: Three different teacher samples were used in the development of the questionnaire. The largest sample was 109 teachers from 10 elementary schools in Tasmania.

Reliability: Alpha coefficients as an estimate of each scales internal consistency were provided. These ranged from a low of 0.70 to 0.91.

Subscales: The design of the instrument into seven subscales include: student support, affiliation, professional interest, staff freedom, participatory decision making, innovation, and resource adequacy. More recently, an eighth subscale, work pressure, has been added. Each subscale is assessed by seven items.

References:
Fisher, D.L. and B.J. Fraser. 1983. Use of WES to assess science teachers' perceptions of school environment of different types of schools. *European Journal of Science Education* 5: 231-233.

Fraser, B.J. and Fisher, D.L. 1986. Using short forms of classroom climate instruments to assess and improve classroom psychosocial environment. *Journal of Research in Science Teaching* 23:387-413.

Moos, R.H. 1979. *Evaluating educational environments*. San Francisco: Jossey-Bass.

School-Level Environment Questionnaire

1. There are many disruptive, difficult students in the school.
2. I seldom receive encouragement from colleagues.
3. Teachers frequently discuss teaching methods and strategies with each other.
4. I am often supervised to ensure that I follow directions carefully.
5. Decisions about the running of the school are usually made by the principal or a small group of teachers.
6. It is very difficult to change anything in this school.
7. The school or department library includes an adequate selection of books and periodicals.
8. There is constant pressure to keep working.
9. Most students are helpful and cooperative to teachers.
10. I feel accepted by other teachers.
11. Teachers avoid talking with each other about teaching and learning.
12. I am not expected to conform to a particular teaching style.
13. I have to refer even small matters to a senior member of staff for a final answer.
14. Teachers are encouraged to be innovative in this school.
15. The supply of equipment and resources is inadequate.
16. Teachers have to work long hours to complete all their work.
17. Most students are pleasant and friendly to teachers.
18. I am ignored by other teachers.
19. Professional matters are seldom discussed during staff meetings.
20. It is considered very important that I closely follow syllabuses and lesson plans.
21. Action can usually be taken without gaining the approval of the subject department head or senior member of staff.
22. There is a great deal of resistance to proposals for curriculum change.
23. Video equipment, tapes and films are readily available and accessible.
24. Teachers don't have to work very hard in this school.
25. There are many noisy, badly-behaved students.
26. I feel that I could rely on my colleagues for assistance if I should need it.
27. Many teachers attend inservice and other professional development courses.
28. There are few rules and regulations that I am expected to follow.
29. Teachers are frequently asked to participate in decisions concerning administrative policies and procedures.
30. Most teachers like the idea of change.
31. Adequate duplicating facilities and services are available to teachers.
32. There is no time for teachers to relax.
33. Students get along well with teachers.
34. My colleagues seldom take notice of my professional views and opinions.
35. Teachers show little interest in what is happening in other schools.
36. I am allowed to do almost as I please in the classroom.
37. I am encouraged to make decisions without reference to a senior member or staff.
38. New courses or curriculum materials are seldom implemented in the school.
39. Tape recorders and cassettes are seldom available when needed.
40. You can take it easy and still get the work done.
41. Most students are well-mannered and respectful to the school staff.
42. I feel that I have many friends among my colleagues at this school.
43. Teachers are keen to learn from their colleagues.
44. My classes are expected to use prescribed textbooks and prescribed resource materials.

45. I must ask my subject department head or senior member of staff before I do most things.
46. There is much experimentation with different teaching approaches.
47. Facilities are inadequate for catering for a variety of classroom activities and learning groups of different sizes.
48. Seldom are there deadlines to be met.
49. Very strict discipline is needed to control many of the students.
50. I often feel lonely and left out of things in the staffroom.
51. Teachers show considerable interest in the professional activities of their colleagues.
52. I am expected to maintain very strict control in the classroom.
53. I have very little say in the running of the school.
54. New and different ideas are always being tried out in this school.
55. Projectors for filmstrips, transparencies and films are usually available when needed.
56. It is hard to keep up with your work load.

Scoring: SD = Strongly Disagree; D = Disagree; N = Neither agree or disagree; A = Agree; SA = Strongly Agree.

Reprinted with permission of the author.

Organizational Climate Index

Stern, G.G. 1970. *People in context: Measuring person-environment congruence in education and industry.* New York: Wiley.

Comments: The OCI is one of a set of indices (CCI, AI, HSCI) developed by George Stern and his associates. They were developed to measure both the personality needs of the individual and the psychological character of the environment (organization). The OCI is a measure of the environmental character of the organization. The Stern indices are based on the 30 Need-Press scales (model) of H.A. Murray who stressed that explained behavior was a function of the relationship between an individual (personality needs) and the organization (environmental press). The OCI is a general instrument that can be used to characterize the psychological climate of a wide variety of organizations. According to Stern, needs are the tendencies that give unity and direction to an individual's behavior. Press describes the conditions that represent obstacles to the expression of a need or make such expression easier. Press can be further differentiated as either *beta press or consensual beta press.* Beta press is the private interpretation that each individual places on events around him. Consensual beta press recognizes that people who share a common ideology also tend to share a common interpretation of events. The OCI measures organizational members' interpretations of events, or beta press. When group scores (mean scores) are developed such scores provide a measure of consensual beta press.

Scale Construction: The OCI (long form) is a 300-item instrument, ten items for each of Murray's 30 need-press scales. The short form, which is included here, is an 80-item instrument.

Sample: The instrument was originally developed with college students and in five public schools in upstate New York. However, the instrument has been used extensively in research since the late 1950s.

Reliability: Reliability assessments are provided with KR-20 estimates of internal consistency. These estimates calculated on 931 public school teachers for the 30 press scales ranged from 0.23 to 0.87. The low estimates suggest that some scales should be treated with caution because of possible attenuation of relationships due to low reliability.

Validity: Primary validity information is in the form of significant differences among the average press scores from different organizational settings. Correlations of OCI factors or profiles with other criteria are also provided.

Factor Analysis: A principal component analysis with an equimax rotation yielded six first-order factors and two second-order factors. The second-order factors are Development Press and Control Press; the first-order are Intellectual Climate, Supportiveness, Orderliness, Achievement standards, Practicalness, and Impulse Control.

References:
Frothingham, E.M. 1988. Teacher collegiality: Its relationship to professionalism and organizational climate in public and private schools. Ph.D. dissertation, New York University.

Meyer, D.E. 1988. The relationship of organizational climate to burnout among faculty in selected community colleges in the midwest. Ed.D. dissertation, Oklahoma State University.

Murray, H.A. 1938. *Explorations in personality*. New York: Oxford University. Press.

Stern, G.G. et al. 1970. The Organizational Climate Index. Syracuse, New York: Evaluation Research Association.

Taylor, J. and D.G. Bowers. 1972. The Survey of Organizations: A machine scored standardized questionnaire instrument. Ann Arbor, MI: Institute for Social Research.

Organizational Climate Index (Short Form)

1. Work programs are well organized and progress systematically from week to week.
2. People here express their feelings openly and enthusiastically.
3. everyone here has a strong sense of being a member of the team.
4. There is a lot of group spirit.
5. Administrative policy, goals, and objectives are carefully explained to everyone.
6. When people here disagree with an administrative decision, they work to get it changed.
7. People here put a great deal of energy into everything they do.
8. Improving one's knowledge of important works of art, music, and drama is encouraged here.
9. One of the values most stressed here is open-mindedness.
10. Social events get a lot of enthusiasm and support.
11. People who have friends of the opposite sex show their affection openly.
12. People find others eager to help them get started.
13. People here spend a great deal of time thinking about and discussing complex problems.
14. The ability to plan ahead is highly valued here.
15. Many social activities are unplanned and spontaneous.
16. People are expected to have a great deal of social grace and polish.
17. Untidy reports or ones that depart from a specified style are almost certain to be returned unaccepted.
18. Most people here go to lots of parties and other social activities.
19. There are many facilities and opportunities for individual creative activity.
20. Most people here love to dance.
21. Personality and pull are more important than competence in getting ahead around here.
22. The administrative staff are often joked about or criticized.
23. Most activities here are planned carefully.
24. People here speak up openly and freely.
25. People here are not only expected to have ideas but to do something about them.
26. Good manners and making a good impression are important here.
27. The activities of charities and social agencies are strongly supported.
28. Criticism is taken as a personal affront in this organization.
29. Neatness in this place is the rule rather than the exception.
30. Male-female relationships sometimes become quite serious.
31. Many people here enjoy talking about poetry, philosophy or religion.
32. Everyone is helped to get acquainted.
33. All work assignments are laid out well in advance, so that people can plan their own schedules accordingly.
34. People here thrive on difficulty-the tougher things get, the harder everyone works.
35. Individuals who are not properly groomed are likely to have this called to their attention.
36. Service to the community is regarded as a major responsibility of the institution.
37. People here are not really concerned with deep philosophical or ethical matters.
38. Good work is really recognized around here.
39. Work is checked to see if tit is done properly and on time.
40. Administrators are practical and efficient in the way they dispatch their business.
41. There are no favorites in this place; everyone gets treated alike.
42. People here can get so absorbed in their work they often lose all sense of time or personal comfort.
43. People frequently do things on the spur of the moment.
44. Proper social forms and manners are not particularly important here.

45. Few people here are challenged by deep thinking.
46. People set high standards of achievement for themselves here.
47. New ideas are always being tried here.
48. People here tend to take the easy way out when things get tough.
49. Administrators put a lot of energy and enthusiasm into directing this program.
50. People here talk about their future imaginatively and with enthusiasm.
51. There is a general idea of appropriate dress which everyone follows.
52. There always seem to be a lot of little quarrels going on here.
53. It's easy to get a group together for games, cokes, movies, etc.
54. The work atmosphere emphasizes efficiency and usefulness.
55. People spend a great deal of time together socially.
56. There is not wasted time here; everything has been planned right to the minute.
57. Discussions about improving society are common here.
58. Unusual or exciting plans are encouraged here.
59. People here feel free to express themselves impulsively.
60. People here expect to help out with fund drives, CARE, Red Cross, etc.
61. There is a specific place for everything and everyone here.
62. People here often get involved in long, serious intellectual discussions.
63. The administrative staff will go out of its way to help you with your work.
64. Many people here read magazines and books involving history, economics or political science.
65. Looking and acting "right" is expected.
66. The people here are easily moved by the misfortunes or distress of others.
67. Everyone has the same opportunity to make good.
68. Communications within the organization is always carried on through formal channels.
69. Most activities here present a real personal challenge.
70. People ask permission before deviating from common policies or practices.
71. There is a recognized group of leaders who receive special privileges.
72. People here feel they must really work hared because of the important nature of their work.
73. Parties are colorful and lively here.
74. Programs here are quickly changed to meet new conditions.
75. People are always carefully dressed and neatly groomed.
76. "Lending a helping hand" could very well be the motto of this place.
77. There is considerable interest in the analysis of value systems and the relativity of societies and ethics.
78. There is a lot of interest in the philosophy and goals of science here.
79. Frank discussions about sec are not uncommon among people here.
80. People here are usually quick to help each other out.

Scoring: T-True. Generally true or characteristic of the organization, is something which occurs or might occur, is the way people tend to feel or act. F-False. Generally false or not characteristic of the organization, is something which is not likely to occur, is not the way people tend to feel or act.

Reprinted with permission of Carl R. Steinhoff.

Communication

Communication Relationships Scale
Receiver Information Scale

Goldhaber, G. et al. 1977. The ICA communication audit survey instrument. International Communication Association.

Comments: This survey is composed of two related questionnaires: the Communication Relationships Scale and the Receiver Information Scale. The Communication Relationships Scale is a 15-item questionnaire which measures communication skills between supervisor and subordinates. It taps behaviors applicable to an organizational setting. The Receiver Information Scale consists of 13 items focusing on organizational topic areas extracted from the Communications Relationships Scale.

Sample: One study used 300 faculty from a midwestern university.

Reliability: The Receiver Information Scale had coefficient alpha estimate of 0.88. The Communication Relationships Scale had four subscales (factors): immediate supervisor, 0.94; personal influence, 0.81; co-workers, 0.76; and top management, 0.88.

Validity: No validity studies were mentioned other than the factor analysis discussed below.

Factor Analysis: A principal component analysis produced four factors for the Communication Relationships Scale. The factor names are listed above under reliability. The Receiver Information Scale is considered to be a unidimensional scale.

References:
Goldhaber, G. et al. 1977. The ICA Communication Audit Survey Instrument: 1977 Organizational Norms. Paper presented at the International Communication Association Convention.

Goldhaber, G. et al. 1978. Organizational communication. *Human Communication Research* 5:79-96.

McDowell, E.E. 1985. Faculty members' perceptions of information adequacy and communication relationships in their world of work. Paper presented at the Speech Communication Association. ERIC ED 263 638.

Communication Relationship Scale

1. My relationship with the chair/head of my department is satisfying.
2. I trust my chair/head.
3. My chair/head listens to me.
4. My chair/head is honest with me.
5. My chair/head is friendly with his/her faculty members.
6. I can tell my chair/head when things are going wrong.
7. My chair/head praises me for a good job.
8. I have a say in decisions that affect my job.
9. I influence operations in my department.
10. I have a part in accomplishing my organization's goals.
11. I trust my co-workers.
12. My co-workers get along with each other.
13. My relationship with my co-workers is satisfying.
14. I trust top management.
15. Top administrators are sincere in their efforts to communicate with faculty members.

Scoring: 1 = Strongly Agree; 2 = Agree; 3 = Uncertain; 4 = Disagree; and 5 = Strongly Disagree.

Reprinted with permission of the author.

Receiving Information Scale

1. How well I am doing in my position
2. My job duties
3. Department policies
4. Pay and benefits
5. How technical changes affect my position
6. Mistakes and failures of my department
7. How I am being judged
8. How my job related problems are being handled
9. How department decisions are made that affect my position
10. Promotion and advancement opportunities in my department
11. Important new program developments in my organization
12. How my job relates to the total department
13. Specific problems faced by administration

Scoring: 1 = Very Little; 2 = Little; 3 = Some; 4 = Great; and 5 = Very Great.

Reprinted with permission of the author.

Communicator Competence Questionnaire

Monge, P.R. et al. nd. Communicator competence in the workplace: Model testing and scale development. Communication Yearbook 5.

Comments: The 12-item CCQ was developed to measure communication competence in either supervisors or subordinates. Supervisors are asked to evaluate their subordinates and subordinates evaluate the supervisor.

Scale Construction: Items were developed to represent encoding and decoding skills appropriate for the workplace. Seven encoding items focus on specific behaviors such as being able to express one's ides clearly, having a good command of the language, and being easy to understand. Five decoding items focus on skills such as listening, responding to messages quickly, and attentiveness.

Sample: Samples were taken from two large firms in the same industry in the midwest. One sample consisted of 220 respondents--supervisor-subordinate dyads. The second sample consisted of 60 staff people of manufacturing firm.

Validity: Convergent validity was assessed by correlating the competence scores on each factor with two global measures of competence. This analysis was conducted for both the supervisor and the subordinate data. The correlation between these measures was 0.74 offering reasonably good evidence for the convergent validity of the scales.

Factor Analysis: An oblique confirmatory factor analysis produced two factors--an encoding factor and a decoding factor. The two factors are free to covary and are significantly correlated.

References:
Level, D.A. and L. Johnson. 1978. Accuracy of information flows within the supervisor/subordinate relationship. *Journal of Business Communication* 15:13-22.

Wiemann, J.M. 1977. Explication and test of a model of communicative competence. *Human Communication Research* 3:195-213.

Communication Competence Questionnaire

1.   My subordinate has a good command of the language.
2.   My subordinate is sensitive to others' needs of the moment.
3.   My subordinate typically gets right to the point.
4.   My subordinate pays attention to what other people say to him or her.
5.   My subordinate can deal with others effectively.
6.   My subordinate is a good listener.
7.   My subordinate's writing is difficult to understand.
8.   My subordinate expresses his or her ideas clearly.
9.   My subordinate is difficult to understand when he or she speaks.
10.   My subordinate generally says the right thing at the right time.
11.   My subordinate is easy to talk to.
12.   My subordinate usually responds to messages (memos, phone calls, reports, etc.) quickly.

Scoring: YES! = very strong agreement; YES = strong agreement; yes = mild agreement; ? = neutral feelings of the language; NO! = very strong disagreement; NO = strong disagreement; no = mild disagreement.

Reprinted with permission of Sage Publications, Inc.

Communication Effectiveness Questionnaire

Viggiano, M.A. 1990. The relationship between the communicator style of the principal and the principal's effectiveness as a communicator in instructional matters. Ed.D. dissertation New York University.

Comments: This instrument is an adaptation, and refinement, of a questionnaire developed by the University of Washington for the Seattle Schools for use in their effective schools project. The instrument is designed to determine teachers' perceptions of the principal's effectiveness as a communicator. Communicator effectiveness is the ability of the principal to communicate clearly to teachers about instructional matters.

Sample: The initial sample was composed of 331 teachers and ten principals.

Reliability: The alpha coefficient for the scale is 0.90.

Validity: A panel of judges, teachers and principals, were used to establish the content validity of the instrument.

References:
DeVito, J.A. 1976. *The interpersonal communication book.* New York: Harper and Row, Publishers.

Norton, R. 1983. *Communication style: Theory, applications and measures.* Beverly Hills: Sage Publications.

Communication Effectiveness Questionnaire

1. My principal provides a clear vision of what our school is all about.
2. My principal conducts formal discussions concerning the improvement of instruction.
3. My principal conducts formal discussions concerning student achievement.
4. Improved instructional practice results from discussion with my principal.
5. My principal provides me with information on current instructional topics.
6. My principal facilitates my participation in staff development opportunities.
7. My principal promotes an ongoing review of instructional materials.
8. My principal uses clearly established criteria for judging my performance in the classroom.
9. My principal provides frequent feedback concerning my classroom performance.
10. My principal is available to address my instructional concerns.

Scoring: A five-point Likert scale ranges from Little or None = 1 to Frequently or Always = 5.

Reprinted with permission from Martha Viggiano.

Conflict

Organizational Communication Conflict Instrument

Putnam, L. and C. Wilson. 1982 Communication strategies in organizational conflict: Reliability and validity of a measurement scale. In M. Burgoon, ed. *Communication Yearbook*. Beverly Hills, CA: Sage.

Comments: The authors contend that the OCCI is different from other conflict assessment instruments in that it focuses on behavioral choices that respondents make rather than a person's individual style of dealing with conflict.

Reliability: Internal consistency was assessed by the alpha coefficient. The three subscales were: nonconfrontation, 0.93; solution-orientation, 0.88, and control, 0.82.

Factor Analysis: Factor analysis produced three factors that account for 56% of the common variance. The nonconfrontation dimension consists of both smoothing and avoidance strategies; solution-orientation consists of compromise and collaborative strategies; and control refers to the polarized behaviors of the individual in group situations.

References:
Schuelke, D. and E. McDowell. 1990. A study of the relationship between willingness to communicate and preferred conflict strategy: Implications for teaching communication and conflict. Paper presented at International Communication Association. ERIC ED 322 561.

Wilson, C. and M. Waltman. 1988. Assessing the Putnam-Wilson Organizational Communication Conflict Instrument (OCCI). *Management Communication Quarterly* 1:367-388.

Organizational Communication Conflict Instrument

1. I blend my ideas with others to create new alternatives for resolving conflict.
2. I shy away from topics that are sources of disputes.
3. I insist that my position be accepted during a conflict.
4. I suggest solutions that combine a variety of viewpoints.
5. I steer clear of disagreeable situations.
6. I avoid a person I suspect of wanting to discuss a disagreement.
7. I look for middle-of-the-road solutions.
8. I give in a little on my ideas when the other person also gives in.
9. I minimize the significance of conflict.
10. I integrate arguments into a solution from issues raised in a dispute.
11. I stress my point by hitting my fist on the table.
12. I will go fifty-fifty to reach a settlement.
13. I raise my voice when trying to get another person to accept my position.
14. I offer creative solutions in discussions of disagreement.
15. I keep quiet about views in order to avoid disagreements.
16. I frequently give in a little if the other person will meet me halfway.
17. I downplay the importance of a disagreement.
18. I reduce disagreements by saying they are insignificant.
19. I meet the opposition at the midpoint of our differences.
20. I assert my opinion forcefully.
21. I dominate arguments until the other person understands my position.
22. I suggest we work together to create solutions to disagreements.
23. I try to use everyone's ideas to generate solutions to problems.
24. I offer tradeoffs to reach solutions to problems.
25. I argue for my stance.
26. I withdraw when someone confronts me about a controversial issue.
27. I sidestep disagreements when they arise.
28. I try to smooth over disagreements by making them appear unimportant.
29. I stand firm in my views during a conflict.
30. I take a tough stand, refusing to retreat.

Scoring: Ranges from Strongly Agree = 1 to Strongly Disagree = 5.

Reprinted with permission of Earl E. McDowell.

Rahim Organizational Conflict Inventory II

Rahim, M.A. and C. Psenicka. 1984. Comparison of reliability and validity of unweighted and factor scales. *Psychological Reports* 55:439-445.

Comments: The 35-item ROCI II measures the degree of interpersonal conflict with superiors, subordinates, and peers.

Sample: Responses were received from 1,219 executives representing 25 different industries. The respondents represented top, middle, and lower management. The sample only included 50 women.

Reliability: The five scales obtained alpha coefficients ranging from 0.72 to 0.77.

Validity: Analysis of variance and discriminant functions analysis were used to determine whether the five conflict scales could discriminate how an executive handles conflict with boss, subordinates, or peers. An attempted was made to cross-validate the discriminant functions which correctly classified 52% of the cases into the three managerial groups.

Factor Analysis: Five factors were extracted with a principal factoring with a varimax rotation. The five factors accounted for 89% of the common variance. Only items with loadings greater than 0.40 were retained on the factor. The five scales (factors) are: integrating, obliging, dominating, avoiding, and compromising.

References:
Ashworth, M.A. 1989. A study of the conflict management styles of principals and superintendents in the public schools of Ohio. Ph.D. dissertation, Bowling Green State University.

Rahim, M.A. 1983. Rahim Organizational Conflict Inventory II. Palo Alto, CA: Consulting Psychologists Press.

Utley, M.E. et al. 1989. Personality and interpersonal conflict management. *Journal of Personality and Individual Differences* 10:287-293.

Rahim Organizational Conflict Inventory II

1. I try to investigate into an issue with my ___ to find a solution acceptable to us.
2. I generally try to satisfy the needs of my ___.
3. I attempt to avoid being "put on the spot" and try to keep my conflict with my ___ to myself.
4. I try to integrate my ideas with those of my ___ to come up with a decision jointly.
5. I give some to get some.
6. I try to work with my ___ to find solutions to a problem which satisfy our expectations.
7. I usually avoid open discussion of my differences with my ___.
8. I usually hold on to my solution to a problem.
9. I try to find a middle course to resolve an impasse.
10. I use my influence to get my ideas accepted.
11. I use my authority to make a decision in my favor.
12. I usually accommodate the wishes of my ___.
13. I give in to the wishes of my ___.
14. I win some and I lose some.
15. I exchange accurate information with my ___ to solve a problem together.
16. I sometimes help my ___ to make a decision in his favor.
17. I usually allow concessions to my ___.
18. I argue my case with my ___ to show the merits of my position.
19. I try to play down our differences to reach a compromise.
20. I usually propose a middle ground for breaking deadlocks.
21. I negotiate with my ___ so that a compromise can be reached.
22. I try to stay away from disagreement with my ___.
23. I avoid an encounter with my ___.
24. I use my expertise to make a decision in my favor.
25. I often go along with the suggestions of my ___.
26. I use "give and take" so that a compromise can be made.
27. I am generally firm in pursuing my side of the issue.
28. I try to bring all our concerns out in the open so that the issues can be resolved in the best possible way.
29. I collaborate with my ___ to come up with decisions acceptable to us.
30. I try to satisfy the expectations of my ___.
31. I sometimes use my power to win a competitive situation.
32. I try to keep my disagreement with my ___ to myself in order to avoid hard feelings.
33. I try to avoid unpleasant exchanges with my ___.
34. I generally avoid an argument with my ___.
35. I try to work with my ___ for a proper understanding of a problem.

Scoring: The word boss, subordinates, or peers appeared in each blank space in the instrument.

Reprinted with permission from C. Psenicka.

Culture

Organizational Culture Assessment Inventory

Steinhoff, C.R. and R.G. Owens. 1988. The Organizational Culture Inventory: A metaphorical analysis of organizational culture in educational settings. Paper presented at American Educational Research Association.

Comments: This instrument was developed as an objective measure of organizational culture. Two major questions were of concern: (1) What are the essential factors which define the metaphor, Organizational Culture? and (2) How can these factors be evaluated objectively in a given organization? Organizational culture is a pattern of basic assumptions developed by a given group as it learns to cope with its problems of external adaptation and internal integration. The study of patterns of these assumptions has focused on control mechanisms, values, norms, history, traditions, ceremonies, rituals, heroes, symbols, and informal networks, as well as internalized solutions to internal and external problems.

Scale Construction: A taxonomy structure of organizational culture was developed from a review of the literature. This taxonomy has six dimensions that define the culture of a school: (1) the history of the organization; (2) values and beliefs of the organization; (3) myths and stories that explain the organization, (4) cultural norms of the organization, (5) traditions, rituals, and ceremonies, and (6) heroes and heroines of the organization.

Sample: The development of the instrument constituted two samples: (1) Several classes of graduate students providing 56 responses representing 47 individual schools. (2) Data were collected from eight elementary schools which represented the major themes identified in the initial analysis.

Data Analysis: The analysis of the initial data produced descriptions of four cultural phenotypes that differentiate in terms of the metaphorical language recognized by respondents as characteristic of the schools in which they work.
1. The family -- Approximately one third of the respondents referred to their schools as the family, home, team, or womb. The principal was described as a parent (strong or weak), nurturer, friend, sibling, or coach.
2. Modern Times -- Many respondents described their schools using the metaphor of the machine. They were described as well oiled machines, political machines, beehives of activity, or rust machines.
3. The Cabaret -- Some respondents described their schools as a circus, a broadway show, a banquet, or a well-choreographed ballet performed by well-appreciated artists.
4. The Little Shop of Horrors -- A small percentage described their school as unpredictable, tension-filled nightmares having the characteristics of Paris during the French Revolution. Teachers in these schools lead isolated lives; there is little social activity.

References:
Owens, R.G. and C.R. Steinhoff. 1989. Towards a theory of organizational culture. *Journal of Educational Administration* 27:6-16.

Organizational Culture Assessment Inventory

1. Every school has a unique history all of its own. Teachers know something of that history even if they have not worked there for a long time, because people talk about things that went on in former times. Some of these events may have been powerful incidents in the community that affected the school, and others may be purely internal matters that might seem unimportant or even mundane to outsiders.

   Please describe in a brief paragraph some of the more important events or trends that helped to shape the character of your school as it is today.

2. Schools usually espouse some official, formal, public set of values and beliefs. Ordinarily these appear in handbooks, newsletters, speeches, and so on. But in day-to-day work, a school may sometimes seem to be operating from values and beliefs that are different from the official public statements. The latter values and beliefs are, of course, often implicitly understood but not often talked about.

   In a brief paragraph, please describe the actual, functional values and beliefs that are important in your school.

3. People who work in schools very often tell stories - perhaps mythical, or apocryphal, or humorous - that help to explain what life in them is really like.

   Briefly describe a common story that is likely to be told to a newcomer by an "old hand" in your school to impress upon the individual "how things are really done around here."

4. Every school has established but unwritten expectations for behavior on the job.

   In a brief paragraph, please describe some of the most important expectations that have to be met in your school in order to get along.

5. Schools often develop informal customs, or rituals, that are more or less unique. For example, in one school that we know of there is a bridge game going on in the teachers' lounge every day with different people sitting in as they come off of hall and cafeteria duty. In another school, the principal has an informal coffee klatch in the school kitchen every morning. and so on.

   In a brief paragraph, please describe any such rituals that are important in the daily life of your school.

6. Schools seem to have at least one person, either now or in the past, who is thought of with great respect (or even reverence) because he or she is/was so outstanding in the life of the school.

   If you can think of such an individual in the history of your school, please describe in a brief paragraph why it is that the individual is so well-regarded.

7. In responding to the previous questions, you have provided a rich description of important aspects of the culture of your school. But the culture of a school is a total entity, even greater than the sum of its parts. We now would like you to summarize the descriptions that you have provided by using metaphors as a way to convey the essence of the culture of your school. A metaphor identifies

one object with another and ascribes to the first object one or more qualities of the second. For example, some administrators speak of the school as a family.

People often use metaphors to succinctly describe complex ideas. For example, when we say that a school is a "well-oiled machine," that metaphor makes clear what that particular school is really like in the eyes of the people who work in it. For another example, for teachers to speak of a principal as being "Dr. Jekyll and Mr. Hyde" tells us a lot about the impact of the behavior of that individual principal on the teachers in that particular school.

In this sense, considering the descriptions that you have already written, what one best metaphor would you use to complete the following sentences:

    a. My school "is" a (an, the)
    b. Please explain why you chose this metaphor.
    c. The principal in my school "is" a (an, the)
    d. Please explain.
    e. The typical teacher in my school "is" a (an, the)
    f. Please explain why you chose this metaphor.
    g. The typical student in my school "is" a (an, the)
    h. Please explain why you chose this metaphor.
    I. The community in which my school is situated "is" a (an, the)
    j. Please explain.

8.   What, in your opinion, would be the metaphor for the ideal school?
9.   What, in your opinion, would be the metaphor for the ideal school principal?
10.   What, in your opinion, would be the metaphor for the ideal teacher?
11.   What, in your opinion, would be the metaphor for the ideal student?
12.   What, in your opinion, would be the metaphor for the ideal school community?

Scoring: Responses are scored on the basis of school metaphor.

Reprinted with permission of the author.

Decision Making

Decisional Participation Scale

Alutto, J.A. and J.A. Belasco. 1972. Patterns of teacher participation in school system decision making. *Educational Administration Quarterly* 9:27-41.

Comments: A 12-item instrument designed to measure a teacher's actual and desired rates of participation in decision making. Individuals can be categorized as decisional deprived, at equilibrium, or saturated.

Sample: Teachers were taken from two school districts in western New York State resulting in a sample of 454 teachers.

Reliability: Test-retest reliability estimates exceeded 0.80 for all sections of the questionnaire.

Validity: The Mohrman study cited below provides information on the validity and factor profile for the 12-item instrument. Three factors were found, one for actual participation and two for deprivation.

Definition of Factors: *Decisional deprivation* means current participation in decision making less than preferred; *Decisional equilibrium* means current participation equal to preferred; and *Decisional saturation* means current participation greater than desired.

References:
Alutto, J.A. and J.A. Belasco. 1974. A typology for participation in organizational decision making. *Administrative Science Quarterly.* 10:117-125.

Mohrman, A.M. et al. 1978. Participation in decision making: A multidimensional perspective. *Educational Administration Quarterly* 14:13-29.

Decisional Participation Scale

1. When a new faculty member is to be hired in your school or department, would you be involved in making such a decision?
    A. If yes, in what capacity?
    B. If you would be involved, with whom would you discuss this matter?
    C. Do you want to be involved in making such decisions?
    D. If you do, in what capacity?
    E. Who do you believe presently has the "final say" in deciding whether or not to hire a new faculty member in a given area?
    F. Who do you believe should have the "final say" in deciding whether or not to hire a new faculty member in a given area?

2. When school or department budgets are planned, would you be involved in their preparation?
    A. If yes, in what capacity?
    B. If you would be involved, with whom would you discuss this matter?
    C. Do you want to be involved in making such decisions?
    D. If you do, in what capacity?
    E. Who do you believe presently has the "final say" in deciding on departmental or school budgets?
    F. Who do you believe should have the "final say" in deciding on departmental or school budgets?

3. When a new textbook is needed for a course in your department of school, would you be involved in making such a decision?
    A. If yes, in what capacity?
    B. If you would be involved, with whom would you discuss this matter?
    C. Do you want to be involved in making such decisions?
    D. If you do, in what capacity?
    E. Who do you believe presently has the "final say" in selecting texts for courses?
    F. Who do you believe should have the "final say" in selecting texts for courses?

4. When one of your students becomes involved in academic or personal problems, would you be involved in deciding how to resolve the difficulties?
    A. If yes, in what capacity?
    B. If you would be involved, with whom would you discuss this matter?
    C. Do you want to be involved in making such decisions?
    D. If you do, in what capacity?
    E. Who do you believe presently has the "final say" in resolving such student problems?
    F. Who do you believe should have the "final say" in resolving such student problems?

5. When individual faculty assignments are considered, would you be involved in making such decisions?
    A. If yes, in what capacity?
    B. If you would be involved, with whom would you discuss this matter?
    C. Do you want to be involved in making such decisions?
    D. If you do, in what capacity?
    E. Who do you believe presently has the "final say" in designating faculty assignments?
    F. Who do you believe should have the "final say" in designating faculty assignments?

6. When a faculty member has a grievance, would you be involved in resolving the problem?
   A. If yes, in what capacity?
   B. If you would be involved, with whom would you discuss this matter?
   C. Do you want to be involved in making such decisions?
   D. If you do, in what capacity?
   E. Who do you feel <u>presently</u> has the "final say" in resolving faculty grievances?
   F. Who do you feel <u>should</u> have the "final say" in resolving faculty grievances?

7. When new instructional methods (e.g. team teaching) are suggested, would you be interested in making the decision whether to adopt them or not?
   A. If yes, in what capacity?
   B. If you would be involved, with whom would you discuss this matter?
   C. Do you want to be involved in making such decisions?
   D. If so, in what capacity?
   E. Who do you believe <u>presently</u> has the "final say" in deciding matters concerning new instructional methods?
   F. Who do you believe <u>should</u> have the "final say" in deciding matters concerning new instructional methods?

8. If new building facilities are needed, would you become involved in making such a decision?
   A. If so, in what capacity?
   B. If you would be involved, with whom would you discuss this matter?
   C. Do you want to be involved in making such decisions?
   D. If you do, in what capacity?
   E. Who do you believe <u>presently</u> has the "final say" concerning the construction of new facilities?
   F. Who do you believe <u>should</u> have the "final say" concerning the construction of new facilities?

9. When there are problems involving community groups (e.g. P.T.A., civil rights groups), would you become involved in eliminating the difficulties?
   A. If yes, in what capacity?
   B. If you would be involved, with whom would you discuss this matter?
   C. Do you want to be involved in making such decisions?
   D. If so, in what capacity?
   E. Who do you believe <u>presently</u> has the "final say" in determining how such difficulties are resolved?
   F. Who do you believe <u>should</u> have the "final say" in determining how such difficulties are resolved?

10. When there are problems with administrative services, (clerks, typists, etc.), would you become involved in resolving such difficulties?
    A. If yes, in what capacity?
    B. If you would be involved, with whom would you discuss this matter?
    C. Do you want to be involved in making such decisions?
    D. If so, in what capacity?
    E. Who do you believe <u>presently</u> has the "final say" about how such problems are resolved?
    F. Who do you believe <u>should</u> have the "final say" about how such matters are resolved?

11. Would you be involved in any decisions concerning faculty members' salaries?
    A. If yes, in what capacity?
    B. If you would be involved, with whom would you discuss this matter?
    C. Do you want to be involved in making such decisions?
    D. If so, in what capacity?
    E. Who do you believe <u>presently</u> has the "final say" in such matters?
    F. Who do you believe <u>should</u> have the "final say" in such matters?

12. Would you be involved in decisions concerning general instructional policy?
    A. If yes, in what capacity?
    B. If you would be involved, with whom would you discuss this matter?
    C. Do you want to be involved in making such decisions?
    D. If so, in what capacity?
    E. Who do you believe <u>presently</u> has the "final say" about instructional policies?
    F. Who do you believe <u>should</u> have the "final say" about instructional policies?

Scoring: Responses are Yes or No for each of the general twelve questions and C; for A and D a brief explanation is required; for B, E and F the title of the appropriate person is required; and also for B the title of the appropriate person next to most often and often is required.

Reprinted with permission of the author.

Shared Decision-Making Survey

King, R.L. and E.J. Meshanko. 1992. Shared decision making in schools: The locus of control. Paper presented at Association of Teacher Educators. Mimeo.

Comments: The survey assesses the degree of involvement of teachers in shared decision making within a school district. It is based on the question: Do teachers have a high personal stake in the decision? The assumption is made that if they have a personal involvement, interest in participation will be high. The survey is based on the literature, philosophy, and research which proposes that it is desirable for teacher participation in decision making in education as well as the corporate world. Corollary terms upon which this survey is based are: school-site management, school-based management, decentralized management, and shared governance.

Sample: The study was based on a stratified random sample which selected nine school districts from 499 in the state of Pennsylvania. All teachers, principals, and school board members responded to the survey. This was 1,935 teachers, 77 principals, and 81 school board members.

Reliability: Reliability estimate was 0.87. Type of reliability was not indicated.

References:
Marcoline, J.F. 1990. A survey of shared decision-making in Pennsylvania: Comparing teacher and administrative perceptions. Ph.D. dissertation, Indiana University of Pennsylvania.

Meshanko, E. 1990. Teacher decision-making: An analysis of teachers, principals, and school board members perspectives. Ph.D. dissertation, Indiana University of Pennsylvania.

Shared Decision-Making Survey

Section I
1. Hiring a faculty member.
2. Selecting new textbooks.
3. Setting or revising school goals.
4. Determine faculty assignments.
5. Determine faculty evaluation procedures.
6. Determine classroom discipline policies.
7. Determine faculty schedules.
8. Determine budget priorities.
9. Determine staff development programs.
10. Determine grading policies.

Scoring: Indicate the extent that teachers in your school district actually participate in the above situations: Not participate = 1; Provide or gather information = 2; Suggest possible alternative decisions = 3; Recommend a decision = 4; and Make the decision = 5.

Section II

11. Hiring a new faculty member.
12. Selecting new textbooks.
13. Setting or revising school goals.
14. Determine faculty.
15. Determine faculty evaluation procedures.
16. Determine classroom discipline policies.
17. Determine faculty schedules.
18. Determine budgeting priorities.
19. Determine staff development programs.
20. Determine grading policies.

Scoring: Please indicate the extent that teachers in your school district would like to participate in the above situations: (see response scale above).

Section III

21. Hiring a new faculty member.
22. Selecting new textbooks.
23. Setting or revising school goals.
24. Determine faculty assignments.
25. Determine faculty evaluation procedures.
26. Determine classroom discipline policies.
27. Determine faculty schedules.
28. Determine budgeting priorities.
29. Determine staff development programs.
30. Determine grading policies.

Scoring: To the extent that teachers are involved in shared decision-making, it indicates the procedure that allows for this involvement: No involvement = 1; Informal discussions with administrators = 2; Formal committees organized as the need arises = 3; On-going formal committee structure without board policy = 4; and Board policy for shared decision making = 5.

Reprinted with permission of the author.

Dogmatism

Dogmatism Scale (Form E)

Rokeach, M. 1960. *The open and closed mind.* New York: Basic Books.

Comments: This 40-item scale assesses individual differences in openness or closedness of belief systems. All the statements express an opinion and all statements are written in the negative. The items are based upon three dimensions of belief systems: belief-disbelief, central-peripheral, and time-perspective. The scale was refined through item analyses. Form E is the final version of the scale. In addition, the scale also assesses general authoritarianism and general intolerance. This is the most frequently cited instrument to measure dogmatism.

Scale Construction: Statements that reflected the characteristics of open and closed systems were written. Some of the items were the result of statements made by people who were considered to be closed-minded, while nine items came from the work of others. The scale went through five revisions. The initial scale contained 57 items; Form B had 43 items; Form C had 36 items; and Form D had 66 items. Forty items were taken from Form D and these became the final version, Form E.

Sample: Reliability data were gathered from samples of 959 university students attending Michigan State University, Ohio State University, and Purdue University in the Midwest; 207 university students attending New York University and Brooklyn College in New York; and 217 university students attending the University College in London as well as another British university. A group of 121 destitute veterans in New York and sample of 60 automobile factory workers participated in Great Britain.

Reliability: Corrected reliability for Form A was 0.70 and 0.75 for Form B. Form C had reliabilities lower than anticipated and therefore, Form D contained 30 new items. The corrected reliability for Form D was 0.91. Twenty-six items were deleted in order to shorten the scale. Form E had a corrected reliability of 0.81 for the British college sample and 0.78 for the British automobile workers. Odd-even reliability coefficients corrected by the Spearman-Brown formula for six samples of American and British college students ranged from 0.68 (Ohio State University) to 0.85 (Ohio State University). Test-retest reliabilities over a five-to six-month period were 0.71 for 58 Ohio State University students, and over a one-month period 0.84 for 17 veterans. Overall, reliabilities ranged from 0.68 to 0.93.

Validity: Two construct validity studies were conducted using known high and low dogmatic groups. In the first study, no significant differences were found between graduate students selected by their college professors to be in one or the other group. However, in the second study, when psychology graduate students selected other students as most and least dogmatic, significant differences were found. Other researchers have conducted studies to establish construct, predictive, concurrent, and criterion validity.

Definition of Dimensions: The scale contains items involving the belief-disbelief dimension (4 items) and items involving the central-peripheral dimension (36 items). The belief-disbelief dimension consists of: *isolation within and between belief* which deals with the *accentuation of differences between the belief and the disbelief systems* (1) and *the coexistence of contradictions within the belief system* (2 and 3) as well as *relative amount of knowledge possessed* (4). The central-peripheral dimension consists of: *specific content of primitive beliefs* which deals with the *beliefs regarding the aloneness, isolation, and helplessness of man* (5, 6, 7, and 8), *beliefs regarding the uncertainty of the future* (9, 10, 11, 12, and 13), *beliefs about self-adequacy and inadequacy* (14), and *self-aggrandizement as a defense against self-inadequacy* (15, 16, and 17). *Formal content of the intermediate belief region* deals with *authoritarianism* (18 and 19), *belief in the cause* (20, 21, 22, 23, 24, 25, and 26), and *intolerance* (27, 28, 29, 30, 31, 32, and 33). *Interrelations among primitive, intermediate, and peripheral beliefs* deals with the *tendency to make a party-line change* (34 and 35), *narrowing* (36), *attitude toward the past, present, and future* (37), and *knowing the future* (38, 39, and 40).

Data Analysis: Means and standard deviations are reported as well as normative data for the original samples on all five forms of the scale.

References:
Esposito, J. 1974. Supervisor personality and task performance. *Journal of Experimental Education* 42:17-20.

Kleiber, D. et al. 1973. The multi-dimensionality of locus of control. *Journal of Clinical Psychology* 29:411-416.

McColskey, W. and others. 1985. Predictors of principals' reliance on formal and informal sources of information. *Evaluation and Policy Analysis* 7:427-436.

Spivey, J.R. 1975. Dogmatism and the secondary social studies teachers' perspective. *Illinois School Research* 11:26-31.

Ward, G. R. et al. 1978. Personality profiles and dogmatism in undergraduate teacher education students. *Psychology in the Schools* 15:33-36.

Dogmatism Scale

1. The United States and Russia have just about nothing in common.
2. The highest form of government is a democracy and the highest form of democracy is run by those who are most intelligent.
3. Even though freedom of speech for all groups is a worthwhile goal, it is unfortunately necessary to restrict the freedom of certain political groups.
4. It is only natural that a person would have a much better acquaintance with ideas he believes in than with ideas he opposes.
5. Man on his own is a helpless and miserable creature.
6. Fundamentally, the world we live in is a pretty lonesome place.
7. Most people just don't give a "damn" for others.
8. I'd like it if I could find someone who would tell me how to solve my personal problems.
9. It is only natural for a person to be rather fearful of the future.
10. There is so much to be done and so little time to do it in.
11. Once I get wound up in a heated discussion I just can't stop.
12. In a discussion I often find it necessary to repeat myself several times to make sure I am being understood.
13. In a heated discussion I generally become so absorbed in what I am going to say that I forget to listen to what the others are saying.
14. It is better to be a dead hero than to be a live coward.
15. While I don't like to admit this even to myself, my secret ambition is to become a great man, like Einstein, or Beethoven, or Shakespeare.
16. The main thing in life is for a person to want to do something important.
17. If given the chance I would do something of great benefit to the world.
18. In the history of mankind there have probably been just a handful of really great thinkers.
19. There are a number of people I have come to hate because of the things they stand for.
20. A man who does not believe in some great cause has not really lived.
21. It is only when a person devotes himself to an ideal or cause that life becomes meaningful.
22. Of all the different philosophies which exist in this world there is probably only one which is correct.
23. A person who gets enthusiastic about too many causes is likely to be a pretty "wishy-washy" sort of person.
24. To compromise with our political opponents is dangerous because it usually leads to the betrayal of our own side.
25. When it comes to differences of opinion in religion we must be careful not to compromise with those who believe differently from the way we do.
26. In times like these, a person must be pretty selfish if he considers primarily his own happiness.
27. The worst crime a person could commit is to attack publicly the people who believe in the same thing he does.
28. In times like these it is often necessary to be more on guard against ideas put out by people or groups in one's own camp than by those in the opposing camp.
29. A group which tolerates too much differences of opinion among its own members cannot exist for long.
30. There are two kinds of people in this world: those who are for the truth and those who are against the truth.
31. My blood boils whenever a person stubbornly refuses to admit he's wrong.
32. A person who thinks primarily of his own happiness is beneath contempt.
33. Most of the ideas which get printed nowadays aren't worth the paper they are printed on.
34. In this complicated world of ours the only way we can know what's going on is to rely on leaders or experts who can be trusted.
35. It is often desirable to reserve judgment about what's going on until one has had a chance to hear the opinions of those one respects.
36. In the long run the best way to live is to pick friends and associates whose tastes and beliefs are the same as one's own.

37. The present is all too often full of unhappiness. It is only the future that counts.
38. If a man is to accomplish his mission in life, it is sometimes necessary to gamble "all or nothing at all."
39. Unfortunately, a good many people with whom I have discussed important social and moral problems don't really understand what's going on.
40. Most people just don't know what's good for them.

Scaling: I agree a little = 1; I agree on the whole = 2; I agree very much = 3; I disagree a little = -1; I disagree on the whole = -2; and I disagree very much = -3. For scoring purposes, 4 is added to each item score, thus creating a 1-to-7 scale.

Interpersonal Relations

Machiavellianism Scales (Mach Scales)

Christie, R. and F.L. Geis. 1970. *Studies in Machiavellianism*. New York: Academic Press.

Comments: The Mach IV examines how an individual deals with other individuals; specifically it assesses how manipulable an individual is in interpersonal relationships. A "Kiddie Mach" is also available. This is one of the most frequently used instruments to measure interpersonal relationships.

Scale Construction: Originally, 71 items were written based on the works of Machiavelli. These items fell into three categories: the nature of interpersonal tactics (32); views of human nature (28); and abstract or generalized morality (11). Sixty items correlated at the 0.05 level with a total Mach score. The ten highest items worded in the Machiavellian direction and the ten highest items worded in the opposite direction were selected for the Mach IV scale.

Sample: The original sample consisted of 1,196 university students in Iowa, New York, and North Carolina.

Reliability: Split-half reliabilities averaged 0.79. Average item-test correlation was 0.38.

Validity: Concurrent validation studies have been conducted using correlations between the Mach IV and the Mach V scales. Information is included about predictive validation studies.

Factor Analysis: Factor analysis yielded three factors: seven items on duplicity (2, 3, 6, 7, 9, 10, and 15); seven items on negativism (1, 5, 8, 12, 13, 18, and 20); and four items on distrust of people (4, 11, 14, and 16).

References:
Richford, M.L. and J.C. Fortune. 1984. The secondary principal's job satisfaction in relation to two personality constructs. *Education* 105:17-20.

Shea, M.T. and J.R. Beatty. 1983. Measuring Machiavellianism with Mach V: A psychometric investigation. *Journal of Personality Assessment* 47:509-513.

Machiavellianism Scales (Mach Scales)

1. Never tell anyone the real reason you did something unless it is useful to do so.
2. The best way to handle people is to tell them what they want to hear.
3. One should take action only when sure it is morally right.
4. Most people are basically good and kind.
5. It is safest to assume that all people have a vicious streak and it will come out when they are given a chance.
6. Honesty is the best policy in all cases.
7. There is no excuse for lying to someone else.
8. Generally speaking, men won't work hard unless they're forced to do so.
9. All in all, it is better to be humble and honest than to be important and dishonest.
10. When you ask someone to do something for you, it is best to give the real reasons for wanting it rather than giving reasons which carry more weight.
11. Most people who get ahead in the world lead clean, moral lives.
12. Anyone who completely trusts anyone else is asking for trouble.
13. The biggest difference between most criminals and other people is that the criminals are stupid enough to get caught.
14. Most men are brave.
15. It is wise to flatter important people.
16. It is possible to be good in all respects.
17. Barnum was wrong when he said that there's a sucker born every minute.
18. It is hard to get ahead without cutting corners here and there.
19. People suffering from incurable diseases should have the choice of being put painlessly to death.
20. Most men forget more easily the death of their father than the loss of their property.

Scaling: Agree Strongly = 3; Agree Somewhat = 2; Agree Slightly = 1; Disagree Slightly = -1; Disagree Somewhat = -2; and Disagree Strongly = -3. Scoring is reversed for the following items: 3, 4, 6, 7, 9, 10, 11, 14, 16, and 17. For scoring purposes. Agree Strongly receives a score of 7; No Response receives a score of 4; and Disagree Strongly receives a score of 1. For reversed items, the scoring is reversed. Since a constant of 20 is added to all scores, scores range from a low of 40 to a high of 160 with 100 being a neutral score.

Reprinted with permission of Delores Kreisman, executor of the Estate of Richard Christie and Academic Press.

Fundamental Interpersonal Relationship Orientation (FIRO-B)

Schutz, W. 1978. *FIRO Awareness Scales Manual*. Palo Alto, CA: Consulting Psychologists Press.

Comments: FIRO-B refers to a theory of interpersonal relations that is helpful in predicting interaction between two individuals. The 54-item FIRO-B examines the behavior that a person exhibits to others and the behavior that a person desires from others in three categories: inclusion, control, and affection. Each of the six Guttman scales contains nine items. The FIRO-B has been replaced with Element B which addresses concerns in the areas of response categories, item wording, and interpretation in scoring. This is one of the most frequently cited instruments to measure interpersonal relationships.

Sample: The original sample consisted of over 1,000 participants. The majority were university students and there was a small sample of Air Force personnel.

Reliability: The reproducibility coefficients for the six scales had a mean of 0.94. Reproducibility coefficients ranged from 0.93 to 0.94. Test-retest reliability coefficients (Harvard sample) over a one-month interval ranged from 0.71 to 0.82, with a mean of 0.76 for the six scales.

Validity: Information about content and concurrent validity is included in Part I of the manual. In addition, FIRO-B scores are provided for 12 occupational groups. Part II contains a review of the research studies and various applications of the FIRO Awareness Scales from 1958-1977.

Definition of Scales: *Inclusion* is defined as the need to form and continue a satisfying relationship with people in terms of interaction and association. Positive inclusion refers to words such as: mingle, communicate, companion, and togetherness. Negative inclusion refers to words such as: outcast, lonely, withdrawn, and ignore. *Control* is defined as the need to form and continue a satisfying relationship with people in terms of control and power. Positive control refers to such words as: power, authority, superior, and leader. Negative control refers to words such as: resistance, anarchy, submissive, and follower. *Affection* is defined as the need to form and continue a satisfying relationship with people in terms of love and affection. Positive affection refers to words such as: like, personal, intimate, and friend. Negative affection refers to words such as: dislike, rejecting, hate, and cool.

References:

Fuqua, A.B. 1983. Professional attractiveness, inside sponsorship, and perceived paternalism as predictors of upward mobility of public school superintendents. Ed.D. dissertation, Virginia Polytechnic Institute and State University.

Lachiondo, D.K. 1985. The effects of selected personal and role variables of assistant principal-disciplinarians on the reported use of due process in student discipline. Ph.D. dissertation, University of Idaho.

Mulinaro, M.E. 1990. Relationship between the interpersonal relationship variables of inclusion, control and openness and self-perceived preferred leadership styles of deans and department chairpersons in the public and private colleges of West Virginia. Ed.D. dissertation, West Virginia University.

Phelps, H.A. 1989. A comparative investigation of the self-perceptions of the behavioral characteristics of principals of selected high schools. Ed.D. dissertation, Temple University.

Fundamental Interpersonal Relationship Orientation (FIRO-B)

1.   I try to be with people.
2.   I let other people decide what to do.
3.   I join social groups.
4.   I try to have close relationships with people.
5.   I tend to join social organizations when I have an opportunity.
6.   I let other people strongly influence my actions.
7.   I try to be included in informal social activities.
8.   I try to have close, personal relationships with people.
9.   I try to include other people in my plans.
10. I let other people control my actions.
11. I try to have people around me.
12. I try to get close and personal with people.
13. When people are doing things together I tend to join them.
14. I am easily led by people.
15. I try to avoid being alone.
16. I try to participate in group activities.
17. I try to be friendly to people.
18. I let other people decide what to do.
19. My personal relations with people are cool and distant.
20. I let other people take charge of things.
21. I try to have close relationships with people.
22. I let other people strongly influence my actions.
23. I try to get close and personal with people.
24. I let other people control my actions.
25. I act cool and distant with people.
26. I am easily led by people.
27. I try to have close, personal relationships with people.
28. I like people to invite me to things.
29. I like people to act close and personal with me.
30. I try to influence strongly other people's actions.
31. I like people to invite me to join in their activities.
32. I like people to act close toward me.
33. I try to take charge of things when I am with people.
34. I like people to include me in their activities.
35. I like people to act cool and distant toward me.
36. I try to have other people do things the way I want them done.
37. I like people to ask me to participate in their discussions.
38. I like people to act friendly toward me.
39. I like people to invite me to participate in their activities.
40. I like people to act distant toward me.
41. I try to be the dominant person when I am with people.
42. I like people to invite me to things.
43. I like people to act close toward me.
44. I try to have other people do things I want done.
45. I like people to invite me to join their activities.
46. I like people to act cool and distant toward me.
47. I try to influence strongly other people's actions.

48. I like people to include me in their activities.
49. I like people to act close and personal with me.
50. I try to take charge of things when I'm with people.
51. I like people to invite me to participate in their activities.
52. I like people to act distant toward me.
53. I try to have other people do things the way I want them done.
54. I take charge of things when I'm with people.

Scaling: Scoring for items 1-16 and 41-54 is: 1 = Never; 2 = Rarely; 3 = Occasionally; 4 = Sometimes; 5 = Often; and 6 = Usually. Scoring for items 17-40 is: 1 = Nobody; 2 = One or Two People; 3 = A Few People; 4 = Some People; 5 = Many People; and 6 = Most People. Scoring can also be relative or normative. More detailed information about scoring is covered in the manual. In addition, scoring templates are available.

Reprinted with permission of Will Schutz Associates.

Element B: Behavior

Schutz, W. 1992. Beyond FIRO-B-Three new theory-derived measures-Element B: Behavior, Element F: Feelings, Element S: Self. *Psychological Reports* 70:915-937.

Comments: Element B is the revised form of the FIRO-B. According to the author, it is a much stronger instrument both theoretically and psychometrically. Element B: Behavior measures three areas of interpersonal behavior: inclusion, control, and openness (openness replaces affection).

Sample: Fifty students in an adult education class participated in the development of Element B. In addition, 43 people from NASA, 23 from army intelligence, and 84 university students completed the instrument in order to obtain stable reproducibility coefficients.

Reliability: The reproducibility coefficients for the six scales had a mean of 0.92. Reproducibility coefficients ranged from 0.89 to 0.93. Since the test-retest reliability coefficient (over a three-week interval) for the FIRO-B had a mean of 0.76 for the six scales, this figure was used as an approximation of the stability of the scales of Element B.

Definition of Scales: *Inclusion* refers to reaching the correct amount of contact with individuals (do things with, share). *Control* refers to reaching the correct amount of control over individuals (take charge, influence). *Openness* refers to reaching the correct amount of openness (disclose, tell true feelings).

Data Analysis: Reproducibility and means for scales of Element B as well as mean scores based on age and sex are provided. Pearson intercorrelations of scales on Element B and FIRO-B are included.

Reference:
Schutz, W. 1987. *Guide to Element B.* Mill Valley, CA: Will Schutz Associates.

Element B

1.   I seek out people to be with.
2.   People decide what to do when we are together.
3.   I am totally honest with my close friends.
4.   People invite me to do things.
5.   I am the dominant person when I am with people.
6.   My close friends tell me their real feelings.
7.   I join social groups.
8.   People strongly influence my actions.
9.   I confide in my close friends.
10.   People invite me to join their activities.
11.   I get other people to do things I want done.
12.   My close friends tell me about private matters.
13.   I join social organizations.
14.   People control my actions.
15.   I am more comfortable when people do not get too close.
16.   People include me in their activities.
17.   I strongly influence other people's actions.
18.   My close friends do not tell me all about themselves.
19.   I am included in informal social activities.
20.   I am easily led by people.
21.   People should keep their private feelings to themselves.
22.   People invite me to participate in their activities.
23.   I take charge when I am with people socially.
24.   My close friends let me know their real feelings.
25.   I include people in my plans.
26.   People decide things for me.
27.   There are some things I do not tell anyone.
28.   People include me in their social affairs.
29.   I get people to do things the way I want them done.
30.   My closest friends keep secrets from me.
31.   I have people around me.
32.   People strongly influence my ideas.
33.   There are some things I would not tell anyone.
34.   People ask me to participate in their discussions.
35.   I take charge when I am with people.
36.   My friends confide in me.
37.   When people are doing things together I join them.
38.   I am strongly influenced by what people say.
39.   I have at least one friend to whom I can tell anything.
40.   People invite me to parties.
41.   I strongly influence other people's ideas.
42.   My close friends keep their feelings a secret from me.
43.   I look for people to be with.
44.   Other people take charge when we work together.
45.   There is a part of myself I keep private.
46.   People invite me to join them when we have free time.
47.   I take charge when I work with people.
48.   At least two of my friends tell me their true feelings.

49. I participate in group activities.
50. People often cause me to change my mind.
51. I have close relationships with few people.
52. People invite me to do things with them.
53. I see to it that people do things the way I want them to.
54. My friends tell me about their private lives.

Scaling: Respondents describe Expressed and Received behavior as well as Perceived (What I See) and Wanted (What I Want) behavior. What I See ranges from disagree to agree, while What I Want ranges from want to don't want. Each scale receives a score from 0 to 9. The higher the score, the greater the agreement. Dissatisfaction is the difference between the scores on What I Want and What I See. Information is provided to convert FIRO-B scores into Element B scores.

Reprinted with permission of Will Schutz Associates.

Job Commitment

Work Commitment Index

Blau, G.J. et al. 1993. On developing a general index of work commitment. *Journal of Vocational Behavior*. 42:298-314.

Comments: The purpose of this research was to design a general work commitment index with distinct work commitment factors similar to the procedure used with job satisfaction to develop the Job Descriptive Index. This index demonstrates that employees view their job, organization, occupation, and work in general differently.

Scale Construction: Work commitment was measured across four facets: career (occupation), job, value, and organization. The 31 items measuring career came from four scales: Blau's (1988) career commitment scale; Gould's (1979) career involvement scale; Greenhaus's (1971) general attitude toward work subscale; and Sekaran's (1982) career salience measure. The 10 items measuring job facet came from Kanungo's (1982) job involvement scale. The 10 items measuring value facet came from Kanungo's measure of work involvement and Blood's (1969) Protestant work ethic scale. The eight items measuring organization facet came from Meyer and Allen's (1984) affective commitment scale.

Sample: The participants in the first study consisted of 407 part-time MBA students from three universities in the Philadelphia area and 383 part-time MBA students (seven weeks later). There were 328 students who completed the survey both times. The participants in the second study consisted of 339 full-time registered nurses from three hospitals in a large eastern city.

Reliability: The alpha coefficients (Cronbach) were 0.91 (occupational commitment), 0.81 (value of work), 0.82 (organizational commitment), and 0.83 (job involvement). Test-retest reliabilities were 0.90 (occupational commitment), 0.91 (job involvement), 0.92 (value of work), and 0.94 (organizational commitment).

Validity: Confirmatory factor analysis was used to test the discriminant validity of the four scales.

Factor Analysis: Although principal components analyses yielded five factors, only four factors were used to develop four separate scales. There were minor differences between the varimax rotation and the oblique rotation. Therefore, the results of the oblique rotation were reported. The four factors are: 11 items on occupational commitment (1-11); seven items on the value of work (12-18); six items on organizational commitment (19-25); and seven items on job involvement (26-31).

Data Analysis: Means, standard deviations, coefficient alpha, test-retest reliabilities, and correlations for the four factors are reported.

References:
Blau, G. 1988. Further exploring the meaning and measurement of career commitment. *Journal of Vocational Behavior* 32:284-297.

Blood, M. 1969. Work values and job satisfaction. *Journal of Applied Psychology* 53:456-459.

Gould, S. 1979. Characteristics of planners in upwardly mobile occupations. *Academy of Management Journal* 22:539-550.

Greenhaus, J. 1971. An investigation of the role of career salience in vocational behavior. *Journal of Vocational Behavior* 1:209-226.

Kanungo, R.N. 1982. Measurement of job and work involvement. *Journal of Applied Psychology* 3:341-349.

Meyer, J. and N. Allen. 1984. Testing the "side-bet theory" of organizational commitment: Some methodological considerations. *Journal of Applied Psychology* 69:372-378.

Sekaran, U. 1982. An investigation of the career salience in dual career families. *Journal of Vocational Behavior* 20:111-119.

Work Commitment Index

The following are not completed items. The respondent completes the statement with the personal pronoun or article as needed.

1. If could, would go into a different occupation
2. Can see self in occupation for many years
3. Occupation choice is a good decision
4. If could, would not choose occupation
5. No money need, still continue in occupation
6. Sometimes dissatisfied with occupation
7. Like occupation too well to give up
8. Education/training not for occupation
9. Have ideal occupation for life work
10. Wish chosen different occupation
11. Disappointed that entered occupation
12. Most important things involve job
13. Job only small part of who I am
14. Live, eat, and breathe my job
15. Most interests centered around my job
16. Most personal life goals are job-oriented
17. Job is very central to my existence
18. Like to be absorbed in job most of time
19. Hard work makes self a better person
20. Wasting time as bad as wasting money
21. Person's worth is how well does job
22. Better to have more responsible job
23. People should get involved in work
24. Work should be central to life
25. Life goals should be work-oriented
26. Don't feel like belong to organization
27. Not emotionally attached to organization
28. Organization has personal meaning for me
29. Do not feel like part of organization
30. Glad to spend rest of days with organization
31. Organization's problems are mine too

Scaling: Strongly Disagree = 1; Moderately Disagree = 2; Slightly Disagree = 3; Slightly Agree = 4; Moderately Agree = 5; and Strongly Agree = 6.

Reprinted with permission of the author.

Organizational Commitment Questionnaire

Mowday, R.T. et al. 1979. The measurement of organizational commitment. *Journal of Vocational Behavior* 14:224-247.

Comments: The 15-item OCQ measures organizational commitment which is defined as "the relative strength of an individual's identification with and involvement in a particular organization." Commitment-related behaviors fall into three categories: belief and acceptance of organizational goals and values; willingness to exert effort for the organization; and a desire to continue membership in the organization. A nine item OCQ is also available.

Sample: The original sample of the OCQ consisted of 2,563 workers from the following nine work organizations: public employees (569), classified university employees (243), hospital employees (382), bank employees (411), telephone company employees (605), scientists and engineers (119), auto company managers (115), psychiatric technicians (60), and retail management trainees (212).

Reliability: The alpha coefficients ranged from 0.82 to 0.93 for psychiatric technicians; 0.84 for scientists and engineers; 0.88 for hospital employees (short form) and bank employees; and 0.90 for public employees, classified university employees (short form), telephone company employees, and auto company managers. The median alpha is 0.90. Test-retest reliabilities for psychiatric technicians over a 2-month interval was 0.53; over a 3-month interval was 0.63; and over a 4-month interval was 0.75.

Validity: Factor analyses conducted on six samples yielded a single factor. Convergent validity was established by correlating the Sources of Organizational Attachment Questionnaire with the OCQ. Convergent validities ranged from 0.63 to 0.74. Discriminate validity was established by comparing the OCQ to one measure of job involvement, one measure of career satisfaction, and one measure of job satisfaction. Predictive validity was established by examining the relationship between performance and organizational commitment. Evidence is provided to support all three validity claims.

Factor Analysis: Factor analyses (varimax rotation) were conducted on the six samples. Each analysis yielded a one-factor solution.

Data Analysis: Means, standard deviations, item analyses correlations, and norms are reported.

References:
Dean, R. and J.P. Wanous. 1983. Reality shock and commitment: A study of new employees' expectations. Paper presented at American Psychological Association. ERIC ED 237 852.

Dornstein, M. and Y. Matalon. 1989. A comprehensive analysis of the predictors of organizational commitment: A study of voluntary army personnel in Israel. *Journal of Vocational Behavior* 34:192-203.

Porter, L.W. et al. 1976. Organizational commitment and managerial turnover: A longitudinal study. *Organizational Behavior and Human Performance* 15:87-98.

Organizational Commitment Questionnaire

1. I am willing to put a great deal of effort beyond that normally expected in order to help this organization be successful.
2. I talk up this organization to my friends as a great organization to work for.
3. I feel very little loyalty to this organization.
4. I would accept almost any type of job assignment in order to keep working for this organization.
5. I find that my values and the organization's values are very similar.
6. I am proud to tell others that I am part of this organization.
7. I could just as well be working for a different organization as long as the type of work was similar.
8. This organization really inspires the very best in me in the way of job performance.
9. It would take very little change in my present circumstances to cause me to leave this organization.
10. I am extremely glad that I chose this organization to work for over others I was considering at the time I joined.
11. There's not too much to be gained by sticking with this organization indefinitely.
12. Often, I find it difficult to agree with this organization's policies on important matters relating to its employees.
13. I really care about the fate of this organization.
14. For me this is the best of all possible organizations for which to work.
15. Deciding to work for this organization was a definite mistake on my part.

Scaling: Strongly Disagree = 1; Moderately Disagree = 2; Slightly Disagree = 3; Neither Disagree nor Agree = 4; Slightly Agree = 5; Moderately Agree = 6; and Strongly Agree = 7. The scoring is reversed for items 3, 7, 9, 11, 12, and 15. Responses are added and divided by 15 to reach an overall score.

Reprinted with permission of Lyman W. Porter.

Job Involvement

Job Involvement Scale

Lodahl, T. and M. Kejner. 1965. The definition and measurement of job involvement. *Journal of Applied Psychology* 49:24-33.

Comments: The 20-item JIS measures job involvement, which is defined as "the degree to which a person's work performance affects his self-esteem." A six-item version consists of the following items: 3, 6, 8, 11, 15, and 18. The JIS is the most frequently cited instrument to measure job involvement. In addition, many instruments were based on their work.

Sample: The original samples consisted of: 137 nursing personnel (head nurses, staff nurses, registered nurses, practical nurses, nurse aides, and orderlies), 70 engineers, and 46 graduate students studying business administration.

Reliability: Corrected split-half correlation coefficients were 0.72 for nurses, 0.80 for engineers, and 0.89 for graduate students.

Validity: Information about discriminant validity is provided. Four sets of data measured the relationship between job involvement and other variables.

Factor Analysis: Multiple factor analytic procedures were performed and a three factor solution was accepted.

Data Analysis: Means and standard deviations are provided.

References:
Chadha, N.K. and R. Kaur. 1987. Correlational study of demographic variables with job involvement and job satisfaction in a public sector organization. *Perspectives in Psychological Researches* 10:11-18.

Chusmir. L.H. 1986. Gender differences in variables affecting job commitment among working men and women. *Journal of Social Psychology* 126:87-94.

Chusmir, L.H. and C.S. Koberg. 1986. Creativity differences among managers. *Journal of Vocational Behavior* 29:240-253.

Saal, F.E. 1978. Job involvement: A multivariate approach. *Journal of Applied Psychology* 63:53-61.

Job Involvement Scale

1. I'll stay overtime to finish a job, even if I'm not paid for it.
2. You can measure a person pretty well by how good a job he does.
3. The major satisfaction in my life comes from my job.
4. For me, mornings at work really fly by.
5. I usually show up for work a little early, to get things ready.
6. The most important things that happen to me involve my work.
7. Sometimes I lie awake at night thinking ahead to the next day's work.
8. I'm really a perfectionist about my work.
9. I feel depressed when I fail at something connected with my job.
10. I have other activities more important than my work.
11. I live, eat, and breathe my job.
12. I would probably keep working even if I didn't need the money.
13. Quite often I feel like staying home from work instead of coming in.
14. To me, my work is only a small part of who I am.
15. I am very much involved personally in my work.
16. I avoid taking on extra duties and responsibilities in my work.
17. I used to be more ambitious about my work than I am now.
18. Most things in life are more important than work.
19. I used to care more about my work, but now other things are more important to me.
20. Sometimes I'd like to kick myself for the mistakes I make in my work.

Scaling: Strongly Agree = 1; Agree = 2; Disagree = 3; and Strongly Disagree = 4. A high score represents low involvement.

Reprinted with permission of the author.

Job Satisfaction

Job Satisfaction Index

Brayfield, A.H. and H.F. Rothe. 1951. An index of job satisfaction. *Journal of Applied Psychology* 35:307-311.

Comments: The 18-item JSI provides an overall index of job satisfaction rather than measuring specific aspects.

Sample: Although different groups were used to develop the index, the final version of the index was given to two samples. The first sample consisted of 231 female office workers. The second sample consisted of 91 (49 men and 42 women) adult night school students attending classes in Personnel Psychology at the University of Minnesota.

Reliability: The scale was administered to 231 female office workers. The range of job satisfaction scores was 35-87. The mean score was 63.8 with a standard deviation of 9.4. The odd-even product moment reliability was 0.77 which was corrected by the Spearman-Brown formula to 0.87.

Validity: According to the authors, the individual items are evidence of face validity. In addition, 77 men who were members of an Army Specialized Training Program in personnel psychology at the University of Minnesota, were responsible for developing approximately 1,000 items. These items were edited and the remaining 246 items were sorted using the criteria established by Thurstone. The 77 adult judges agreed that the items expressed a feeling of satisfaction or dissatisfaction with a job and should therefore be included. An outside criterion was also used to establish validity. The scale was given to 91 adult night school students in classes in Personnel Psychology at the University of Minnesota. The 91 participants were then separated into two groups, personnel and non-personnel, based upon their employment. A comparison was made between the means of the two groups. Significant differences (0.05 level) were found between the two groups. Therefore, the evidence for the scale's validity is based upon the nature of the items, the method used to develop the scale, and its ability to differentiate between groups.

References:
Camp, W.G. 1987. Student misbehavior and job satisfaction of vocational agriculture teachers: A path analysis. ERIC ED 279 791.

Jones, J.J. 1983. The relationship between selected predictor variables and perceived job satisfaction of Oklahoma public school superintendents. Ed.D. Dissertation, Oklahoma State University

Tharrington, D.E. 1992. Perceived principal leadership behavior and reported teacher job satisfaction. Ed.D. dissertation, University of North Carolina, Chapel Hill.

Job Satisfaction Index

1. My job is like a hobby to me.
2. My job is usually interesting enough to keep me from getting bored.
3. It seems that my friends are more interested in their jobs.
4. I consider my job rather unpleasant.
5. I enjoy my work more than my leisure time.
6. I am often bored with my job.
7. I feel fairly well satisfied with my present job.
8. Most of the time I have to force myself to go to work.
9. I am satisfied with my job for the time being.
10. I feel that my job is no more interesting than others I could get.
11. I definitely dislike my work.
12. I feel that I am happier in my work than most other people.
13. Most days I am enthusiastic about my work.
14. Each day of work seems like it will never end.
15. I like my job better than the average worker does.
16. My job is pretty uninteresting.
17. I find real enjoyment in my work.
18. I am disappointed that I ever took this job.

Scaling: Strongly Agree = 1; Agree = 2; Undecided = 3; Disagree = 4; Strongly Disagree = 5. The scoring for items 1, 2, 5, 7, 9, 12, 13, 15, and 17 is reversed. The scores range from a low of 18 to a high of 90. The lower the score, the lower the level of job satisfaction.

Reprinted with permission of the author.

Teacher Job Satisfaction Questionnaire

Lester, P.E. 1984. Development of an instrument to measure teacher job satisfaction. Ph.D. dissertation, New York University.

Comments: The 77-item TJSQ is based on the work of Maslow and Herzberg. The TJSQ has been translated into Spanish, French, Arabic, and Mandarin. It has been used mainly in doctoral dissertations over the last decade.

Sample: A random sample of 620 teachers from elementary, junior high school, and senior high schools in New York City, Westchester, Nassau, and Suffolk Counties (New York) participated.

Reliability: The alpha coefficient (Cronbach) for entire scale is 0.93. Coefficients of internal consistency are 0.92 (supervision), 0.82 (colleagues and work itself), 0.83 (working conditions), 0.80 (pay), 0.73 (responsibility), 0.81 (advancement), 0.71 (security), and 0.74 (recognition). Coefficients for scales range from 0.71 (security) to 0.92 (supervision). The alpha coefficient for each factor, means, standard deviations, and alpha, if item deleted are provided in tabular form.

Validity: Content validation was performed through a panel of judges reducing the original number of items from 120 to 77. Statements with less than 80% agreement were either rewritten or rejected. The items were edited into a form specifically geared to teachers in an educational setting. Vaguely defined words, words with double meanings, emotionally loaded words, double negatives, and unclear words were eliminated, resulting in clear, concise, and direct statements of no more than 20 words. Approximately 50% of the items were written in a positive form, and 50% in a negative form to avoid response set bias. The data were cross-validated using a split-sample technique. Construct validity was obtained through factor analysis.

Factor Analysis: A nine factor orthogonal varimax solution was accepted using criterion of eigenvalues greater than or equal to unity. The nine factors are: 14 items on supervision (19, 73, 47, 11, 27, 71, 52, 34, 65, 70, 14, 62, 6, and 56); 10 items on colleagues (22, 57, 77, 17, 48, 35, 43, 63, 60, and 45); seven items on working conditions 64, 20, 40, 18, 31, 29, and 10); seven items on pay (53, 2, 72, 42, 67, 5, and 76); eight items on responsibility (75, 69, 74, 44, 24, 39, 21, and 61); nine items on work itself (30, 28, 51, 33, 8, 3, 54, 13, and 55); five items on advancement (59, 37, 1, 23, and 9); three items on security (25, 15, and 32); and three items on recognition (16, 7, and 58). The following eleven items had factor loadings below 0.30 (4, 12, 26, 36, 38, 41, 46, 49, 50, 66, and 68) and therefore, were not included in any further statistical analysis. They are filler items. Factor loading, communalities, item reversals, eigenvalues, etc. are reported.

Definitions of Factors: *Supervision* refers to supervisory style, which may be defined in terms of task-oriented behavior and person-oriented behavior. Task-oriented behavior requires direction and coordination of group activities to achieve the goals of the organization. Person-oriented behavior requires trust, respect, support, friendship, openness, and attempts to improve the environment. *Colleagues* are the teaching work group and the social aspects of the school setting. The teachers in the work group give and receive support and seek cooperation in the achievement of a common purpose or goal. The similarity of attitudes, the performance of jobs, the formation of personal relationships among fellow teachers, and an increase in self-esteem, are all aspects of social interaction. *Working Conditions* refer to the physical conditions of the work environment, as well as the overall aspects of the school organization as defined and communicated by its administrative policies. *Pay* refers to the annual income which may serve as indicator of recognition and achievement, or of failure. *Respon-*

sibility is the desire to be accountable for one's own work, to help one's students learn, and the opportunity to take part in policy or decision-making activities. *Work Itself* is the job of teaching or the tasks related to the job. It involves the freedom to institute innovative materials and to utilize one's skills and abilities in designing one's work (creativity) as well as the freedom to experiment and to influence or control what goes on in the job (autonomy). *Advancement* or promotion refers to a change in status or position, which may be equated with greater wages and power. *Security* refers to the school's policies regarding tenure, seniority, layoffs, pension, retirement, and dismissal. *Recognition* involves the attention, appreciation, prestige, and esteem of supervisors, colleagues, students, and parents.

Data Analysis: The means and standard deviations for each of the nine factors of the TJSQ were analyzed by location (urban and suburban), size of district (small/large), county, school level, and school level within district. One-way analyses of variance were also performed with each of the personal and demographic variables and the nine factors of the TJSQ. The results of demographic analyses are provided.

References:
Coates, B.R. 1992. The effect of shared decision-making on teacher job satisfaction and teacher professionalism. Ed.D. dissertation, United States International University.

Ford, S.W. 1987. The relationship between expectations and realities of job satisfaction for elementary school teachers. Ed. D. dissertation, University of Colorado, Boulder.

Johnston, R.H. 1991. The relationship between job satisfaction of Colorado middle school teachers and selected school and teacher characteristics. Ph.D. dissertation, University of Southern Mississippi.

Raisnai, R.B. 1988. A study of relationship of organizational climate and teachers' and schools' selected demographic characteristics to teacher job satisfaction as perceived by the teachers in selected Michigan public secondary schools. Ph.D. dissertation, Michigan State University.

Rauch, L.E. 1990. The relationship between participative decision-making and job satisfaction of elementary, middle, and secondary public school teachers. Ed.D. dissertation, University of San Francisco.

Teacher Job Satisfaction Questionnaire

1. Teaching provides me with an opportunity to advance professionally.
2. Teacher income is adequate for normal expenses.
3. Teaching provides an opportunity to use a variety of skills.
4. When instructions are inadequate, I do what I think is best.
5. Insufficient income keeps me from living the way I want to live.
6. My immediate supervisor turns one teacher against another.
7. No one tells me that I am a good teacher.
8. The work of a teacher consists of routine activities.
9. I am not getting ahead in my present teaching position.
10. Working conditions in my school can be improved.
11. I receive recognition from my immediate supervisor.
12. If I could earn what I earn now, I would take any job.
13. I do not have the freedom to make my own decisions.
14. My immediate supervisor offers suggestions to improve my teaching.
15. Teaching provides for a secure future.
16. I receive full recognition for my successful teaching.
17. I get along well with my colleagues.
18. The administration in my school does not clearly define its policies.
19. My immediate supervisor gives me assistance when I need help.
20. Working conditions in my school are comfortable.
21. Teaching provides me the opportunity to help my students learn.
22. I like the people with whom I work.
23. Teaching provides limited opportunities for advancement.
24. My students respect me as a teacher.
25. I am afraid of losing my teaching job.
26. Teaching involves too many clerical tasks.
27. My immediate supervisor does not back me up.
28. Teaching is very interesting work.
29. Working conditions in my school could not be worse.
30. Teaching discourages originality.
31. The administration in my school communicates its policies well.
32. I never feel secure in my teaching job.
33. Teaching does not provide me the chance to develop new methods.
34. My immediate supervisor treats everyone equitably.
35. My colleagues stimulate me to do better work.
36. My students come to class inadequately prepared.
37. Teaching provides an opportunity for promotion.
38. My immediate supervisor watches me closely.
39. I am responsible for planning my daily lessons.
40. Physical surroundings in my school are unpleasant.
41. I do not have the freedom to use my judgment.
42. I am well paid in proportion to my ability.
43. My colleagues are highly critical of one another.
44. I do have responsibility for my teaching.
45. My colleagues provide me with suggestions or feedback about my teaching.
46. Teaching provides me an opportunity to be my own boss.
47. My immediate supervisor provides assistance for improving instruction.

48. I do not get cooperation from the people I work with.
49. My immediate supervisor is not afraid to delegate work to others.
50. Behavior problems interfere with my teaching.
51. Teaching encourages me to be creative.
52. My immediate supervisor is not willing to listen to suggestions.
53. Teacher income is barely enough to live on.
54. I am indifferent toward teaching.
55. The work of a teacher is very pleasant.
56. I receive too many meaningless instructions from my immediate supervisor.
57. I dislike the people with whom I work.
58. I receive too little recognition.
59. Teaching provides a good opportunity for advancement.
60. My interests are similar to those of my colleagues.
61. I am not responsible for my actions.
62. My immediate supervisor makes available the material I need to do my best.
63. I have made lasting friendships among my colleagues.
64. Working conditions in my school are good.
65. My immediate supervisor makes me feel uncomfortable.
66. I prefer to have others assume responsibility.
67. Teacher income is less than I deserve.
68. I go out of my way to help my colleagues.
69. I try to be aware of the policies of my school.
70. When I teach a good lesson, my immediate supervisor notices.
71. My immediate supervisor explains what is expected of me.
72. Teaching provides me with financial security.
73. My immediate supervisor praises good teaching.
74. I am not interested in the policies of my school.
75. I get along well with my students.
76. Pay compares with similar jobs in other school districts.
77. My colleagues seem unreasonable to me.

Scaling: Strongly Disagree = 1; Disagree = 2; Neutral (neither disagree or agree) = 3; Agree = 4; and Strongly Agree = 5. Scoring is reversed for the following 22 unfavorable items (27, 52, 65, 6, 56, 57, 77, 48, 43, 40, 18, 74, 61, 30, 33, 54, 13, 23, 9, 25, 32, and 58).

Reprinted with permission of the author.

Job Descriptive Index

Smith, P.C. et al. 1969. *The measurement of satisfaction in work and retirement*. Chicago: Rand McNally.

Comments: The original 72-item JDI contained five scales. The JDI was revised in 1985 by substituting several items. The revised JDI has a new scale that measures satisfaction with the job in general. The complete forms, scoring key, instructions, and norms can be obtained from Dr. Patricia C. Smith, Department of Psychology, Bowling Green State University, Bowling Green, OH 43403. Additional scales include the 18-item Job in General Scale which assesses global job satisfaction and the 18-item Stress in General Scale which measures overall job stress. An updated (1990) manual is available that explains the methodology in developing and revising the JDI and the JIG as well as the administration, scoring, and reporting results of the JDI, the revised JDI, and the JIG. The JDI is one of the most frequently used instruments to measure job satisfaction.

Sample: Although the original sample consisted of 988 people from seven different organizations, additional studies were conducted with 2,662 people from 21 different organizations.

Reliability: Corrected split-half correlations were 0.84 (work), 0.80 (pay), 0.86 (promotions), 0.87 (supervision), and 0.88 (co-workers). Means and standard deviations for male and female workers are also provided.

Validity: A multitrait-multimethod matrix assessed convergent and discriminant validity.

Scales: The original JDI contained the following five scales: co-workers (18), pay (9), supervision (18), work (18), and opportunities for promotion (9).

References:
Collier, D.O. 1992. Developmental changes in predictors of job satisfaction for female elementary school teachers. Ph.D. dissertation, Old Dominion University.

Glick, N.L. 1992. Job satisfaction among academic administrators. *Research in Higher Education* 33:625-639.

Secumski-Kiligian, E.A. 1993. The relationship between elementary school teachers' job satisfaction, principals' managerial styles and student achievement. Ed.D. dissertation, Wayne State University.

Warr, C.N. 1991. Job satisfaction and intent to leave present employment among secondary teachers in vocational/technical education in the United States. Ed.D. dissertation, University of Georgia.

Wilcox, H.D. 1992. The relationship between the teachers' perception of the high school principal's leadership style and the correlates job satisfaction and morale. Ed.D. dissertation, University of Akron.

Job Descriptive Index

Think of the work you do at present. How well does each of the following words or phrases describe your work? In the blank beside each word below, write

Y for "Yes" if it describes your work
N for "No" if it does NOT describe it
? if you cannot decide

WORK ON PRESENT JOB

Routine
Satisfying
Good

Think of the kind of supervision that you get on your job. How well does each of the following words or phrases describe this? In the blank beside each word below, write

Y for "Yes" if it describes the supervision you get on your job
N for "No" if it does NOT describe it
? if you cannot decide

SUPERVISION

Impolite
Praises good work
Doesn't supervise enough

Think of the pay you get now. How well does each of the following words or phrases describe your present pay? In the blank beside each word below, write

Y for "Yes" if it describes your pay
N for "No" if it does NOT describe it
? if you cannot decide

PRESENT PAY

Income adequate for normal expenses
Insecure
Less than I deserve

Think of the majority of the people that you work with now or the people you meet in connection with your work. How well does each of the following words or phrases describe these people? In the blank beside each word below, write

Y for "Yes" if it describes the people you work with
N for "No" if it does NOT describe them
? if you cannot decide

CO-WORKERS (PEOPLE)

Boring
Responsible
Intelligent

Think of the opportunities for promotion that you have now. How well does each of the following words or phrases describe these? In the blank beside each word below, write

Y for "Yes" if it describes your opportunities for promotion
N for "No" if it does NOT describe them
? if you cannot decide

OPPORTUNITIES FOR PROMOTION

Dead-end job
Unfair promotion policy
Regular promotions

Think of your job in general. All in all, what is it like most of the time? In the blank beside each word or phrase below, write

Y for "Yes" if it describes your job
N for "No" if it does NOT describe it
? if you cannot decide

JOB IN GENERAL

Undesirable
Better than most
Rotten

Scaling: Each scale is written on a separate page. For positive items, a Yes receives 3 points; ? receives 1 point; and No receives no points. For negative items the scoring system is reversed. The scores on each scale are tallied separately.

Reprinted with permission of Bowling Green State University, Department of Psychology, Bowling Green, OH 43403.

Minnesota Satisfaction Questionnaire

Weiss, D.J. et al. 1967. *Manual for the Minnesota Satisfaction Questionnaire*. Minneapolis, MN: Industrial Relations Center, University of Minnesota.

Comments: The 100-item MSQ measures actual satisfaction with intrinsic and extrinsic aspects of the work environment. In addition to the MSQ, the Minnesota Importance Questionnaire was developed to assess the importance of various aspects to potential satisfaction. A 20-item short form of the MSQ was created by taking one item (highest correlation) from each of the 20 scales. The MSQ is one of the most frequently used instruments to measure job satisfaction.

Scale Construction: The Work Adjustment Project used the Hoppock Job Satisfaction Blank, the 54-item Employee Attitude Scale created by the Industrial Relations Center, and 22 additional items to measure satisfaction. These eighty items were used to design various satisfaction instruments. However, these instruments focused primarily on extrinsic satisfaction. A new instrument, the MSQ, was developed to measure intrinsic and extrinsic aspects of job satisfaction. Each of the 20 scales contains five items.

Sample: The original samples consisted of 1,793 employees from 25 occupations. One hundred and ninety-one suburban elementary school teachers from kindergarten to grade six participated in the study.

Reliability: Hoyt reliability coefficients for 27 normative groups ranged from 0.93 (advancement and recognition) to 0.78 (responsibility). For the group of 191 teachers, the Hoyt reliability coefficients were 0.90 (ability utilization and recognition), 0.79 (achievement and social status), 0.85 (activity), 0.92 (advancement), 0.83 (authority), 0.90 (company policies/practices, compensation, and social service), 0.81 (co-workers, independence, and supervision-technical), 0.86 (creativity), 0.75 (moral values and responsibility), 0.74 (security), 0.84 (supervision-human relations), 0.76 (variety), 0.91 (working conditions), and 0.87 (general satisfaction). Test-retest correlation coefficients for a one-week interval ranged from 0.66 (co-workers) to 0.91 (working conditions) for 75 night school students. Test-retest correlation coefficients for a one-year interval ranged from 0.35 (independence) to 0.71 (ability utilization) for 115 workers.

Validity: Construct validity for the MSQ is supported by the validation studies of the Minnesota Importance Questionnaire which is based on the Theory of Work Adjustment. A detailed description is provided in the Manual for the Minnesota Satisfaction Questionnaire. Concurrent validity was established by studying group differences in satisfaction. One-way analysis of variance and Bartlett's test of homogeneity of variance were performed on 25 occupational groups. Group differences were statistically significant at the 0.001 level for both means and variances on all 21 MSQ scales.

Scales: The twenty scales and their corresponding items are: ability utilization (7, 27, 47, 67, and 87); achievement (19, 39, 59, 79, and 99); activity (20, 40, 60, 80, and 100); advancement (14, 34, 54, 74, and 94); authority (6, 26, 46, 66, and 86); company policies and practices (9, 29, 49, 69, and 89); compensation (12, 32, 52, 72, and 92); co-workers (16, 36, 56, 76, and 96); creativity (2, 22, 42, 62, and 82); independence (4, 24, 44, 64, and 84); moral values (3, 23, 43, 63, and 83); recognition (18, 38, 58, 78, and 98); responsibility (17, 37, 57, 77, and 97); security (11, 31, 51, 71, and 91); social service (1, 21, 41, 61, and 81); social status (8, 28, 48, 68, and 88); supervision-human relations (10, 30, 50, 70, and 90); supervision-technical (15, 35, 55, 75, and 95); variety (5, 25, 45, 65, and 85); and working conditions (13, 33, 53, 73, and 93). It is also possible to include a general satisfaction scale. This scale consists of 20 items, one from each of the 20 scales (24, 25, 28, 30, 35, 43, 51, 61, 66, 67, 69, 72, 74, 77, 82, 93, 96, 98, 99, and 100).

Definition of Scales: *Ability utilization* refers to the chance to do something that makes use of my abilities. *Achievement* refers to the feeling of accomplishment I get from the job. *Activity* refers to being able to keep busy all the time. *Advancement* refers to the chances for advancement on this job. *Authority* refers to the chance to tell other people what to do. *Company policies and practices* refer to the way company policies are put into practice. *Compensation* refers to my pay and the amount of work I do. *Co-workers* refer to the way my co-workers get along with each other. *Creativity* refers to the chance to try my own methods of doing the job. *Independence* refers to the chance to work alone on the job. *Moral values* refers to being able to do things that don't go against my conscience. *Recognition* refers to the praise I get for doing a good job. *Responsibility* refers to the freedom to use my own judgment. *Security* refers to the way my job provides for steady employment. *Social service* refers to the chance to do things for other people. *Social status* refers to the chance to be "somebody" in the community. *Supervision-human relations* refers to the way my boss handles his men. *Supervision-technical* refers to the competence of my supervisor in making decisions. *Variety* refers to the chance to do different things from time to time. *Working conditions* refer to the actual working conditions. The short form of the MSQ is comprised of the 20 scale items listed above.

Factor Structure: Intercorrelations for 14 norm groups are presented. The intercorrelation matrices were factor analyzed using a principal factors solution. Two factors were extracted for the teacher group. The first factor was intrinsic satisfaction which accounted for about two-thirds of the common variance. The second factor was extrinsic satisfaction (two supervision scales, co-workers, and recognition) and accounted for about one-third of the common variance.

Data Analysis: Means, standard deviations, standard errors of measurement, and normative data are presented for all groups. In addition, MSQ scale intercorrelations and factor analyses are reported.

References:
Bowers, B.L. 1991. The relationship of staff development/inservice education and teachers' job satisfaction in selected middle schools. Ph.D. dissertation, University of Minnesota.

Lawson, D.L. 1993. Job satisfaction and the Missouri career ladder program. Ph.D. dissertation, University of Mississippi.

Prest, G.S. 1993. A study of instructional assistants' job satisfaction and supervising teachers' leadership behavior. Ed.D. dissertation, University of Minnesota.

Thompson, J.M. and M.D. Blain. 1992. Presenting feedback on the Minnesota Importance Questionnaire and the Minnesota Satisfaction Questionnaire. *Career Development Quarterly* 41:62-66.

Wagner, C.R. 1991. Mentoring and job satisfaction in eleven northeast Minnesota school districts. Ph.D. dissertation, University of Minnesota.

Minnesota Satisfaction Questionnaire

On my present job, this is how I feel about:

1. The chance to be of service to others.
2. The chance to try out some of my own ideas.
3. Being able to do the job without feeling it is morally wrong.
4. The chance to work by myself.
5. The variety in my work.
6. The chance to have other workers look to me for direction.
7. The chance to do the kind of work that I do best.
8. The social position in the community that goes with the job.
9. The policies and practices toward employees of this company.
10. The way my supervisor and I understand each other.
11. My job security.
12. The amount of pay for the work I do.
13. The working conditions (heating, lighting, ventilation. etc.) on this job.
14. The opportunities for advancement on this job.
15. The technical "know-how" of my supervisor.
16. The spirit of cooperation among my co-workers.
17. The chance to be responsible for planning my work.
18. The way I am noticed when I do a good job.
19. Being able to see the results of the work I do.
20. The chance to be active much of the time.
21. The chance to be of service to people.
22. The chance to do new and original things on my own.
23. Being able to do things that don't go against my religious beliefs.
24. The chance to work alone on the job.
25. The chance to do different things from time to time.
26. The chance to tell other workers how to do things.
27. The chance to do work that is well suited to my abilities.
28. The chance to be "somebody" in the community.
29. Company policies and the way in which they are administered.
30. The way my boss handles his men.
31. The way my job provides for a secure future.
32. The chance to make as much money as my friends.
33. The physical surroundings where I work.
34. The chances of getting ahead on this job.
35. The competence of my supervisor in making decisions.
36. The chance to develop close friendships with my co-workers.
37. The chance to make decisions on my own.
38. The way I get full credit for the work I do.
39. Being able to take pride in a job well done.
40. Being able to do something much of the time.
41. The chance to help people.
42. The chance to try something different.
43. Being able to do things that don't go against my conscience.
44. The chance to be alone on the job.
45. The routine in my work.

46. The chance to supervise other people.
47. The chance to make use of my best abilities.
48. The chance to "rub elbows" with important people.
49. The way employees are informed about company policies.
50. The way my boss backs his men up (with top management).
51. The way my job provides for steady employment.
52. How my pay compares with that for similar jobs in other companies.
53. The pleasantness of the working conditions.
54. The way promotions are given out on this job.
55. The way my boss delegates work to others.
56. The friendliness of my co-workers.
57. The chance to be responsible for the work of others.
58. The recognition I get for the work I do.
59. Being able to do something worthwhile.
60. Being able to stay busy.
61. The chance to do things for other people.
62. The chance to develop new and better ways to do the job.
63. The chance to do things that don't harm other people.
64. The chance to work independently of others.
65. The chance to do something different every day.
66. The chance to tell people what to do.
67. The chance to do something that makes use of my abilities.
68. The chance to be important in the eyes of others.
69. The way company policies are put into practice.
70. The way my boss takes care of complaints brought to him by his men.
71. How steady my job is.
72. My pay and the amount of work I do.
73. The physical working conditions of the job.
74. The chances for advancement on this job.
75. The way my boss provides help on hard problems.
76. The way my co-workers are easy to make friends with.
77. The freedom to use my own judgment.
78. The way they usually tell me when I do my job well.
79. The chance to do my best at all times.
80. The chance to be "on the go" all the time.
81. The chance to be of some small service to other people.
82. The chance to try my own methods of doing the job.
83. The chance to do the job without feeling I am cheating anyone.
84. The chance to work away from others.
85. The chance to do many different things on the job.
86. The chance to tell others what to do.
87. The chance to make use of my abilities and skills.
88. The chance to have a definite place in the community.
89. The way the company treats its employees.
90. The personal relationship between my boss and his men.
91. The way layoffs and transfers are avoided in my job.
92. How my pay compares with that of other workers.
93. The working conditions.
94. My chances for advancement.
95. The way my boss trains his men.

96. The way my co-workers get along with each other.
97. The responsibility of my job.
98. The praise I get for doing a good job.
99. The feeling of accomplishment I get from the job.
100. Being able to keep busy all the time.

Scaling: I am not satisfied = 1; I am only slightly satisfied = 2; I am satisfied = 3; I am very satisfied = 4; and I am extremely satisfied = 5.

Reprinted with permission of Vocational Psychology Research, University of Minnesota.

Leadership

Least Preferred Coworker

Fiedler, F.E. 1967. *A theory of leadership effectiveness*. New York: McGraw-Hill.

Comments: The 15-item LPC is a semantic differential instrument based on Fiedler's contingency theory of leadership effectiveness. It includes three dimensions: the quality of leader-member relations; degree of task structure; and a measure of leader-position power.

Scale Construction: The LPC is a brief and straightforward scale which uses a semantic differential format with 15 bipolar adjectives. In responding to the scale, individuals are instructed to think of a coworker with whom they **work least well**. It employees an eight-point Likert type response anchor. For each pair of bipolar adjectives (pleasant-unpleasant, friendly-unfriendly), the positive adjective receives the higher score. A person's LPC score is the sum of the ratings. Established norms indicate that a score of 63 or less constitutes a low LPC response, and a score of 73 or higher, a high LPC score. A high LPC score represents a more generalized interpersonally-oriented leader style. The low LPC is considered to be a more task-oriented style.

Sample: The development of the LPC was based on large samples of adults (2,000 or more subjects) across a variety of adult populations.

Reliability: Split-half reliability estimates ranged from 0.86 to 0.92. Median test-retest reliability co-efficients ranged from 0.67 to 0.81.

Validity: Extensive construct validity studies have documented that high LPC leaders are interpersonally oriented and that low LPC scores constitute a task-oriented leader style.

Factor Analysis: Fiedler employed a number of factor analytic studies in the development of the LPC. This information is documented in some detail in the references cited below.

References:
Fiedler, F.E. and M.M. Chemers. 1984. *Improving leadership effectiveness*. New York: Wiley.

Fiedler, F.E. and J.E. Garcia. 1987. *New approaches to effective leadership*. New York: Wiley.

Least Preferred Co-Worker Scale

1.	Pleasant	Unpleasant
2.	Friendly	Unfriendly
3.	Rejecting	Accepting
4.	Helpful	Frustrating
5.	Unenthusiastic	Enthusiastic
6.	Tense	Relaxed
7.	Distant	Close
8.	Cold	Warm
9.	Cooperative	Uncooperative
10.	Supportive	Hostile
11.	Quarrelsome	Harmonious
12.	Self-Assured	Hesitant
13.	Efficient	Inefficient
14.	Gloomy	Cheerful
15.	Open	Guarded

Scoring: See description above.

Reprinted with permission of the author.

Locus of Control

Internal Control Index

Duttweiler, P.C. 1984. The Internal Control Scale: A newly developed measure of locus of control. *Educational and Psychological Measurement* 44:209-221.

Comments: The 28-item ICI was developed in four stages and was constantly revised based upon the results of each stage of development. It has two stable factors, internal consistency, norms for demographic categories from college students, and convergent validity.

Scale Construction: The pretesting stage consisted of identifying those aspects related to internal locus of control (autonomy, cognitive processing, delay of gratification, resistance to influence attempts, and self-confidence). Items were developed based on clarity and conciseness. The tryout test was administered to a sample of 548 junior college, continuing education, college, and university students. After item analysis and factor analyses, 28 items were selected for the field test administration, which included 684 people similar to the tryout sample. Analyses of variance, item analysis, and factor analyses were conducted to further refine the ICI.

Sample: The replication sample consisted of 133 students from Gainesville Junior College.

Reliability: Alpha coefficients of 0.84 for the field test and 0.85 for the Gainesville replication study were reported. Item total-score correlations for both samples are provided.

Validity: Convergent validity was established by correlating the ICI with Mirels' Factor I of Rotter's I-E Scale (significant at the 0.001 level).

Factor Analysis: A varimax rotation with both the field test sample and the Gainesville Junior College replication sample (133 students) resulted in a two-factor solution. The two factors are confidence in one's own ability and autonomous behavior. For the field test, 14 items loaded on confidence in one's own ability (3, 4, 5, 7, 9, 10, 13, 15, 16, 18, 20, 21, 25, and 28), whereas 13 items loaded on the same factor for the Gainesville replication sample (1, 3, 7, 9, 10, 12, 13, 15, 16, 19, 20, 23, and 28). For the field test, 13 items loaded on autonomous behavior (2, 6, 8, 11, 12, 14, 17, 19, 22, 23, 24, 26, and 27), whereas 14 items loaded on the same factor for the Gainesville replication sample (1, 2, 6, 8, 11, 14, 16, 18, 20, 21, 22, 24, 26, and 27).

Data Analysis: Field test means and standard deviations on the ICI are presented by age group, sex, race, educational level, and socio-economic level.

References:
MacDonald, A.P., Jr. 1973. Measures of internal-external control. In J.P. Robinson and P.R. Shaver (Eds.) *Measures of social psychological attitudes.* Ann Arbor: University of Michigan.

Mirels, H.L. 1970. Dimensions of internal versus external control. *Journal of Consulting and Clinical Psychology* 34:226-228.

Internal Control Index

1. When faced with a problem I try to forget it.
2. I need frequent encouragement from others to keep me working at a difficult task.
3. I like jobs where I can make decisions and be responsible for my own work.
4. I change my opinion when someone I admire disagrees with me.
5. If I want something I work hard to get it.
6. I prefer to learn the facts about something from someone else rather than have to dig them out for myself.
7. I will accept jobs that require me to supervise others.
8. I have a hard time saying "no" when someone tries to sell me something I don't want.
9. I like to have a say in any decisions made by any group I'm in.
10. I consider the different sides of an issue before making any decisions.
11. What other people think has a great influence on my behavior.
12. Whenever something good happens to me I feel it is because I've earned it.
13. I enjoy being in a position of leadership.
14. I need someone else to praise my work before I am satisfied with what I've done.
15. I am sure enough of my own opinions to try and influence others.
16. When something is going to affect me I learn as much about it as I can.
17. I decide to do things on the spur of the moment.
18. For me, knowing I've done something well is more important than being praised by someone else.
19. I let other peoples' demands keep me from doing things I want to do.
20. I stick to my opinions when someone disagrees with me.
21. I do what I feel like doing not what other people think I ought to do.
22. I get discouraged when doing something that takes a long time to achieve results.
23. When part of a group I prefer to let other people make all the decisions.
24. When I have a problem I follow the advice of friends or relatives.
25. I enjoy trying to do difficult tasks more than I enjoy trying to do easy tasks.
26. I prefer situations where I can depend on someone else's ability rather than just my own.
27. Having someone important tell me I did a good job is more important to me than feeling I've done a good job.
28. When I'm involved in something I try to find out all I can about what is going on even when someone else is in charge.

Scaling: Rarely = 5; Occasionally = 4; Sometimes = 3; Frequently = 2; and Usually = 1. The scoring is reversed for the following items: 3, 5, 7, 9, 10, 12, 13, 15, 16, 18, 20, 21, 25, and 28.

Reprinted with permission of the author.

Teacher Locus of Control

Rose, J.S. and F.J. Medway. 1981. Measurement of teachers' beliefs in their control over student outcome. *Journal of Educational Research* 74:185-189.

Comments: The 28-item TLC assesses teachers' perceptions about internal or external classroom control. The scale is internally consistent and has higher correlations with classroom teaching behaviors than Rotter's I-E scale.

Scale Construction: The original TLC contained 32 positive or success situations and 32 negative or failure situations. Three judges examined the items and categorized them as I+ or I-. They also looked at the clarity of the items. After each administration of the TLC, items were kept if they loaded on the appropriate scale, and if their biserial correlations with the total scale were significant at the 0.05 level. Out of the 28 items, fourteen items describe positive (success) situations, while the other 14 describe negative (failure) situations.

Sample: Prior to the final version of the TLC, four samples that included 183 elementary school teachers completed three versions of the scale. The final sample consisted of 89 female teachers who taught the fourth grade.

Reliability: KR20 reliabilities were 0.71 (student success) and 0.81 (student failure).

Validity: One validation study examined the relationship between locus of control and the implementation of innovative educational practices. A second validation study looked at the relationship between the scores on the TLC and the classroom behavior of fourth grade teachers. The results of both validation studies demonstrated that the TLC was a better predictor of teacher and student behavior than Rotter's I-E scale (a more general assessment of control beliefs).

Factor Analysis: A principal factoring with a varimax rotation yielded two factors: student success (I+) and student failure (I-).

Data Analysis: Means and standard deviations are reported for the sample of 89 teachers. In addition, t-tests were performed to see if there were any significant differences related to teachers' race, socioeconomic level of the students, and the geographic location of the school. The only significant relationship was found on the I+ scale. Teachers in low SES schools scored significantly higher on the I+ scale than teachers in high SES schools.

References:
Rose, J.S. 1978. Relationships among teacher locus of control, teacher and student behavior, and student achievement. Ph.D. dissertation, University of South Carolina.

Thomson, J.R. Jr. and H.M. Handley. 1990. Relationship between teacher self-concept and teacher efficacy. Paper presented at Mid-South Educational Research Association. ERIC ED 327 508.

Teacher Locus of Control

1. When the grades of your students improve, it is more likely
   a. because you found ways to motivate the students, or
   b. because the students were trying harder to do well.

2. Suppose you had difficulties in setting up learning centers for students in your classroom. Would this probably happen
   a. because you lacked the appropriate materials, or
   b. because you didn't spend enough time in developing activities to go into the center?

3. Suppose your students did not appear to be benefiting from a more individualized method of instruction. The reason for this would probably be
   a. because you were having some problems managing this type of instruction, or
   b. because the students in your class were such that they needed a more traditional kind of approach.

4. When a student gets a better grade on his report card than he usually gets, is it
   a. because the student was putting more effort into his schoolwork, or
   b. because you found better ways of teaching that student?

5. If the students in your class became disruptive and noisy when you left them alone in the room for five minutes, would this happen
   a. because you didn't leave them interesting work to do while you were gone, or
   b. because the students were more noisy that day than they usually are?

6. When some of your students fail a math test, it is more likely
   a. because they weren't attending to the lesson, or
   b. because you didn't use enough examples to illustrate the concept.

7. Suppose you were successful at using learning centers with your class of 30 students. Would this occur
   a. because you worked hard at it, or
   b. because your students easily conformed to the new classroom procedure?

8. When a student pulls his or grade up from a "C" to a "B," it is more likely
   a. because you came up with an idea to motivate the student, or
   b. because the student was trying harder to do well.

9. Suppose you are teaching a student a particular concept in arithmetic or math and the student has trouble learning it. Would this happen
   a. because the student wasn't able to understand it, or
   b. because you couldn't explain it very well?

10. When a student does better in school than he usually does, is it more likely
    a. because the student was trying harder, or
    b. because you tried hard to encourage the student to do better?

11. If you couldn't keep your class quiet, it would probably be
    a. because the students came to school more rowdy than usual, or
    b. because you were so frustrated that you weren't able to settle them down.

12. Suppose a play put on by your class was voted the "Best Class Play of the Year" by students and faculty in your school. Would it be
    a. because you put in a lot of time and effort as the director, or
    b. because the students were cooperative.

13. Suppose it were the week before Easter vacation and you were having some trouble keeping order in your classroom. This would more likely happen
    a. because you weren't putting extra effort into keeping the students under control, or
    b. because the students were more uncontrollable than usual.

14. If one of your students couldn't do a class assignment, would it be
    a. because the student wasn't paying attention during the class lesson, or
    b. because you gave the student an assignment that wasn't on his or her level?

15. Suppose you wanted to teach a series of lessons on Mexico, but the lessons didn't turn out as well as you had expected. This would more likely happen
    a. because the students weren't that interested in learning about Mexico, or
    b. because you didn't put enough effort into developing the lessons.

16. Suppose a student who does not typically participate in class begins to volunteer his or her answers. This would more likely happen
    a. because the student finally encountered a topic of interest to him or her, or
    b. because you tried hard to encourage the student to volunteer his or her answers.

17. Suppose one of your students cannot remain on task for a particular assignment. Would this be more likely to happen
    a. because you gave the student a task that was somewhat less interesting than most tasks, or
    b. because the student was unable to concentrate on his or her schoolwork that day?

18. Suppose you were unable to devise an instructional system as requested by the principal, which would accommodate the "needs of individual students" in your class. This would most likely happen
    a. because there were too many students in your class, or
    b. because you didn't have enough knowledge or experience with individualized instructional programs.

19. If the students in your class perform better than they usually do on a test, would this happen
    a. because the students studied a lot for the test, or
    b. because you did a good job of teaching the subject area?

20. When the performance of a student in your class appears to be slowly deteriorating, it is usually
    a. because you weren't trying hard enough to motivate him or her, or
    b. because the student was putting less effort into his or her schoolwork.

21. Suppose a new student was assigned to your class, and this student had a difficult time making friends with his or her classmates. Would it be more likely
    a. that most of the other students did not make an effort to be friends with the new student, or
    b. that you were not trying hard enough to encourage the other students to be more friendly toward the newcomer?

22. If the students in your class performed better on a standardized achievement test given at the end of the year compared to students you had last year, it would probably be
    a. because you put more effort into teaching this year, or

b. because this year's class of students were somewhat smarter than last year's.

23. Suppose, one day, you find yourself reprimanding one of your students more often than usual. Would this be more likely to happen
    a. because that student was misbehaving more than usual that day, or
    b. because you were somewhat less tolerant than you usually are?

24. Suppose one of your underachievers does his or her homework better than usual. This would probably happen
    a. because the student tried hard to do the assignment, or
    b. because you tried hard to explain how to do the assignment.

25. Suppose one of your students began to do better schoolwork than he usually does. Would this happen
    a. because you put much effort into helping the student do better, or
    b. because the student was trying harder to do well in school?

Scoring: The TLC uses a forced-choice format. Half of the items represent positive (success) situations, while the other half represent negative (failure) situations. Separate scores are obtained for student success (I+) and student failure (I-).

Reprinted with permission of the Helen Dwight Reid Educational Foundation. Published by Heldref Publications, 1319 18th Street, NW. Washington, D.C. 20036-1802.

Internal-External Locus of Control Scale

Rotter, J.B. 1966. Generalized expectancies for internal versus external control of reinforcement. *Psychological Monographs: General and Applied* 80 (Whole No. 609).

Comments: The 29-item I-E Scale assesses "generalized expectancies for internal versus external control of reinforcement." Item analysis, factor analysis, and reliability tests demonstrate the internal consistency of the scale. The I-E Scale has been used to develop validate other instruments. It is one of the most frequently used instruments to measure locus of control.

Scale Construction: The original I-E scale contained 100 forced-choice items, each one comparing an external belief with an internal one. Based upon item analysis and factor analysis, the revised scale contained 60 items. Item correlations with the Marlowe-Crowne Social Desirability Scale, validity data from two studies, and reliability data resulted in reducing the scale to 23 items. The final version of the scale contains 23 forced-choice items plus six filler items.

Sample: Biserial item correlations are reported for a sample of 200 men and 200 women enrolled in psychology courses at Ohio State University. In addition to students at Ohio State, other samples consisted of 10th, 11th, and 12th graders, a national stratified sample, prisoners at the Colorado Reformatory, elementary psychology students at Kansas State University, and Ohio Federal prisoners.

Reliability: The KR20 reliability coefficient was 0.70 for the sample of 200 men and 200 women. Test-retest reliability after one month was 0.72 and after two months was 0.55. Reliability data are provided for all of the samples.

Validity: Discriminant validity is supported by the low correlations with intelligence, social desirability, and political liberalness. Evidence of construct validity is found in the predicted differences in behavior for people above and below the median of the I-E Scale and from correlations with behavioral criteria. Numerous studies are discussed to support construct validity.

Factor Analysis: The two factor analyses that were performed support the unidimensionality of the scale.

Data Analysis: Biserial item correlations of each item with total score, excluding that item are presented. Means and standard deviations for various samples are also provided.

References:

Jones, B.J.W. 1993. Career socialization, locus-of-control and perceptions of sex role stereotypes among female administrators in Georgia's technical institutes. Ph.D. dissertation, Georgia State University.

Sillonis, R. 1991. The relationship between locus-of-control and self-esteem among K-12 public school principals and school effectiveness. Ed.D. dissertation, University of San Francisco.

Sims, B.J. 1992. Elementary school site implementation of centrally mandated policy: An interpretation of teacher locus-of-control, school climate, and principal leadership style. Ph.D. dissertation, University of California, Berkeley.

Internal-External Locus of Control Scale

1. a. Children get into trouble because their parents punish them too much.
   b. The trouble with most children nowadays is that their parents are too easy with them.

2. a. Many of the unhappy things in people's lives are partly due to bad luck.
   b. People's misfortunes result from the mistakes they make.

3. a. One of the major reasons why we have wars is because people don't take enough interest in politics.
   b. There will always be wars, no matter how hard people try to prevent them.

4. a. In the long run people get the respect they deserve in this world.
   b. Unfortunately, an individual's worth often passes unrecognized no matter how hard he tries.

5. a. The idea that teachers are unfair to students is nonsense.
   b. Most students don't realize the extent to which their grades are influenced by accidental happenings.

6. a. Without the right breaks one cannot be an effective leader.
   b. Capable people who fail to become leaders have not taken advantage of their opportunities.

7. a. No matter how hard you try some people just don't like you.
   b. People who can't get others to like them don't understand how to get along with others.

8. a. Heredity plays the major role in determining one's personality.
   b. It is one's experiences in life which determine what they're like.

9. a. I have often found that what is going to happen will happen.
   b. Trusting to fate has never turned out as well for me as making a decision to take a definite course of action.

10. a. In the case of the well-prepared student there is rarely if ever such a thing as an unfair test.
    b. Many times exam questions tend to be so unrelated to course work that studying is really useless.

11. a. Becoming a success is a matter of hard work; luck has little or nothing to do with it.
    b. Getting a good job depends mainly on being in the right place at the right time.

12. a. The average citizen can have an influence in government decisions.
    b. This world is run by the few people in power, and there is not much the little guy can do about it.

13. a. When I make plans, I am almost certain that I can make them work.
    b. It is not always wise to plan too far ahead because many things turn out to be a matter of good or bad fortune anyhow.

14. a. There are certain people who are just no good.
    b. There is some good in everybody.

15. a. In my case getting what I want has little or nothing to do with luck.
    b. Many times we might just as well decide what to do by flipping a coin.

16. a. Who gets to be the boss often depends on who was lucky enough to be in the right place first.
    b. Getting people to do the right thing depends upon ability, luck has little or nothing to do with it.

17. a. As far as world affairs are concerned, most of us are the victims of forces we can neither understand nor control.
    b. By taking an active part in political and social affairs, the people can control world events.

18. a. Most people don't realize the extent to which their lives are controlled by accidental happenings.
    b. There really is no such thing as "luck."

19. a. One should always be willing to admit mistakes.
    b. It is usually best to cover up one's mistakes.

20. a. It is hard to know whether or not a person really likes you.
    b. How many friends you have depends on how nice a person you are.

21. a. In the long run the bad things that happen to us are balanced by the good ones.
    b. Most misfortunes are the result of lack of ability, ignorance, laziness, or all three.

22. a. With enough effort we can wipe out political corruption.
    b. It is difficult for people to have much control over the things politicians do in office.

23. a. Sometimes I can't understand how teachers arrive at the grades they give.
    b. There is a direct connection between how hard I study and the grades I get.

24. a. A good leader expects people to decide for themselves what they should do.
    b. A good leader makes it clear to everybody what their jobs are.

25. a. Many times I feel that I have little influence over the things that happen to me.
    b. It is impossible for me to believe that chance or luck plays an important role in my life.

26. a. People are lonely because they don't try to be friendly.
    b. There's not much use in trying too hard to please people, if they like you, they like you.

27. a. There is too much emphasis on athletics in high school.
    b. Team sports are an excellent way to build character.

28. a. What happens to me is my own doing.
    b. Sometimes I feel that I don't have enough control over the direction my life is taking.

29. a. Most of the time I can't understand why politicians behave the way they do.
    b. In the long run the people are responsible for bad government on a national as well as on a local level.

Scoring: A forced-choice format is used. The total score is calculated by adding the number of external beliefs selected (2a, 3b, 4b, 5b, 6a, 7a, 9a, 10b, 11b, 12b, 13b, 15b, 16a, 17a, 18a, 20a, 21a, 22b, 23a, 25a, 26b, 28b, and 29a).

Perceived Control at School Scale

Adelman, H.S. et al. 1986. An instrument to assess students' perceived control at school. *Educational and Psychological Measurement* 46:1005-1017.

Comments: The 16-item PCSS measures students' perceived control at school. Data on reliability, validity, and factor structure are provided. Variations based upon sample characteristics have been found.

Scale Construction: Twelve items were written based on five areas of control in which schools are different. Four items were added as a reliability check to see if there were differences based on positively and negatively worded items. The pilot PCSS consisted of 16 items. Two forms of the PCSS were developed (one for the current school and one for the previous school).

Sample: Four samples were used. Two samples consisted of 107 special education students and the other two samples consisted of 113 regular education students. A description of the samples is provided.

Reliability: For the total special education samples the alpha coefficient was 0.80, while the alpha coefficient for the total regular education samples was 0.69. The alpha coefficient for all four samples was 0.65. Test-retest reliability over a two-week interval was 0.80 for special education students and 0.55 for regular education students.

Validity: To establish construct validity, the PCSS was correlated with the Nowicki-Strickland Locus of Control Scale. In addition, differences in group responses were used to further establish construct validity.

Factor Analysis: Principal components factor analysis with a varimax rotation yielded five factors for the special education samples and six factors for the regular education samples (there was overlapping). The five factors are: five items on personal power/decision making (14, 12, 1, 15, and 3); four items on self-determination (8, 11, 7, and 10); four items on others interference with autonomy (2, 16, 5, and 13); two items on powerlessness (4 and 6); and two items on impersonal interference with autonomy (9 and 10). Factor loadings are presented.

References:
Nichols, B.K. 1985. Self-perceptions of control and esteem as related to participation in a leadership training program. Ph.D. dissertation. University of California, Los Angeles.

Taylor, L., Adelman, H.S. and Kaser-Boyd, N. 1984. Attitudes toward involving minors in decisions. *Professional Psychology: Research and Practice* 15:436-449.

Perceived Control at School Scale

At school, how much of the time do you feel...

1. you have a say in deciding about what the rules should be?
2. people don't let you be yourself and act the way you really are?
3. you have a say in deciding about what should happen to you if you break a rule?
4. you can't influence what is happening to you?
5. people want you to be yourself and to act the way you really are?
6. people don't let you take part in making decisions?
7. you have a choice about what you are doing or learning?
8. you can influence what is happening to you?
9. the rules make you do things you don't agree with?
10. no matter what you do you probably won't get what you want?
11. you have very little choice about what you are doing or learning?
12. you are able to change something if you don't like it?
13. others make your decisions for you?
14. you get to do things in the way you think is right for you?
15. people want you to take part in making decisions?
16. people don't treat you fairly?

Scoring: Never = 1; Not very often = 2; Slightly less than half the time = 3; Slightly more than half the time = 4; Very Often = 5; and Always = 6. Scoring is reversed on the following items: 2, 4, 6, 9, 10, 11, 13, and 16. Perceived control scores can range from 16 to 96.

Reprinted with permission of the author.

Mentoring

Questionnaire for Beginning Teachers
Questionnaire for Mentor Teachers

Reiman, A.J. and R.A. Edelfelt. 1991. The opinions of mentors and beginning teachers. Research Report, North Carolina State University. ERIC ED 329 519.

Comments: The questionnaires were designed to study beginning teachers and their mentors. They were developed to check the influence of long-term mentor training, with a focus on developmental supervision, and to examine the degree to which the intent of the North Carolina Certification Program was being carried out.

Scale Construction: Questionnaire items were created from an earlier study where ideas and themes were explored through interview techniques. Parallel forms of the instrument were developed for the mentor teacher and for the beginning teacher. The questionnaires employed a discrepancy model of investigation and scoring. The items with the largest discrepancy between respondents were critically analyzed. The respondents were instructed to indicate on a four-point scale the degree to which each condition in the questionnaire was operative in their situation.

Sample: Questionnaires were sent to 22 mentor teachers and to 16 beginning teachers.

Reference:
School-based mentoring: Untangling the tensions between theory and practice. Research Report 90-7, North Carolina State University.

Questionnaire for Beginning Teachers

1. I have had adequate time to plan.
2. My mentor provided assistance with classroom management.
3. My mentor provided help with instructional concerns.
4. My mentor provided assistance with personal concerns.
5. I received help from the district office on salary and certification questions.
6. My mentor was in my classroom.
7. I was receptive to criticism.
8. Feedback from classroom observations was helpful.
9. My teaching assignment was realistic for a beginner.
10. I discussed all aspects of teaching with my mentor.
11. My mentor helped me keep current professionally.
12. I had opportunities to talk with other novice teachers.
13. I got help from colleagues.
14. I sought feedback from students.
15. There was time to reflect on my teaching.
16. I got adequate clerical support.
17. I found satisfaction in teaching.
18. Professional development opportunities were provided.
19. I have been helped to develop my own teaching style.
20. I followed the textbook in my teaching.
21. I have been helped to develop a repertoire of teaching strategies.
22. I felt a part of the school community.
23. Teaching included mundane duties.
24. The materials I needed for teaching were available.
25. I got help and encouragement from my principal.
26. I was assessed by administration on the Teacher Performance Appraisal Instrument.
27. The climate in my school supported a good learning environment for students.
28. The climate in our school supported a good learning environment for me as a beginning teacher.
29. I have thought that I would have liked to have been involved in the selection of my mentor.
30. I had opportunities to visit and observe exemplary teachers.
31. I had opportunities to read and to review educational research and theory with my mentor.
32. My mentor is empathic.
33. My mentor can describe teaching concepts in a way that is understandable.
34. My mentor has acted on my behalf.
35. I participated in decisions on school policy.
36. Teaching was what I thought it would be.
37. I think I will be teaching five years from now.
38. I felt pressured to teach in certain ways.
39. We used technology to great advantage in our school.
40. There were opportunities to exchange ideas with colleagues.
41. Students were responsive to the way I taught.
42. Motivating students was very difficult.
43. Classroom management was a problem for me.
44. I communicated with parents.
45. Our school functioned in an efficient and productive manner.
46. The rules and requirements in our school were reasonable.

Questionnaire for Mentor Teachers

I have enough time to work with my ICT.

I confer with my ICT.

I make formal observations of my ICT.

I make informal observations of my ICT.

I visit my ICT's classroom.

I consult with my ICT on

      discipline.

      classroom management.

      school routines.

      the content being taught.

      changing the way teachers and students work together.

      finding materials.

      selecting materials.

      making materials.

      developing curriculum.

      skills in questioning.

      cooperative learning.

      personal concerns.

I support my ICT in

      maintaining his or her well being.

      fostering self-evaluation.

      increasing student self-direction.

      and decision making.

      individualizing instruction.

      finding effective ways to group.

      students for learning.

I help my ICT understand

      the community.

      the goals of school.

      different cultures, races, and lifestyles.

      democratic values as they apply in school.

      instructional theory and research.

      dialects and language.

      usage.

      the issues in promotion and retention.

      the initial certification program.

      managing time.

      school policy.

      school district policy.

I assist my ICT with

      identifying student needs.

      identifying student interests.

      motivating students.

teaching basic skills.
planning lessons to achieve.
measurable learning outcomes.
working with the high-risk child.
working with exceptional children.
developing critical thinking.
employing democratic values.
fostering problem solving.
helping students help each other.
developing homework assignments.
evaluating student learning.
designing teacher-made tests.
interpreting standardized test scores.
reporting student achievement.
communicating with parents.
relating local issues to the curriculum.
planning professional development.

I challenge my ICT to
be an active listener.
employ positive reinforcement.
analyze his or her teaching.
reflect on teaching.
encourage original expression.
evaluate his or her teaching.
use technology.
use computers.
develop learning centers.
document student learning.
stay current professionally.
promote equal opportunity.

I encourage ICT reflection through
conferences.
journal writing.
audiotaping.
videotaping.

I have been able to use the knowledge and techniques learned in mentor training.
I do demonstration teaching.
I use developmental theory in my work with my ICT.
I use the research of Bruce Joyce in my work with my ICT.
I vary the amount of structure employed in working with my ICT.

Scoring: Scoring is identical for both questionnaires. Never or hardly ever = 1; Sometimes = 2; Frequently = 3; and Always or almost always = 4.

Reprinted with permission of the authors. © Reiman and Edelfelt, 1990. Questionnaire for Beginning Teachers and Questionnaire for Mentor Teachers.

Morale

Purdue Teacher Opinionnaire

Bentley, R.R. and A.M. Rempel. 1970. *Purdue Teacher Opinionnaire*. Lafayette, IN: Purdue Research Foundation, Purdue University.

Comments: The 100-item PTO not only provides a total score that indicates a general level of teacher morale, but also ten sub-scale scores that provide meaningful information about the various components of teacher morale. The PTO is the most frequently cited instrument to measure morale.

Scale Construction: Originally, the 145-item PTO contained items in eight areas: teaching as an occupation; relationships with students; relationships with other teachers; administrative policies and procedures; relationships with community; curriculum factors; working conditions; and economic factors. KR reliability coefficients ranged from 0.79 to 0.98, with an overall reliability coefficient of 0.96.

Sample: The original sample of 3, 023 consisted of high school teachers from 60 schools in Indiana (stratified random sample) and 16 schools in Oregon (eastern part of the state).

Reliability: The following test-retest correlations are reported: 0.88 (teacher rapport with principal); 0.84 (satisfaction with teaching); 0.80 (rapport among teachers); 0.81 (teacher salary); 0.77 (teacher load); 0.76 (curriculum issues); 0.81 (teacher status); 0.78 (community support of education); 0.80 (school facilities and services); and 0.62 (community pressures). The correlations range from 0.62 (community pressures) to 0.88 (teacher rapport with principal) with a median correlation of 0.87. In addition, norms are available for all school levels.

Validity: The PTO discriminates not only among different schools, but also among the individual teachers within a particular school. In addition, principals completed the PTO the way they thought their faculty would respond. Differences between the median scores for teachers and principals was not significant.

Factor Analysis: Originally, a principal components analysis and an oblique rotation of the extracted factors were performed (570 teachers). The results yielded eight factors. Then, additional factor analytic procedures were conducted to high, middle, and low teacher morale groups. Ten factors were identified instead of eight. The ten factors are: 20 items on teacher rapport with principal (2, 3, 5, 7, 12, 33, 38, 41, 43, 44, 61, 62, 69, 70, 72, 73, 74, 92, 93, and 95); 20 items on satisfaction with teaching (19, 24, 26, 27, 29, 30, 46, 47, 50, 51, 56, 58, 60, 76, 78, 82, 83, 86, 89, and 100); 14 items on rapport among teachers (18, 22, 23, 28, 48, 52, 53, 54, 55, 77, 80, 84, 87, and 90); seven items on teacher salary (4, 9, 32, 36, 39, 65, and 75); 11 items on teacher load (1, 6, 8, 10, 11, 14, 31, 34, 40, 42, and 45); five items on curriculum issues (17, 20, 25, 79, and 88); eight items on teacher status (13, 15, 35, 37, 63, 64, 68, and 71); five items on community support of education (66, 67, 94, 96, and 97); five items on school facilities and services (16, 21, 49, 57, 59); and five items on community pressures (81, 85, 91, 98, and 99). The PTO Supplement contains two new factors: teacher rapport with school board (10 items) and teacher rapport with superintendent (10 items).

Definition of Factors: *Teacher rapport with principal* deals with the teacher's feelings about the principal (his/her professional competency), his/her interest in teachers and their work, his/her ability to communicate, and his/her skill in human relations. *Satisfaction with teaching* deals with teacher relationships with students and feelings of satisfaction with teaching. *Rapport among teachers* deals with a teacher's relationships with other teachers. *Teacher salary* deals with the teacher's feelings about salary and salary policies. *Teacher load* deals with record-keeping, clerical work, community demands on teacher time, extra-curricular load, and keeping up-to-date professionally. *Curriculum issues* deal with teacher reactions to the adequacy of the school program in meeting student needs. *Teacher status* deals with the prestige, security, and benefits of teaching. *Community support of education* deals with the extent to which the community understands and is willing to support a sound educational program. *School facilities and services* deal with the adequacy of facilities, supplies, and equipment as well as the efficiency of the procedures for obtaining materials and services. *Community pressures* deal with community expectations with respect to the teacher's personal standards, his/her participation in outside-school activities, and his/her freedom to discuss controversial issues in the classroom.

Data Analysis: Test-retest correlations, frequency distribution of test-retest correlations for individual schools by factor and total scores, means and standard deviations, inter-factor correlations, median scores by factors, percentile distribution of school medians by factors, and percentile distribution of school medians by items are reported.

References:
Carroll, D.F.O. 1992. Teacher morale as related to school leadership behavior. Ed.D. dissertation, East Tennessee State University.

Moyes, W.E. 1992. Career ladder participation and secondary school teacher morale. Ed.D. dissertation, University of Missouri, Columbia.

Pikos, S. 1993. Perceptions of building administrators and teachers at the secondary level on the role of the teacher in sh

Purdue Teacher Opinionnaire

1. Details, "red tape," and required reports absorb too much of my time.
2. The work of individual faculty members is appreciated and commended by our principal.
3. Teachers feel free to criticize administrative policy at faculty meetings called by our principal.
4. The faculty feels that their salary suggestions are adequately transmitted by the administration to the school board.
5. Our principal shows favoritism in his relations with the teachers in our school.
6. Teachers in this school are expected to do an unreasonable amount of record-keeping and clerical work.
7. My principal makes a real effort to maintain close contact with the faculty.
8. Community demands upon the teacher's time are unreasonable .
9. I am satisfied with the policies under which pay raises are granted.
10. My teaching load is greater than that of most of the other teachers in our school.
11. The extra-curricular load of the teachers in our school is unreasonable.
12. Our principal's leadership in faculty meetings challenges and stimulates our professional growth.
13. My teaching position gives me the social status in the community that I desire.
14. The number of hours a teacher must work is unreasonable.
15. Teaching enables me to enjoy many of the material and cultural things I like.
16. My school provides me with adequate classroom supplies and equipment.
17. Our school has a well-balanced curriculum.
18. There is a great deal of griping, arguing, taking sides, and feuding among our teachers.
19. Teaching gives me a great deal of personal satisfaction.
20. The curriculum of our school makes reasonable provision for student individual differences.
21. The procedures for obtaining materials and services are well defined and efficient.
22. Generally, teachers in our school do not take advantage of one another.
23. The teachers in our school cooperate with each other to achieve common, personal, and professional objectives.
24. Teaching enables me to make my greatest contribution to society.
25. The curriculum of our school is in need of major revisions.
26. I love to teach.
27. If I could plan my career again, I would choose teaching.
28. Experienced faculty members accept new and younger members as colleagues.
29. I would recommend teaching as an occupation to students of high scholastic ability.
30. If I could earn as much money in another occupation, I would stop teaching.
31. The school schedule places my classes at a disadvantage.
32. The school tries to follow a generous policy regarding fringe benefits, professional travel, professional study, etc.
33. My principal makes my work easier and more pleasant.
34. Keeping up professionally is too much of a burden.
35. Our community makes its teachers feel as though they are a real part of the community.
36. Salary policies are administered with fairness and justice.
37. Teaching affords me the security I want in a position.
38. My school principal understands and recognizes good teaching procedures.
39. Teachers clearly understand the policies governing salary increases.
40. My classes are used as a "dumping ground" for problem students.
41. The lines and methods of communication between teachers and the principal in our school are well developed and maintained.
42. My teaching load in this school is unreasonable.
43. My principal shows a real interest in my department.
44. Our principal promotes a sense of belonging among the teachers in our school.
45. My heavy teaching load unduly restricts my non-professional activities.
46. I find my contacts with students, for the most part, highly satisfying and rewarding.
47. I feel that I am an important part of this school system.

48. The competency of teachers in our school compares favorably with that of teachers in other schools that I know.
49. My school provides the teachers with adequate audio-visual aids and projection equipment.
50. I feel successful and competent in my present position.
51. I enjoy working with student organizations, clubs, and societies.
52. Our teaching staff is congenial to work with.
53. My teaching associates are well prepared for their jobs.
54. Our school faculty has a tendency to form into cliques.
55. The teachers in our school work well together.
56. I am at a disadvantage professionally because other teachers are better prepared to teach than I am.
57. Our school provides adequate clerical services for the teachers.
58. As far as I know, the other teachers think I am a good teacher.
59. Library facilities and resources are adequate for the grade or subject area which I teach.
60. The "stress and strain" resulting from teaching makes teaching undesirable for me.
61. My principal is concerned with the problems of the faculty and handles these problems sympathetically.
62. I do not hesitate to discuss any school problem with my principal.
63. Teaching gives me the prestige I desire.
64. My teaching job enables me to provide a satisfactory standard of living for my family.
65. The salary schedule in our school adequately recognizes teacher competency.
66. Most of the people in this community understand and appreciate good education.
67. In my judgment, this community is a good place to raise a family.
68. This community respects its teachers and treats them like professional persons.
69. My principal acts as though he is interested in me and my problems.
70. My school principal supervises rather than "snoopervises" the teachers in our school.
71. It is difficult for teachers to gain acceptance by the people in this community.
72. Teachers' meetings as now conducted by our principal waste the time and energy of the staff.
73. My principal has a reasonable understanding of the problems connected with my teaching assignment.
74. I feel that my work is judged fairly by my principal.
75. Salaries paid in this school system compare favorably with salaries in other systems with which I am familiar.
76. Most of the actions of students irritate me.
77. The cooperativeness of teachers in our school helps make my work more enjoyable.
78. My students regard me with respect and seem to have confidence in my professional ability.
79. The purposes and objectives of the school cannot be achieved by the present curriculum.
80. The teachers in our school have a desirable influence on the values and attitudes of their students.
81. This community expects its teachers to meet unreasonable personal standards.
82. My students appreciate the help I give them with their school work.
83. To me there is no more challenging work than teaching.
84. Other teachers in our school are appreciative of my work.
85. As a teacher in this community my nonprofessional activities outside of school are unduly restricted.
86. As a teacher, I think I am as competent as most other teachers.
87. The teachers with whom I work have high professional ethics.
88. Our school curriculum does a good job of preparing students to become enlightened and competent citizens.
89. I really enjoy working with my students.
90. The teachers in our school show a great deal of initiative and creativity in their teaching assignments.
91. Teachers in our community feel free to discuss controversial issues in their classes.
92. My principal tries to make me feel comfortable when he visits my classes.
93. My principal makes effective use of the individual teacher's capacity and talent.

94. The people in this community, generally, have a sincere and wholehearted interest in the school system.
95. Teachers feel free to go to the principal about problems of personal and group welfare.
96. This community supports ethical procedures regarding the appointment and reappointment of the teaching staff.
97. This community is willing to support a good program of education.
98. Our community expects the teachers to participate in too many social activities.
99. Community pressures prevent me from doing my best as a teacher.
100. I am well satisfied with my present teaching position.

Scoring: Agree = 4; Probably Agree = 3; Probably Disagree = 2; and Disagree = 1. The scoring is reversed for the following items: 1, 5, 6, 8, 10, 11, 14, 18, 25, 30, 31, 34, 40, 42, 45, 54, 56, 60, 71, 72, 76, 79, 81, 85, 98, and 99.

Reprinted with permission of the Purdue Research Foundation. West Lafayette, IN. 47906.

Staff Morale Questionnaire

Smith, K.R. 1971. The validation of a morale measuring instrument. *Journal of Educational Administration* 9:32-37.

Comments: A new 72-item SMQ has been developed for teachers based on the three factors currently identified. The SMQ has been used in Great Britain, Australia, Indonesia, New Zealand, New Guinea, Canada, Israel, and the United States.

Scale Construction: The original 50-item SMQ based on the work of Cattell and Stice examined five areas: group cohesion; tenacity and fortitude; leadership synergy; adventurous striving; and personal reward. Originally, there were ten items in each category. When the 50-item questionnaire was factor analyzed, three factors emerged.

Sample: Teachers from six schools in Florida participated (four schools were identified as high morale schools and two schools were identified as low morale schools). Four hundred and fifteen secondary school teachers in Singapore completed the 24-item SMQ. Seven items from the original 50-item SMQ were added to the 24-item SMQ. Four months later, an additional 305 secondary school teachers in six schools in Singapore completed the SMQ.

Validity: The purpose of the Singapore study was to provide construct validation of the three factors in the SMQ. The factor loadings for the SMQ are provided.

Factor Analysis: A varimax rotation yielded seven factors. The first three factors are labeled as: leadership synergy, cohesive pride, and personal challenge. Ten items loaded on leadership synergy (9, 10, 11, 12, 13, 14, 15, 16, 26, and 29); nine items loaded on cohesive pride (1, 2, 3, 4, 8, 18, 20, 22, and 25), and five items loaded on personal challenge (23, 24, 27, 30, and 31). A second factor analysis was performed with the second sample. A varimax rotation yielded three factors: leadership synergy (1, 2, 7, 8, 9, 10, 11, 12, 13, 14, 18, 21, 22, 24, and 25); cohesive pride (3, 4, 5, 6, 15, and 17); and personal challenge (16, 19, 20, 23, 26, and 27).

Definition of Factors: *Cohesive pride* means that the staff works together to achieve the objectives of the school; it exemplifies cooperation. *Personal challenge* relates to the incentives that are received from job satisfaction; it assesses how a group uses its potentiality for freedom. *Leadership/synergy* describes the energy of the group and is viewed as the most important morale factor.

References:
Smith, K.R. 1976. Morale: A refinement of Stogdill's model. *Journal of Educational Administration* 14:87-93.

Smith, K.R. 1987. One hundred dissertations: A review of the University of New England Morale Research Project. *Journal of Educational Administration* 25:101-125.

Williams, K.W. and T.J. Lane. 1975. Construct validation of a Staff Morale Questionnaire. *Journal of Educational Administration* 13:90-97.

Wong, R.Y.L. 1991. Construct validation of the Staff Morale Questionnaire-The Singapore Scene. *Journal of Educational Administration* 29:71-80.

Staff Morale Questionnaire

1. I would rather teach with my present colleagues than with any other group of teachers in another school.
2. In this school teachers have a sense of belonging and of being needed.
3. The teachers in this school co-operate with each other to achieve common professional objectives.
4. Every teacher on this staff contributes towards the achievement of the school's aims.
5. I would perform my duties equally well and continuously under less pleasant conditions than I have at present.
6. I do school work beyond my normal working hours.
7. When I believe that suggestions made by my immediate supervisor are of little value, I ignore them.
8. Members of this staff can be relied upon to work with steady persistence.
9. On the whole, how much chance is given to you in this school to show what you can really do?
10. How well are you kept informed about what is going on in your school?
11. How do you feel after your immediate supervisor has talked to you about a mistake or weakness in your work?
12. How well are school policies and the reasons for them explained to you?
13. How well do you think your school is run?
14. The principal seems to want everything to depend solely on his judgment.
15. Our principal encourages teachers to participate in the formulating of major school projects.
16. Duties delegated to teachers are clearly and explicitly defined.
17. To what extent do teachers in your school pursue in-service or university courses?
18. In general, teachers on this staff show a great deal of originality and initiative in their teaching.
19. To me there is no more challenging profession than teaching.
20. Teachers in this school display confidence and keenness when called upon for a special effort.
21. In general, I have tried to be innovative in my teaching techniques on my own initiative.
22. Teachers in this school are convinced of the importance of the school's objectives.
23. The teaching I am doing at present gives me a feeling of success and pride.
24. I feel that I am an important part of my present school.
25. There is no complaining, arguing and taking of sides among my colleagues.
26. To what extent do you feel that your colleagues act as a unified staff rather than as a collection of independent individuals?
27. Keeping up to date professionally is too much of a burden.
28. Are you provided with the best possible equipment consistent with your school's aims and finances?
29. Would your immediate supervisor support you and back you up if something went wrong which was not your fault?
30. To what extent would you wish to share in the organization and running of your school?
31. To what extent do past successes in teaching cause you to strive for similar success in the future?

Scoring: A four-point scale is used ranging from 1 to 4.

Reprinted with permission of Kevin B. Smith, PO Box 440, Armidale NSW 2350, Australia.

Motivation

Job Diagnostic Survey

Hackman, J.R. and G.R. Oldham. 1974. Job Diagnostic Survey. Tests in Microfiche, ETS Test Collection, Princeton, NJ.

Comments: The JDS has satisfactory psychometric characteristics. Internal consistency reliabilities are satisfactory and the scale items are able to discriminate. According to the authors, the JDS may be used to determine if motivation and satisfaction are really problematic; is the job low in motivation potential; what specific aspects of the job are causing the difficulty; how ready are the employees for change; and what special problems and opportunities are present in the existing work system? The JDS is the most frequently cited instrument to measure motivation.

Scale Construction: It took over two years to develop and refine the JDS, which is based on the work of Turner and Lawrence (1965) and Hackman and Lawler (1971). According to the theory which is the basis for the JDS, positive personal and work outcomes are obtained when three critical psychological states exist. The three critical psychological states are created by the existence of five core dimensions. Using the theory, a motivating potential score can be computed. The JDS has been revised three times over the last two years.

Sample: The original sample consisted of 658 blue collar, white collar, and professional workers from seven industrial and service companies representing 62 distinct jobs. Demographic characteristics are included. Overall, over 1,500 employees from 15 distinct companies representing 100 jobs have participated.

Reliability: Internal consistency reliabilities were: 0.71 (skill variety, feedback from the job itself, and job choice format), 0.59 (task identity), 0.66 (task significance and autonomy), 0.78 (feedback from agents), 0.59 (dealing with others), 0.74 (experienced meaningfulness of the work), 0.72 (experienced responsibility for the work), 0.76 (knowledge of results, general satisfaction, and internal work motivation), 0.56 (social satisfaction), 0.79 (supervisory satisfaction), 0.84 (growth satisfaction), and 0.88 (would like format). Median off-diagonal correlations are also reported.

Validity: The substantive validity of the JDS is described in more detail in another report by Hackman and Oldham (1974). Overall, the variables assessed by the JDS relate to each other as predicted by the theory that is the foundation of the survey. In addition, the job dimensions are related to behavioral measures of absenteeism and supervisory ratings of performance effectiveness.

Job Measures: The JDS measures five core dimensions (skill variety, task identity, task significance, autonomy, and feedback from the job itself) and two additional dimensions (feedback from agents and dealing with others). Section one contains seven items, while Section two contains 14 items (two items for each dimension) The JDS also examines three psychological states (experienced meaningfulness of the work, experienced responsibilities for work outcomes, and knowledge of results) and three affective reactions to the job (general satisfaction, internal work motivation, and satisfaction with job security, pay and other compensation, peers and co-workers, supervision, and opportunities for personal growth and development). Section three contains 15 items, while Section five contains ten items. Section four contains 14 items that relate to the five specific types of satisfaction. Finally, the JDS measures individual growth need strength. Section six contains 11 items in a would like format, while Section seven contains 12 items in a job choice format.

Data Analysis: Means, standard deviations, and the results of one-way analyses of variance are reported. Between-job differences are statistically significant for all of the JDS scale scores. Intercorrelations among the JDS scales are presented.

References:

Burk, M.P. 1991. A study of clinical supervision and the job satisfaction of elementary teachers in Oklahoma. Ed.D. dissertation, Oklahoma State University.

Dyer, L.S. 1992. A study relating job satisfaction, personal values, and personal characteristics to teacher absenteeism. Ed.D. dissertation, Oklahoma State University.

Hackman, J.R. and G.R. Oldham. 1974. Motivation through the design of work: Test of a theory (Technical Report No. 6). New Haven, CT: Yale University.

Matheson, R.R. 1992. A comparative study of the perceived job satisfaction of site administrators in San Diego city schools. Ed.D. dissertation, University of San Diego.

Morton, J.T. 1991. A test of the job characteristics model of motivation in public schools. Ed.D. dissertation, Rutgers University, State University of New Jersey, New Brunswick.

Job Diagnostic Survey Section One

1. To what extent does your job require you to *work closely with other people* (either clients, or people in related jobs in your organization)?
   1. Very little; dealing with other people is not at all necessary in doing the job.
   4. Moderately; some dealing with others is necessary.
   7. Very much; dealing with other people is an absolutely essential and crucial part of doing the job.

2. How much *autonomy* is there in your job? That is, to what extent does your job permit you to decide *on your own* how to go about doing the work?
   1. Very little; the job gives me almost no personal "say" about how and when the work is done.
   4. Moderate autonomy; many things are standardized and not under my control, but I can make some decisions about the work.
   7. Very much; the job gives me almost complete responsibility for deciding how and when the work is done.

3. To what extent does your job involve doing a *"whole" and identifiable piece of work*? That is, is the job a complete piece of work that has an obvious beginning and end? Or is it only a small *part* of the overall piece of work, which is finished by other people or by automatic machines?
   1. My job is only a tiny part of the overall piece of work; the results of my activities cannot be seen in the final product or service.
   4. My job is a moderate-sized "chunk" of the overall piece of work; my own contribution can be seen in the final outcome.
   7. My job involves doing the whole piece of work, from start to finish; the results of my activities are easily seen in the final product or service.

4. How much *variety* is there in your job? That is, to what extent does the job require you to do many different things at work, using a variety of your skills and talents?
   1. Very little; the job requires me to do the same routine things over and over again.
   4. Moderate variety.
   7. Very much; the job requires me to do many different things, using a number of different skills and talents.

5. In general, how *significant or important* is your job? That is, are the results of your work likely to significantly affect the lives or well-being of other people?
   1. Not very significant; the outcomes of my work are *not* likely to have important effects on other people.
   4. Moderately significant.
   7. Highly significant; the outcomes of my work can affect other people in very important ways.

6. To what extent do *managers or co-workers* let you know how well you are doing on your job?
   1. Very little; people almost never let me know how well I am doing.
   4. Moderately; sometimes people may give me "feedback"; other times they may not.
   7. Very much; managers or co-workers provide me with almost consistent "feedback" about how well I am doing.

7. To what extent does *doing the job* itself provide you with information about your work performance? That is, does the actual *work itself* provide clues about how well you are doing aside from any "feedback" co-workers or supervisors may provide?

1. Very little; the job itself is set up so I could work forever without finding out how well I am doing.

4. Moderately; sometimes doing the job provides "feedback" to me; sometimes it does not.

7. Very much; the job is set up so that I get almost constant "feedback" as I work about how well I am doing.

Scoring: Various seven-point scales are used for the seven sections of the JDS. Section one of the JDS measures the seven job dimensions. Very Little: the job requires me to do the same routine things over and over again = 1; Moderate Variety = 4; and Very Much: the job requires me to do many different things, using a number of different skills and talents = 7.

Job Diagnostic Survey Section Two

1. The job requires me to use a number of complex or high-level skills.
2. The job requires a lot of cooperative work with other people.
3. The job is arranged so that I do *not* have the chance to do an entire piece of work from beginning to end.
4. Just doing the work required by the job provides many chances for me to figure out how well I am doing.
5. The job is quite simple and repetitive.
6. The job can be done adequately by a person working alone--without talking or checking with other people.
7. The supervisors and co-workers on this job almost *never* give me any "feedback" about how well I am doing in my work.
8. This job is one where a lot of other people can be affected by how well the work gets done.
9. The job denies me any chance to use my personal initiative or judgment in carrying out the work.
10. Supervisors often let me know how well they think I am performing the job.
11. The job provides me the chance to completely finish the pieces of work I begin.
12. The job itself provides very few clues about whether or not I am performing well.
13. The job gives me considerable opportunity for independence and freedom in how I do the work.
14. The job itself is *not* very significant or important in the broader scheme of things.

Scoring: Section two also measures the seven job dimensions. Very Inaccurate = 1; Mostly Inaccurate = 2; Slightly Inaccurate = 3; Uncertain = 4; Slightly Accurate = 5; Mostly Accurate = 6; and Very Accurate = 7.

Job Diagnostic Survey Section Three

1. It's hard, on this job, for me to care very much about whether or not the work gets done right.
2. My opinion of myself goes up when I do this job well.
3. Generally speaking, I am very satisfied with this job.
4. Most of the things I have to do on this job seem useless or trivial.
5. I usually know whether or not my work is satisfactory on this job.
6. I feel a great sense of personal satisfaction when I do this job well.
7. The work I do on this job is very meaningful to me.
8. I feel a very high degree of *personal* responsibility for the work I do on this job.
9. I frequently think of quitting this job.

10. I feel bad and unhappy when I discover that I have performed poorly on this job.
11. I often have trouble figuring out whether I'm doing well or poorly on this job.
12. I feel I should personally take the credit or blame for the results of my work on this job.
13. I am generally satisfied with the kind of work I do on this job.
14. My own feelings generally are *not* affected much one way or the other by how well I do on this job.
15. Whether or not this job gets done right is clearly *my* responsibility.

Scoring: Section three measures general satisfaction and internal work motivation. Disagree Strongly = 1; Disagree = 2; Disagree Slightly = 3; Neutral = 4; Agree Slightly = 5; Agree = 6; and Agree Strongly = 7.

Job Diagnostic Survey Section Four

1. The amount of job security I have.
2. The amount of pay and fringe benefits I receive.
3. The amount of personal growth and development I get in doing my job.
4. The people I talk to and work with on my job.
5. The degree of respect and fair treatment I receive from my boss.
6. The feeling of worthwhile accomplishment I get from doing my job.
7. The chance to get to know other people while on the job.
8. The amount of support and guidance I receive from my supervisor.
9. The degree to which I am fairly paid for what I contribute to this organization.
10. The amount of independent thought and action I can exercise in my job.
11. How secure things look for me in the future in this organization.
12. The chance to help other people while at work.
13. The amount of challenge in my job.
14. The overall quality of the supervision I receive in my work.

Scoring: Section four measures specific satisfactions. Extremely Dissatisfied = 1; Dissatisfied = 2; Slightly Dissatisfied = 3; Neutral = 4; Slightly Satisfied = 5; Satisfied = 6; and Extremely Satisfied = 7.

Job Diagnostic Survey Section Five

1. Most people on this job feel a great sense of personal satisfaction when they do the job well.
2. Most people on this job are very satisfied with the job.
3. Most people on this job feel that the work is useless or trivial.
4. Most people on this job feel a great deal of personal responsibility for the work they do.
5. Most people on this job have a pretty good idea of how well they are performing their job.
6. Most people on this job find the work very meaningful.
7. Most people on this job feel that whether or not the job gets done right is clearly their own responsibility.
8. People on this job often think of quitting.
9. Most people on this job feel bad or unhappy when they find that they have performed the work poorly.
10. Most people on this job have trouble figuring out whether they are doing a good or a bad job.

Scoring: Section five measures the three psychological states as well as general satisfaction and internal work motivation. It also measures general satisfaction and internal work motivation. Disagree Strongly = 1; Disagree = 2; Disagree Slightly = 3; Neutral = 4; Agree Slightly = 5; Agree = 6; and Agree Strongly = 7.

Job Diagnostic Survey Section Six

1.   High respect and fair treatment from my supervisor.
2.   Stimulating and challenging work.
3.   Chances to exercise independent thought and action in my job.
4.   Great job security.
5.   Very friendly co-workers.
6.   Opportunities to learn new things from my work.
7.   High salary and good fringe benefits.
8.   Opportunities to be creative and imaginative in my work.
9.   Quick promotions.
10.   Opportunities for personal growth and development in my job.
11.   A sense of worthwhile accomplishment in my work.

Scoring: Section six measures individual growth need strength Would like having this only a moderate amount (or less) = 4; Would like having this very much = 7; and Would like having this extremely much = 10.

Job Diagnostic Survey Section Seven

1.   a. A job where the pay is very good.
     b. A job where there is considerable opportunity to be creative and innovative.

2.   a. A job where you are often required to make important decisions.
     b. A job with many pleasant people to work with.

3.   a. A job in which greater responsibility is given to those who do the best work.
     b. A job in which greater responsibility is given to loyal employees who have the most   seniority.

4.   a. A job in an organization which is in financial trouble--and might have to close down   within the
        year
     b. A job in which you are not allowed to have any say whatever in how your work is   scheduled,
        or in the procedures to be used in carrying it out.

5.   a. A very routine job.
     b. A job where your co-workers are not very friendly.

6.   a. A job with a supervisor who is often very critical of you and your work in front of other   people.
     b. A job which prevents you from using a number of skills that you worked hard to develop.

7.   a. A job with a supervisor who respects you and treats you fairly.
     b. A job which provides constant opportunities for you to learn new and interesting things.

8.   a. A job where there is a real chance you could be laid off.
       b. A job with very little chance to do challenging work.

9.   a. A job in which there is a real chance for you to develop new skills and advance in the organization.
       b. A job which provides lots of vacation time and an excellent fringe benefit package.

10.   a. A job with little freedom and independence to do your work in the way you think best.
       b. A job where the working conditions are poor.

11.   a. A job with very satisfying team-work.
       b. A job which allows you to use your skills and abilities to the fullest extent.

12.   a. A job which offers little or no challenge.
       b. A job which requires you to be completely isolated from co-workers.

Scoring: Section seven measures individual growth need strength Strongly prefer A = 1; Slightly Prefer A = 2; Neutral = 3; Slightly Prefer B = 4; and Strongly Prefer B = 5. A scoring key for the JDS is provided. In addition, a short form of the JDS is available.

Reprinted with permission of the author.

Educational Works Components Study

Miskel, C.G. and L.E. Heller. 1973. The Educational Work Components Study: An adapted set of measures for work motivation. *Journal of Experimental Education* 42:45-50.

Comments: The Work Components Study was developed by Borgatta (1967) for industrial settings. Miskel and Heller modified the WCS for public schools. The theoretical foundation for the WCS is the two-factor theory of motivation (Herzberg et al., 1959). The 56-item EWCS contains six factors.

Sample: The sample of 745 consisted of 153 seniors and 42 graduate students in a school of education as well as 118 administrators and 432 teachers from three public school districts. A stratified random sampling procedure was used.

Reliability: Alpha coefficients (Cronbach) for the WCS ranged from 0.68 to 0.83. For school personnel, alpha coefficients for the EWCS ranged from 0.73 to 0.83. The estimates of internal consistency were 0.80 (potential for personal challenge and development), 0.73 (competitiveness desirability), 0.79 (tolerance for work pressure), 0.81 (conservative security), 0.82 (willingness to seek reward in spite of uncertainty vs. avoidance), and 0.83 (surround concern).

Validity: Factor analysis was undertaken to determine the factorial stability of the EWCS.

Factor Analysis: Varimax orthogonal and maxplane oblique R-factor analysis procedures were performed yielding six factors. The six factors are: eight items on potential for personal challenge and development (13, 24, 31, 34, 39, 42, 45, and 56); seven items on competitiveness desirability and reward of success (3, 11, 21, 35, 37, 49, and 52); nine items on tolerance for work pressure (7, 12, 18, 22, 27, 28, 43, 48, and 50); 11 items on conservative security (2, 10, 14, 15, 20, 26, 33, 36, 41, 47, and 54); 10 items on willingness to seek reward in spite of uncertainty vs. avoidance of uncertainty (1, 4, 6, 9, 19, 25, 32, 40, 46, and 53); and 11 items on surround concern (5, 8, 16, 17, 23, 29, 30, 38, 44, 51, and 55).

Definition of Factors: *Potential for personal challenge and development* measures the desirability of a job that provides for creativity, responsibility, and measures personal ability. *Competitiveness desirability and reward of success* measures job situations where pay is based on merit, competition is keen, and, accomplishment is emphasized. *Tolerance for work pressure* measures job situations where the work load may be excessive and the individual may have to take work home. *Conservative security* measures whether or not the person plays it safe and has job security. *Willingness to seek reward in spite of uncertainty vs. avoidance of uncertainty* measures the person's willingness to do interesting work although the person could lose his/her position. *Surround concern* measures the individual's concern for hygiene factors.

References:
Borgatta, E.F. et al. 1968. The Work Components Study: A revised set of measures for work motivation. *Multivariate Behavioral Research* 3:403-414.

Dunton, D.D. 1983. A study of demographic characteristics and stated attitudes towards work of new and re-entry teachers in selected Illinois districts. Ed.D. dissertation, University of Illinois, Urbana-Champaign.

Fuqua, A.B. 1983. Professional attractiveness, inside sponsorship, and perceived paternalism as predictors of upward mobility of public school superintendents. Ed.D. dissertation, Virginia Polytechnic Institute and State University.

Hatley, P.R. 1991. Work motivation and job satisfaction of principals and assistant principals in Missouri public high schools. Ed.D. dissertation, University of Missouri, Columbia.

Miskel, C. 1977. Principals' attitudes toward work and co-workers, situational factors, perceived effectiveness and innovation effort. *Educational Administration Quarterly* 13:51-70.

Educational Work Components Study Questionnaire

1. I could get fired easily, but the work would be very interesting.
2. The emphasis would be on carrying out clearly outlined school district policies.
3. Salary increases would be strictly a matter of how much you accomplished for the school district.
4. I could not be sure I could keep my job as long as I want it.
5. The lighting is good.
6. The school district is not stable.
7. Trouble might come up that I would have to take care of myself, even outside regular hours.
8. The community has good recreational facilities.
9. The school district has in the recent past been having a hard time holding its position.
10. The job is managing a small group of people doing routine jobs.
11. The school district is known to be involved in heavy competition.
12. The work might be excessive sometimes.
13. There is opportunity for creative work.
14. The work would be routine, but would not be hard to do.
15. I would work as a member of a more-or-less permanent group.
16. The climate would be pleasant.
17. The community would be a wonderful place to raise a family.
18. The schedule of hours might have to be flexible in response to the amount of work.
19. The work might run out, but it would be extremely interesting while it lasted.
20. The pay is not too high, but the job is secure.
21. Persons are supposed to "get the boot" if they don't make good and keep making good.
22. I might sometimes have to take work home with me.
23. The physical working conditions would be attractive.
24. I would have a chance to really accomplish something, even if others wouldn't know about it.
25. I could get fired easily.
26. The work is routine, but the initial salary is high.
27. The work might build up "pressures" on me.
28. The nature of the job changes because the school district changes.
29. The fringe benefits are very good.
30. The ventilation is modern.
31. There would be emphasis on individual ability.
32. There is little permanency of positions.
33. I would be under civil service.
34. The school district is located in a university center and would encourage further specialized work.

35. There are opportunities to earn bonuses.
36. Promotions come automatically.
37. Competition would be open and encouraged.
38. The community would have a good social and cultural life.
39. I would have a chance to further my formal education.
40. I could get fired easily, but the rewards would be high.
41. The work is routine, but highly respected in the community.
42. I would always have a chance to learn something new.
43. There might occasionally be some physical danger.
44. The supervisors are nice people.
45. The work itself keeps changing and I need to change to keep up with it.
46. The job is insecure.
47. The salary increases are regularly scheduled.
48. The work might come in big pushes.
49. There is emphasis on the actual production record.
50. I might be on call when there is pressure to get jobs done.
51. The retirement plan is good.
52. Salary increases would be a matter of how much effort you put in.
53. Rewards are high, and the work interesting, but if one loses his job it is very difficult to get another one.
54. There would be emphasis on satisfying superiors by carrying out school policy.
55. I would have nice people for co-workers.
56. There would be emphasis on originality.

Scoring: Respondents are asked "How desirable would you consider each of the following items in a job for you? A job in which..." Extremely Undesirable. Would never take the job = 1. Undesirable. Would avoid the job = 2. Neither Desirable or Undesirable = 3. Desirable. Would favor the job = 4. Extremely Desirable = 5. Would favor job greatly.

Reprinted with permission of the author.

Needs

Higher Order Need Strength Measure B

Hackman, J.R. and G.R. Oldham. 1974. *The Job Diagnostic Survey: An instrument for the diagnosis of jobs and the evaluation of job redesign projects.* New Haven, CT: Yale University, Department of Administrative Sciences, Technical Report No. 4.

Comments: This 12-item measure, part of the Job Diagnostic Survey (Section seven), assesses a worker's interest in getting "growth satisfaction" from work. Higher order needs include: participation in decision making, the use of a variety of valued skills and abilities, freedom and independence, challenge, expression of creativity, and the opportunity for learning. Lower order needs include: high pay, fringe benefits, job security, friendly co-workers, and considerate supervision. Participants are asked to select between growth needs and other needs.

Scale Construction: See description of the Job Diagnostic Survey.

Sample: Overall, more than 1,500 people from 100 different jobs in 15 companies were surveyed. The respondents included blue-collar, white-collar, and professional workers.

Reliability: Internal consistency reliability for the "would like" format was 0.88 and 0.71 for the job choice format.

Validity: See description of the Job Diagnostic Survey.

Data Analysis: Means and variances of JDS scores for growth need strength are presented.

References:
Cameron, G.J. 1984. The effects of clinical and traditional supervision methods on the satisfaction levels of higher and lower-order need teachers. Ed.D. dissertation, University of San Diego.

Dunham, R.B. 1976. The measurement and dimensionality of job characteristics. *Journal of Applied Psychology* 61:404-409.

Katz, R. 1978. Job longevity as a situational factor in job satisfaction. *Administrative Science Quarterly* 23:204-223.

Pastor, M.C. and D.A. Erlandson. 1982. A study of higher order need strength and job satisfaction in secondary public school teachers. *Journal of Educational Administration* 20:172-183.

Higher Order Need Strength Measure B

1. a. A job where the pay is very good.
    b. A job where there is considerable opportunity to be creative and innovative.

2. a. A job where you are often required to make important decisions.
    b. A job with many pleasant people to work with.

3. a. A job in which greater responsibility is given to those who do the best work.
    b. A job in which greater responsibility is given to loyal employees who have the most   seniority.

4. a. A job in an organization which is in financial trouble--and might have to close down   within   the year.
    b. A job in which you are not allowed to have any say whatever in how your work is   scheduled, or in the procedures to be used in carrying it out.

5. a. A very routine job.
    b. A job where your co-workers are not very friendly.

6. a. A job with a supervisor who is often very critical of you and your work in front of other   people.
    b. A job which prevents you from using a number of skills that you worked hard to develop.

7. a. A job with a supervisor who respects you and treats you fairly.
    b. A job which provides constant opportunities for you to learn new and interesting things.

8. a. A job where there is a real chance you could be laid off.
    b. A job with very little chance to do challenging work.

9. a. A job in which there is a real chance for you to develop new skills and advance in the organization.
    b. A job which provides lots of vacation time and an excellent fringe benefit package.

10. a. A job with little freedom and independence to do your work in the way you think best.
    b. A job where the working conditions are poor.

11. a. A job with very satisfying team-work.
    b. A job which allows you to use your skills and abilities to the fullest extent.

12. a. A job which offers little or no challenge.
    b. A job which requires you to be completely isolated from co-workers.

Scoring: Strongly Prefer A = 1; Slightly Prefer A = 2; Neutral = 3; Slightly Prefer B = 4; and Strongly Prefer B = 5. A score over 3.00 signifies a predominance of higher order need choices, while a score under 3.00 signifies a predominance of lower order need choices.

Reprinted with permission of the author.

Management Position Questionnaire

Porter, L.W. 1961. A study of perceived need satisfactions in bottom and middle management jobs. *Journal of Applied Psychology* 45:1-10.

Comments: The MPQ contains 15 management position characteristics that relate to need satisfaction. Overall, these items correspond to Maslow's need hierarchy: security, social, esteem, autonomy, and self-actualization. No items related to physiological needs were included, and two other items related to pay and to the feeling of being-in-the-know were added. The MSQ examines the differences among needs within various levels of management. Several instruments grew out of the MPQ.

Sample: The original sample consisted of 64 bottom-level (lowest level of management in an organization) and 75 middle-level (above the first level of supervision) managers from three organizations. A description of the three organizations is provided.

Data Analysis: Data reflecting the differences between perceived amount of present fulfillment of needs and the amount of fulfillment believed should be available are reported for both bottom-level and middle-level positions. In addition, data reflecting the importance of these needs for both groups are also presented.

References:
Brown, F. 1973. The job satisfaction of administrators within a multi-ethnic setting. Paper presented at American Educational Research Association. ERIC ED 090 654.

Mitchell, V.F. and P. Moudgill. 1976. Measurement of Maslow's need hierarchy. *Organizational Behavior and Human Performance* 16:334-349.

Porter, L.W. 1962. Job attitudes in management: I. perceived deficiencies in need fulfillment as a function of job level. *Journal of Applied Psychology* 46:375-384.

Trusty, F.M. and T.J. Sergiovanni. 1966. Perceived need deficiencies of teachers and administrators: A proposal for restructuring teacher roles. *Educational Administration Quarterly* 2:168-180.

Van Maanen, J. 1975. Police socialization: A longitudinal examination of job attitudes in an urban police department. *Administrative Science Quarterly* 20:207-228.

Management Position Questionnaire

1. The *feeling of security* in my management position
2. The *opportunity,* in my management position, *to give help to other people*
3. The *opportunity to develop close friendships* in my management position
4. The *feeling of self-esteem* a person gets from being in my management position
5. The *prestige* of my management position *inside* the company (that is, the regard received from others in the company)
6. The *prestige* of my management position *outside* the company (that is, the regard received from others not in the company)
7. The *authority* connected with my management position
8. The *opportunity for independent thought and action* in my management position
9. The *opportunity,* in my management position, *for participation in the setting of goals*
10. The *opportunity,* in my management position, *for participation in the determination of methods and procedures*
11. The *opportunity for personal growth and development* in my management position
12. The *feeling of self-fulfillment* a person gets from being in my management position (that is, the feeling of being able to use one's own unique capabilities, realizing one's potentialities)
13. The *feeling of worthwhile accomplishment* in my management position
14. The *pay* for my management position
15. The feeling of *being-in-the-know* in my management position

Scoring: Each item is rated on a seven-point scale ranging from 1 (minimum) to 7 (maximum). Respondents are asked to give three ratings for each item in terms of: How much of the characteristic is there now connected with your management position? How much of the characteristic do you think should be connected with your management position? How important is this position characteristic to you?

Reprinted with permission of the author.

Manifest Needs Questionnaire

Steers, R.M. and D.N. Braunstein. 1976. A behaviorally-based measure of manifest needs in work settings. *Journal of Vocational Behavior* 9:251-266.

Comments: The MNQ, which measures four of Murray's needs, demonstrates evidence of convergent and discriminant validity. The authors cite the following as three limitations of the MNQ: additional organizations need to be surveyed; the MNQ is a research instrument and should not be used to make decisions about selection or placement; and the instrument only measures four needs.

Scale Construction: Items were written for four needs (achievement, affiliation, autonomy, and dominance) based upon the research of Murray (1938). Some items were worded negatively. A panel of judges examined the items for appropriateness, clarity, and content validity. Then, three studies were conducted to validate the MNQ. The first study was a pilot study. The 20-item MNQ contains five statements for each need.

Sample: The original sample consisted of 96 management students who were working in business, government, and education.

Reliability: Alpha coefficients (Cronbach) were 0.66 (achievement), 0.56 (affiliation), 0.61 (autonomy), and 0.83 (dominance). Test-retest reliabilities over a two week interval with 41 people were 0.72 (achievement), 0.75 (affiliation), 0.77 (autonomy), and 0.86 (dominance).

Validity: The scores on the MNQ were compared with the scores on the Personality Research Form (Jackson, 1967) to establish convergent and discriminant validity. In addition, four independent judges rated 49 participants to establish discriminant validity. The MNQ was also used to predict work group preferences.

Data Analysis: Means, standard deviations, and off-diagonal correlations are reported for the four scales. Point biserial correlations between MNQ scores and eight work group preferences are provided.

References:
Chusmir, L.H. 1988. An update on the internal consistency of the Manifest Needs Questionnaire. *Psychology: A Journal of Human Behavior* 25:14-18.

Chusmir, L.H. and J.N. Hood. 1986. Relationship between Type A behavior pattern and motivational needs. *Psychological Reports* 58:783-794.

Dreher, G.F. and R.R. Mai-Dalton. 1983. A note on the internal consistency of the Manifest Needs Questionnaire. *Journal of Applied Psychology* 68:194-196.

Mowday, R.T. and D.G. Spencer. 1981. The influence of task and personality characteristics on employee turnover and absenteeism incidents. *Academy of Management Journal* 24:634-642.

Steers, R.M. and D.G. Spencer. 1977. The role of achievement motivation in job design. *Journal of Applied Psychology* 62:472-479.

Manifest Needs Questionnaire

1. I do my best work when my job assignments are fairly difficult.
2. When I have a choice, I try to work in a group instead of by myself.
3. In my work assignments, I try to be my own boss.
4. I seek an active role in the leadership of a group.
5. I try very hard to improve on my past performance at work.
6. I pay a good deal of attention to the feelings of others at work.
7. I go my own way at work, regardless of the opinions of others.
8. I avoid trying to influence those around me to see things my way.
9. I take moderate risks and stick my neck out to get ahead at work.
10. I prefer to do my own work and let others do theirs.
11. I disregard rules and regulations that hamper my personal freedom.
12. I find myself organizing and directing the activities of others.
13. I try to avoid any added responsibilities on my job.
14. I express my disagreements with others openly.
15. I consider myself a "team player" at work.
16. I strive to gain more control over the events around me at work.
17. I try to perform better than my co-workers.
18. I find myself talking to those around me about non-business related matters.
19. I try my best to work alone on a job.
20. I strive to be "in command" when I am working in a group.

Scoring: Always, Almost Always, Usually, Sometimes, Seldom, Almost Never, and Never. Scoring is reversed for items 8, 10, 13, 14, and 15.

Reprinted with permission of the author.

Organizational Assessment

Quality of School Life Scale

Epstein, J.L. and J.M. McPartland. 1977. Administration and technical manual for the Quality of School Life Scale. The Johns Hopkins University, Baltimore. Mimeo.

Comments: The 27-item QSL is a multi-dimensional measure of student reactions to school in general, to their classwork, and to their teachers. It is designed for use with students in grades 4-12. It will help teachers, administrators, and researchers measure students' reactions, to describe and monitor the conditions of school life, and to make decisions about the success of school programs.

Scale Construction: The instrument uses multiple choice, true-false, and Likert-type formats, alternately, in order (according to the authors) to minimize response set. Of the 27 items which make up the instrument, 14 items use a true-false response, nine items use multiple choice, and four items use a Likert response.

Sample: The sample consisted of 1,060 elementary students and 3,206 secondary students from one school district in Maryland.

Reliability: Reliability estimates for the total instrument and for the subscales ranged between 0.80 and 0.89 for the various student groups.

Validity: Evidence for concurrent and discriminate validity was obtained from questionnaire items, open-ended written comments, peer and teacher nominations (known group method) and achievement tests. Correlations are provided of the QSL with school performance and participation, family background variables, and educational and occupational plans. In general, students who report high satisfaction with the quality of their school experience are those who are comfortable with the demands and opportunities of the school setting, are industrious and ambitious, have more positive self-evaluations, and receive positive evaluation from teachers and parents.

Factor Analysis: A principal components analysis with a varimax rotation was performed to check the dimensionality among the 27 items. Four interpretable factors emerged. Two of these correspond to the SAT and COM subscales, two other factors divided the TCH subscale into two parts. However, after several statistical tests and comparisons, the TCH subscale was retained as a single dimension.

Definition of Subscales: Three subscales were derived: *Satisfaction with School* (SAT) subscale examines students' general reactions to school. Students who are positive in their evaluation of school life may be more likely to experience feelings of general well-being. *Commitment to Classwork* (COM) subscale deals with the level of student interest in classwork. *Reactions to Teachers* (TCH) subscale examines student evaluations of instructional and personal interactions with teacher. Overall the quality of school experiences may influence student behavior and attitudes.

References:

Epstein, J.L. and J.M. McPartland. 1976. Quality of School Life Scale. Chicago, IL: Riverside Publishing Company.

Epstein, J.L. and J.M. McPartland. 1976. The concept and measurement of the Quality of School Life. *American Educational Research Journal* 13:15-30.

Quality of School Life Scale

Sample Items:

1. I like school very much.
2. Most of the time I do not want to go to school.
3. The school and I are like : Good Friends; Friends; Distant Relatives; Strangers; Enemies.
4. Work in class is just buys work and a waste of time.
5. In class, I often count the minutes till it ends.
6. In my classes I get so interested in an assignment or project that I don't want to stop work. Everyday; quite often; hardly ever; never.
7. The things I get to work on in most of my classes are: Great stuff-really interesting to me; Good stuff-pretty interesting to me; OK-school work is school work; Dull stuff-not very interesting to me; Trash-a total loss for me.
8. I wish I could have the same teachers next year.
9. Most of my teachers want me to do things their way and not my own way.
10. Teachers here have a way with students that makes us like them.
11. Thinking of my teachers this term, I really like: All of them; Most of them; Half of them; One or two of them; None of them.

Scoring: The SAT subscale score is the sum of the points received for items 3, 7, 11, 19, 24; COM subscale is items 1, 5, 9, 13, 15, 17, 20, 22, 23, 25, 27; and TCH subscale is items 2, 4, 6, 8, 10, 12, 14, 16, 18, 21, 26.

Reprinted with permission of the authors. Scale available from Riverside Publishing Company, 8420 Bryn Mawr Avenue, Chicago, IL 60631.

Profile of a School
Profile of Organizational Characteristics

Likert, R. 1980. Survey of Organizations. Rensis Likert Associates, Inc. San Diego, CA: University Associates.

Comments: Likert developed three instruments designed to evaluate various aspects of organizations. The three instruments are based on his Systems Four concept of organizational/administrative behavior. System One is characterized as exploitive-authoritative organizational behavior; System Two benevolent authoritative; System Three consultative; and System Four allows for group participation in decision making and organizational activities.

Scale Construction: The *Profile of a School* is a 64-item instrument with parallel forms designed to be used with students, teachers, administrators, central office staff, and school board members. Its greatest value is the ability to compare scores and responses, one-on-one, across all members of a school system concerning their perceptions of the organizational functioning of a school district.

The *Profile of Organizational Characteristics* is 43-item inventory which covers eight organizational variables: the leadership process used; the character of motivational forces; the character of the communication process; the character of the interaction-influence process; aspects of the decision-making process; the nature of goal setting or ordering; aspects of organizational control; and the performance goals and training practices. This profile is intended to describe the nature of managerial systems used in industrial organizations. Sample items from this instrument are provided below.

Reliability: The testing (technical) manuals associated with each instrument provide ample information on the development of each scale. They also provide reliabilities, validity information, and other psychometric qualities of each scale. All reliability estimates ranged in the low to mid 90s.

References:
Barney, D.G. 1990. An integrative assessment of department head supervisory system-teacher conflict-teacher job satisfaction. Ph.D. dissertation, Marquette University.

Likert, R. 1967. *The human organization.* New York: McGraw Hill.

McGarry, G.T. 1980. Impact of a training program in a state agency. Ed.D. dissertation, Boston University School of Education.

Peoples, P.J. 1990. The relationship among school context factors and leadership style factors of principals of effective and other high schools in southern California. Ed.D. dissertation, University of Southern California.

Tomlin, M.E. 1988. A study to determine if secondary school teachers trained in "teacher expectations and student achievement" have a different perception of the organizational climate of their schools than teachers not so trained. Ed.D. dissertation, University of Wyoming.

Vizzini, C.T. Jr. 1989. The relationship of role conflict and ambiguity as a function of organizational characteristics: A study of curriculum supervisors in the public schools of North Carolina. Ed.D. dissertation, University of North Carolina, Chapel Hill.

Profile of a School

1. How often is your behavior seen by your students as friendly and supportive?
2. How often do you seek to be friendly and supportive to your students?
3. How much confidence and trust do you have in your students?
4. How much trust and confidence do your students have in you?
5. How much interest do your students feel you have in their success as students?
6. How free do your students feel to talk to you about academic matters such as their work, course content, teaching plans, and methods?
7. How free do your students feel to talk to you about non-academic school matters such as student activities, rules of conduct, and discipline?
8. How often do you seek and use your students' ideas about academic matters?
9. How often do you seek and use your students' ideas about non-academic school matters?
10. How much do your students feel that you are trying to help them with their problems?
11. How much influence do you think students have on academic matters?
12. How much influence do you think students have on non-academic matters?
13. How much influence do you think students should have on academic matters?
14. How much influence do you think students should have on non-academic matters?
15. To what extent are students involved in major decisions affecting them?
16. What is the general attitude of your students concerning class, school or personal matters?
17. How accurate is information given to you by your students concerning class, school or personal matters?
18. How do students view communications from you?
19. How do students view communications from the principal?
20. How well do you know the problems faced by your students in their school work?
21. What is the character and amount of interaction in your classroom?
22. To what extent do your students help each other when they want to get something done?
23. To what extent do your students look with pleasure on coming to school?
24. To what extent do you look forward to your teaching day?
25. To what extent do your students feel excited about learning?
26. How often do you see your principal's behavior as friendly and supportive?
27. How much confidence and trust does your principal have in you?
28. How much confidence and trust do you have in your principal?
29. How free do you feel to talk to your principal about academic and non-academic school matters?
30. How often do you try to be friendly and supportive to your principal?
31. How often do you try to be friendly and supportive to other teachers?
32. How often are your ideas sought and used by the principal about academic and non-academic school matters?
33. In your job, how often is it worthwhile or a waste of time for you to do your very best?
34. How much influence do you think teachers have on academic and non-academic school matters?
35. How much influence do you think teachers should have on academic and non-academic school matters?
36. How much influence do you think principals have on academic and non-academic school matters?
37. How much influence do you think principals should have on academic and non-academic school matters?

38. How much influence do you think central office staff has on academic and non-academic school matters?
39. How much influence do you think central office staff should have on academic and non-academic school matters?
40. How often are students' ideas sought and used by the principal about academic matters?
41. How often are students' ideas sought and used by the principal about non-academic school matters?
42. How much do you feel that your principal is interested in your success?
43. How often does your principal use group meetings to solve school problems?
44. To what extent does your principal make sure that planning and the setting of priorities are well done?
45. To what extent does your principal try to provide you with the materials and space you need to do your job well?
46. To what extent does your principal give you useful information and ideas?
47. To what extent are you encouraged to be innovative in developing better educational practices and course content?
48. What is your general attitude toward your school?
49. What is the direction of the flow of information about academic and non-academic school matters?
50. How do you view communications from the principal?
51. How accurate is upward communication to the principal?
52. How well does your principal know the problems faced by teachers?
53. What is the character and amount of interaction in your school between the principal and teachers?
54. What is the character and amount of interaction in your school among teachers?
55. In your school, it is "every man for himself" or do principal, teachers, and students work as a team?
56. How are decisions made in your school system?
57. At what level are decisions made about academic matters?
58. To what extent are you involved in major decisions related to your work?
59. How much does your principal try to help you with your problems?
60. How much help do you get from the central staff?
61. To what extent are decision-makers aware of problems, particularly at lower levels?
62. How high are your principal's goals for educational performance?
63. Who holds high performance goals for your school?
64. Who feels responsible for achieving high performance goals in your school?
65. To what extent is there student resistance to high performance goals in your school?

Scoring: A series of descriptive terms is used to define, broadly, four positions along the continuum. For example: Very Little (1 and 2); Some (3 and 4); Considerable (5 and 6); and Very Great (7 and 8).

Reprinted with permission of Jane Gibson Likert.

Profile of Organizational Characteristics

Sample Items:

1. How much confidence and trust is shown in subordinates?
2. How free do they feel to talk to superiors about job?
3. How often are subordinates' ideas sought and used constructively?
4. Is predominant use made of 1 fear, 2 threats, 3 punishment, 4 rewards, 5 involvement?
5. Where is responsibility felt for achieving organization's goals?
6. How much cooperative teamwork exists?
7. What is the usual direction of informational flow?
8. How is downward communication accepted?
9. How accurate is upward communication?
10. How well do superiors know problems faced by subordinates?
11. At what level are decisions made?
12. Are subordinates involved in decisions related to their work?
13. What does the decision-making process contribute to motivation?
14. How are organizational goals established?
15. How much covert resistance to goals is present?
16. How concentrated are review and control functions?
17. Is there an informal organization resisting the formal one?
18. What are cost, productivity and other control data used for?

Scoring: A series of descriptive terms is used to define four positions along the continuum. For example: System 1 (Virtually None); System 2 (Some); System 3 (Substantial amount); and System 4 (A Great Deal).

Reprinted with permission of Jane Gibson Likert.

Position Analysis Questionnaire

Mecham, R.C. et al. 1969. Users manual for the Position Analysis Questionnaire. University Book Store, 360 W. State St., Lafayette, IN 47906.

Comments: According to the authors, the PAQ is a structured job analysis questionnaire which provides quantified information about the nature of jobs. It differs from most check list instruments in that the items describe job characteristics, or job contexts, which may be found in a wide variety of occupational areas. The instrument generates data which may be applied in employee selection and placement, job evaluation and classification, performance appraisal, determining the similarity of jobs, and the like. The analysis is carried out by numerically rating the degree to which each of 194 job elements (items) applies to the job or position being rated. Based on this rating, it is possible to compare jobs, quantitatively, in terms of similarities, or differences, as to their job dimension profiles.

Reliability: The PAQ has extensive manuals and technical documentation which provide complete and detailed information on the development of the scales and the approach, or application, in utilizing the questionnaire. In addition, complete information is provided on reliability and validity of the scales.

Questionnaire Divisions: The questionnaire is divided into six major divisions. (1) Information input: where and how does the worker get the information that he uses in performing the job? (2) Mental processes: What reasoning, decision making, planning, and information processing activities are involved in performing the job? (3) Work output: What physical activities does the worker perform and what tools are required in performing the job? (4) Relationships with other persons: What relationships with other people are required in performing the job? (5) Job Context: In what physical and social contexts is the work performed? (6) Other job characteristics: What activities, conditions, or characteristics other than those described above are relevant to the job?

These six divisions are further divided into sections and subsections. Each is composed of a group of related job elements (items within the questionnaire).

References:
Mecham, R.C. 1974. Comparison of job evaluation methods. *Journal of Applied Psychology* 59:633-637.

Position Analysis Questionnaire

Sample Items:

1. Reasoning in problem solving
2. Amount of planning/scheduling
3. Advising
4. Negotiating
5. Persuading
6. Instructing
7. Interviewing
8. Routine information exchange
9. Nonroutine information exchange
10. Public speaking
11. Job-required personal contact
12. Supervision of nonsupervisory personnel
13. Direction of supervisory personnel
14. Coordinates activities
15. Staff functions
16. Supervision received
17. Frustrating situations
18. Strained personal contacts
19. Personal sacrifice
20. Interpersonal conflict situations
21. Non-job-required social contact
22. Updating job knowledge
23. Working under distractions.
24. Recognition
25. Attention to detail
26. Time pressure of situation
27. Following set procedures
28. Repetitive activities

Scoring: Each category contains a six-point rating scale that measures importance to this job. N = Does Not Apply; 1 = Very Minor; 2 = Low; 3 = Average; 4 = High; and 5 = Extreme.

Organizational Structure

Structural Properties Questionnaire

Bishop, L.K. and J.R. George. 1973. Organizational structure: A factor analysis of structural characteristics of public elementary and secondary schools. *Educational Administration Quarterly* 9:66-80.

Comments: The 45-item SPQ was designed to measure the structural (bureaucratic) characteristics of elementary and secondary schools based on three conceptual areas proposed by Hage--*complexity, centralization, and formalization.* A prerequisite of structure is the need to have policies, programs, standing orders, procedures, and operating instructions which enable organizational members to behave in a prescribed manner. It includes the following factors: faculty involvement in decision making, the degree of administrative control, the uniform adherence to rules and regulations, the exercise of professional latitude, or restrictions applied to various modes of organizational interactions.

Scale Construction: An original 350-item pool was developed based on the operational definition associated with the three structural properties and appropriate to an educational setting. Through a variety of psychometric procedures, the instrument has undergone four major revisions. It uses a modified four-category Likert response scale.

Sample: The final version (Form Four) of the instrument was based on a sample of 1,367 teachers located in 45 schools including elementary and secondary. The sample included rural, suburban, and urban areas from states in the midwest and northeast. The size and regional diversity of the sample further enhances the representatives of the data, and supports the stability of the factor structure and factor scores associated with the instrument.

Reliability: The Cronbach coefficient alpha for the entire scale was 0.94. Individual coefficients for the 12 subscales ranged from 0.74 to 0.85.

Validity: Several panels of judges were used to determine the content validity of the final 45-item instrument. In each case, 100% agreement was necessary in order for an item to be retained. A criterion-related validity study was conducted by comparing two school districts (known-groups method)--one considered to be highly structured (bureaucratic), the other significantly less structured. Comparisons of average responses of teachers on all 12 scales indicated the ability of the test to discriminate without exception between the two types of organizational structures (all tests of statistical significance for t-tests of comparisons on all scales were 0.05 or smaller). In the development of the 45-item instrument a number of factor analytic solutions were explored including principal components, principal axes, and image factoring in conjunction with varimax and oblique rotations. Each solution yielded substantial congruence in the item loadings.

Factor Analysis and Scoring: A 12 factor orthogonal (varimax) principal component analysis was selected for the final solution and for scoring. This factor solution accounted for 57% of the common variance. The scoring program used factor score coefficient weighted Z scores which facilitates comparisons between groups on the various factors. Using a linear coefficient weighted equation (factor loadings are used as weights) to calculate factor scores allows for supressor effects of certain variables to enter into the factor estimation.

Definition of Factors: The 12 factors derived from the analysis can be unambiguously assigned to one of the three structural characteristics proposed by Hage. *Centralization* (how power is distributed among organizational positions): Participation in Decision making I & II and Hierarchy of Authority I & II; *Formalization* (how rules are used in an organization): Role Specificity and Standardization I, II, & III and Rule Observation-Professional Latitude I & II; *Complexity* (the degree of professional activity required and supported): Specialization, Professional Activity and Professional Training.

Data Analysis: Means, standard deviations, and comparative data among the 45 school districts and 1,376 teachers are provided.

References:
Bishop, L.K. et al. 1967. Structural Properties Questionnaire - Form 1. Claremont Graduate School, California. Working paper.

Bishop, L.K. and J.R. George. 1971. Relationship of organizational structure and teacher personality characteristics to organizational climate. *Administrative Science Quarterly* 16:467-475.

Murphy, M.J. 1979. Structural characteristics and organizational design decision. Paper presented at American Educational Research Association. ERIC ED 170 937.

Murphy, M.J. and L.K. Bishop. 1975. Defining organizational properties of schools: A focus on structure. Paper presented at American Educational Research Association.

Structural Properties Questionnaire
Form 4

Who has the greatest influence in decisions about:

1.	The instructional program?	1. Teachers
2.	Teaching methods?	2. Department or Grade Chairmen
3.	Textbook selection?	3. Consultants or Specialists
4.	Curricular offerings?	4. Administrators

1. Rarely
2. Sometimes
3. Often
4. Very Frequently

5. Teachers are required to follow suggested instructional sequences and unit plans as closely as possible.
6. Principals in your district must refer most non-routine decisions to someone higher up for the final O.K.
7. Rules and regulations concerning teacher behavior are uniformly applied.
8. Days in the school calendar are allotted exclusively to teachers for professional activities.
9. Academic degrees are an important consideration in recruitment of administrative staff.
10. Teachers are required to follow an adopted course of study.
11. Vice-principals and department chairmen in your school must refer most non-routine decisions to someone higher up for a final O.K.
12. Teachers' responsibilities and lines of authority within the school are well-defined.
13. Teaching in your school is a good job for someone who likes to be "his own boss."
14. Teachers receive help from an instructional media specialist in the use of audio-visual equipment.
15. Teachers make visitations to schools outside of the district.
16. Advanced degrees are an important consideration in promotion.
17. Teachers are evaluated according to a formalized procedure.
18. Even small matters often have to be referred to someone higher up for a final answer.
19. At this school, procedures for disciplining students are well-defined.
20. How things are done is left up to the person doing the work.
21. Teachers attend professional conferences during the school year.
22. Academic degrees are an important consideration in recruitment of instructional staff.
23. Teachers are allowed to teach only those subjects which are included in the course-of-study.
24. There can be little action taken here until a superior approves decision.
25. Teachers' activities are governed by written rules and regulations.
26. Most people here make their own rules on the job.
27. Teachers are required to do paper work which could be done by a school office staff.
28. Teachers are allowed to teach outside of their major areas of study.
29. Teachers are required to maintain lesson plans.
30. People here are allowed to do almost as they please.
31. Teachers are allowed to teach outside of their major and minor area of study.
32. Teachers in our school must refer most non-routine decisions to someone higher up for a final O.K.

33. Administrators strictly follow established rules and regulations in dealing with the teaching staff.
34. The Principal's activities are governed by written rules and regulations.
35. A teacher can make his own decisions concerning instructional problems without checking with anybody else.
36. Teachers here teach out of their field of specialization.
37. Any decision I make has to have my superior's approval.
38. Teachers are required to submit lesson plans.
39. The Principal is willing to by-pass regulations to help teachers.
40. Teachers are required to go through channels (chain of command) for routine decisions.
41. The Principal is willing to by-pass regulations to help pupils.
42. Teachers' daily activities must have the approval of a superior.
43. Teachers in this school are closely supervised.
44. Teachers are allowed to violate minor rules and regulations.
45. Rules requiring teachers to sign in and out are strictly followed.

Scoring: Very frequently = 4; Often = 3; Sometimes = 2; Rarely = 1.

Reprinted with permission of the author.

Power

School Participant Empowerment Scale

Short, P.M. and J.S. Rinehart. 1992. School Participant Empowerment Scale. Auburn University. Mimeo.

Comments: The SPES, a refined 38 item instrument, was developed to measure school participant (teacher) empowerment. It was designed to measure several themes such as trust, communication, structures for involvement, risk taking, and critical incidents. In addition, such themes as opportunities for decision making, control over daily schedule, opportunities for growth and development can be empowering aspects of a teacher's job.

Scale Construction: To generate items for the original instrument, teachers were asked to list ways in which they felt empowered in the schools in which they taught. This process yielded 110 items of which 75 were judged to represent empowerment components based on the literature and past research of empowerment.

Sample: The sample consisted of 211 secondary teachers from high schools in three geographic regions--south, southwest, and the midwest. Schools ranged in size from 70 teachers to 125 teachers.

Reliability: The total scale (38 items) alpha coefficient was 0.94. Coefficients for each of the subscales were decision making 0.89; professional growth 0.83; status 0.86; self-efficacy 0.84; autonomy 0.81; and impact 0.82.

Validity: Content validity was determined by a panel of four judges which rated the overall representativeness of each item. From this analysis, 68 items reached general agreement. The 68-item instrument was submitted to a factor analysis from which a final 38 items were retained on six factors.

Factor Analysis: A principal component analysis followed by an oblique rotation was used. Only those items with a factor loading of 0.600 or higher were retained on the factor. This yielded six factors which accounted for about 51% of the common variance. The six dimensions produced by the factor analysis are decision making (10 items); professional growth (six items); status (six items); self-efficacy (six items); autonomy (four items); and impact (six items).

References:
Short, P.M. and J.T. Greer. 1989. Increasing teacher autonomy through shared governance: Effects on policy making and student outcomes. Paper presented at American Educational Research Association.

Short, P.M., J.T. Greer, and R. Michael. 1991. Restructuring schools through empowerment. *Journal of School Leadership* 1:5-25.

School Empowerment Survey

1. I am given the responsibility to monitor programs.
2. I function in a professional environment.
3. I believe that I have earned respect.
4. I believe that I am helping kids become independent learners.
5. I have control over daily schedules.
6. I believe that I have the ability to get things done.
7. I make decisions about the implementation of new programs in the school.
8. I am treated as a professional.
9. I believe that I am very effective.
10. I believe that I am empowering students.
11. I am able to teach as I choose.
12. I participate in staff development.
13. I make decisions about the selection of other teachers for my school.
14. I have the opportunity for professional growth.
15. I have the respect of my colleagues.
16. I feel that I am involved in an important program for children.
17. I have the freedom to make decisions on what is taught.
18. I believe that I am having an impact.
19. I am involved in school budget decisions.
20. I work at a school where kids come first.
21. I have the support and respect of my colleagues.
22. I see students learn.
23. I make decisions about curriculum.
24. I am a decision maker.
25. I am given the opportunity to teach other teachers.
26. I am given the opportunity to continue learning.
27. I have a strong knowledge base in the areas in which I teach.
28. I believe that I have the opportunity to grow by working daily with students.
29. I perceive that I have the opportunity to influence others.
30. I can determine my own schedule.
31. I have the opportunity to collaborate with other teachers in my school.
32. I perceive that I am making a difference.
33. Principals, other teachers, and school personnel solicit my advice.
34. I believe that I am good at what I do.
35. I can plan my own schedule.
36. I perceive that I have an impact on other teachers and students.
37. My advice is solicited by others.
38. I have an opportunity to teach other teachers about innovative ideas.

Scoring: 1 = Strongly Disagree; 2 = Disagree; 3 = Neutral; 4 = Agree; 5 = Strongly Agree

Reprinted with permission of the author.

Zones of Indifference Instrument

Wilkes, S.T. and J.M. Blackbourn. 1981. The design of an instrument to measure zones of indifference of teachers to directives issued by administrators. Mississippi State University. ERIC ED 212 063.

Comments: The 78-item instrument measures the zones of indifference of teachers to directives issued by administrators. Zones of indifference describe the extent to which people will respond to orders or directives issued by authority figures. It suggests that some orders are clearly unacceptable, while some are neutral, and others are unquestionably acceptable. It is also suggested that this "zone of indifference" will be wider or narrower with different organizational members. The difference in the size of the zone is created by the degree to which inducements exceed consequences which determine the individual's adhesion to the organization.

Scale Construction: One hundred twenty-five teachers submitted items which eventually were categorized into two sets of items. One set explained variables describing teacher-determined practices while the other dealt with administrator-determined policy. This produced an initial instrument of 134 items.

Sample: The initial instrument of 134 items was field tested with 104 teachers in four states. Through a variety of factor analytic procedures, the 134 items were reduced to a final 78-item instrument comprising a two factor solution.

Reliability: Alpha coefficient for the total instrument was 0.95. The two subscales (factors) were 0.92 for each subscale.

Validity: Other than the factor analyses conducted, no other information on obtaining validity of the instrument was reported.

Factor Analysis: Responses to the 134-item instrument were submitted to several principal component analyses which reduced the instrument to 80 items and three factors. Only items with loadings of 0.40 or higher were retained. With the use of image analysis and orthogonal rotation the instrument was reduced to two factors: factor 1 deals with teacher determined practices and factor 2 deals with administrator determined policy. Examples of items with high loadings on the two factors are as follows: teacher determined practices (45, 126, 128, 46, 57) and administrator determined policy (121, 102, 97, 123, 114).

References:
Barnard, C.I. 1948. *The functions of the executive*. MA: Harvard University Press.

Kunz, D.W. 1973. Leader behavior of principals and the professional zone of acceptance of teachers. Ed.D. dissertation, Rutgers University.

Zones of Indifference

Indicate how you would respond to the following directives issued by an administrator that would:

1. Provide for the enforcement by teachers of general rules governing student conduct at school.
2. Attempt to structure discussion of school policy, problems or procedure by teachers with members of the community unless a positive approach is evident.
3. Establish heating and cooling regulations for the classroom.
4. Establish a procedure for teachers to "sign-in" and "sign-out" for the school day.
5. Give directions to advance a student to another level when the present progress of the student is not satisfactory.
6. Prescribe procedure for the conduct of club activities.
7. Require attendance at staff-development activities.
8. Instruct teachers to attend open house activities.
9. Establish grading procedures to be used by teachers.
10. Give directions for the changing of classroom bulletin boards at regular intervals.
11. Structure a daily morning devotional activity in the classroom.
12. Require supervision of students after school hours for those students who have to stay after school to make up assignments.
13. Require participation in the teacher evaluation program.
14. Designate specific topics to be taught at specific times.
15. Require teachers to have students recite "The Lord's Prayer" in the homeroom or classroom.
16. Make assignment to study committees of the school.
17. Require attendance at P.T.A. meetings.
18. Require participation in a curriculum study group.
19. Require a six week grade report to the administration.
20. Question non-attendance of teachers at professional meetings.
21. Provide additional time for student classroom assignment conferences.
22. Structure seating arrangement of students in assemblies.
23. Insist upon personal comments on grade sheets in each instance of a decline in student achievement.
24. Require ability grouping of students.
25. Dictate the use of only adopted textbooks in the classroom.
26. Be related to membership in professional organizations.
27. Place ultimate concern on the student.
28. Determine method to be used in the handling of classroom discipline problems.
29. Prohibit students from using the library during class time without teacher supervision.
30. Require the grading of English usage in all subjects taught.
31. Direct teachers to alter records to indicate accreditation compliance.
32. Require a written proposal for all planned field trips.
33. Require written goals and objectives of teachers.
34. Prescribe testing schedules and procedures.
35. Specify methods to be used in teacher-parent relations.
36. Require maintenance of accurate school classroom records.
37. Suggest the use of a teacher's name to order supplies for other teachers.
38. Schedule the use of planning time for supervising another teacher's class who is out on some school activity.
39. Establish a policy of student grade reduction for unexcused absences and tardiness.
40. Forbid the use of tobacco by teachers at school.

41. Determine the time of the teachers' workday.
42. Direct teachers to meet the parents for conference.
43. Require extra assignments that would reduce time for classroom instruction.
44. Require long-range lesson plans.
45. Select teaching procedures to be utilized in the classroom.
46. Structure the standardization of classroom furniture arrangement.
47. Provide for the monitoring of student behavior on the way to school and from school by teachers.
48. Prohibit the consumption of refreshment by teachers in the classroom.
49. Instruct teachers to teach content without regard to student acquisition level.
50. Require attendance at faculty meetings.
51. Prevent teachers from leaving school.
52. Require teacher participation in a census of school age children during or after school hours.
53. Question student religious beliefs and home life.
54. Establish directives requiring teachers to supervise school bus loading/unloading of students.
55. Establish a bi-monthly teaching meeting practice.
56. Provide a list of discipline cases handled by the teacher in the classroom.
57. Require teachers to perform tasks that maintenance or custodial personnel are hired to do.
58. Schedule male/female teacher supervision of restrooms.
59. Require teachers to purchase season football tickets.
60. Establish conditions under which corporal punishment could be administered.
61. Determine the test exemption policy.
62. Excuse students from classes to attend other school sponsored activities.
63. Allow the expenditure of school funds for extra-curricular activities.
64. Provide guidelines outlining student assignment requirements for classroom work.
65. Direct teachers to escort sick students home.
66. Involve altering a student's grade.
67. Be related to teacher involvement in political activities.
68. Direct all teachers to be on duty in the halls during the changing of classes.
69. Determine the amount of planning time per week.
70. Notify teachers of grade/subject assignments.
71. Establish the practice of planning individual student lesson prescriptions.
72. Require a teacher to supervise two classes in the same period in separate rooms.
73. Constitute running errands for the administration which are unrelated to the school program.
74. Assign school related duties outside the classroom involving no students.
75. Attempt to restrict topics that could be discussed in the lounge area.
76. Outline the policy concerning attendance at work.
77. Require a very low noise level to be maintained in the classroom.
78. Instruct teachers to accept a student into class after the suspension of a student.
79. Prohibit the keeping of report cards in the classroom.
80. Establish the policy of paying substitute teachers for sponsoring club activities or other extra-curricular activities.
81. Limit the number of graduate courses a teacher could be enrolled in after school hours.
82. Schedule duty assignments at times other than the required school day.
83. Allow the public to use classroom after hours.
84. Instruct each class to contribute a specified amount of money to the school activity fund.
85. Assign a student with the disciplinary record to your instructional group.
86. Prevent the early dismissal of classes by teachers.
87. Instruct teachers to monitor student classroom appearance in keeping with the school dress code.

88. Assign selected teachers to duties that are not assigned to the entire faculty.
89. Restrict students from restraining students from participation in the activity period.
90. Not allow athletes to participate in sports due to academic problems.
91. Require submission of lesson plans weekly by teachers.
92. Require strict adherence to the curriculum guide and/or daily lesson plan.
93. Structure teacher dress practices.
94. Direct all teachers to attend all school functions.
95. Structure student dress practices.
96. Require the issuance of student failure reports by teachers.
97. Require a standing position while teaching class.
98. Schedule teachers to supervise school-related meetings at school.
99. Provide the procedure for recording student absences.
100. Require attendance at an administrator/teacher conference.
101. Require the submission of absentee and tardy reports every period of the school day.
102. Make assignments of teachers as sponsors to student club activities.
103. Require teachers to use the school cafeteria for lunch.
104. Provide guidelines determining advancement and retention practices.
105. Require the use of a teaching syllabus.
106. Provide guidelines concerning the manner by which sick leave should be utilized by teachers.
107. Schedule teacher to supervise P.E. classes during an unassigned period.
108. Schedule the utilization of teacher aids in the classroom instead of substitute teachers when the regular teacher is not present.
109. Establish the format for written lesson plans.
110. Schedule teachers to move to different rooms for instructional purposes.
111. Direct a teacher to alter attendance reports of students.
112. Determine specific staff development activities.
113. Require teachers to perform information gathering that other professionals are employed to do.
114. Prohibit teachers from leaving the school during school hours.
115. Schedule work days prior to the commencement of school without pay and not specified by contract.
116. Require the keeping of an extensive record of library books that are issued to students.
117. Result in the lowering of grades for poor conduct by students.
118. Establish written job descriptions for teachers.
119. Indicate that classroom materials had been selected by the administration.
120. Require teacher direction of a staff development activity.
121. Direct teachers to refrain from expressing opinions about community problems.
122. Require an instant gathering of data for office purposes.
123. Prohibit the use of corporal punishment as a method of punishment.
124. Determine the length of exams to be administered.
125. Require the maintenance of discipline of students at all times in the classroom.
126. Establish the practice for teachers to collect student activity fees.
127. Structure teacher arrival at school prior to the designated time for the beginning of the school day.
128. Schedule classroom activities by the principal.
129. Prohibit the wearing of jeans by teachers.
130. Involve a teacher administering corporal punishment to another teacher's student.
131. Require the presence of teachers with students in the cafeteria.
132. Prohibit a teacher from being employed in another job.
133. Provide an individual teacher personnel file in the office.
134. Suggest an explanation by the teacher of personal life activities.

Scoring: 1 = A directive you would comply with without question; 2 = A directive you would comply with but mentally question the authority of the administrator to issue; 3 = A directive issued by the administrator that you mentally question the authority of, but alter the application more in keeping with what you think should be done; and 4 = A directive issued by the administrator that you question mentally and refuse compliance with unless forced to do so.

Reprinted with permission of the author.

Professional Performance

Professional Orientation Scale

Corwin, R.G. 1963. The development of an instrument for examining staff conflicts in the public schools. U.S. Office of Education, Dept. of Health Education and Welfare, Contract No. 1934.

Comments: The scale originally contained 45 items as developed by Corwin. Corwin's scales were designed to analyze staff conflict in public schools. Later work by Kuhlman modified the original Corwin 45-item scale into a 24-item instrument. Fifteen items comprise the *Bureaucratic Orientation Scale* and nine items comprise the *Professional Orientation Scale.*

Sample: The scale was administered to a sample of 322 prospective elementary and secondary school teachers from four New Jersey colleges in spring of the year at the completion of their undergraduate teacher preparation training. A follow-up of the same sample was made one year later after they completed their first year of teaching.

Reliability: A split-half reliability estimate for the entire scale was 0.83. Individual subscale reliabilities for the five factors are not provided.

Factor Analysis: The 15-item BOS scale was factor analyzed yielding a five-factor solution which measures five aspects of bureaucratic orientation. The factors were named: organizational control, subordination-standardization, rule orientation, community orientation, and organizational loyalty. The author indicates that a total BOS score, across the 15 Likert-type items, provides an overall index of bureaucratic orientation.

References:
Corwin, R.G. 1970. *Militant professionalism.* New York: Appleton.

Kuhlman, E.L. and H.K. Hoy. 1974. The socialization of professionals into bureaucracies. *Journal of Educational Administration* 2:18-27.

Bureaucratic and Professional Orientation Scales
Form B-P

1. Teachers should subscribe to and diligently read the standard professional journals.
2. Rules stating when the teachers should arrive and depart from the building should be strictly enforced.
3. Unless he/she is satisfied that it is best for the student, a teacher should <u>not</u> do what he/she is told to do.
4. Personnel who openly criticize the administration should be encouraged to go elsewhere.
5. Teachers should be active members of at least one professional teaching association and should attend most conferences and meetings of the association.
6. Teachers should be obedient, respectful and loyal to the principal.
7. Teachers should be completely familiar with the written descriptions of the rules, procedures, manuals and other standard operating procedures for running the class.
8. The criterion of a good school should be one that serves the needs of the local community.
9. A teacher should consistently practice her ideas of the best educational practices even though the administration prefers other views.
10. There should be definite rules specifying the topics that are not appropriate for discussion in a classroom.
11. It should be permissible for the teacher to violate a rule if he/she is sure that the best interests of the students will be served in doing so.
12. Teachers should not publicly advocate a position on the place of religion in the school which differs greatly from the majority of the community.
13. A good teacher should not do anything that he/she believes may jeopardize the interests of the students regardless of who tells him or what the rule states.
14. In case of a dispute in the community over whether a controversial textbook or controversial speaker should be permitted in the school, the teacher should look primarily to the judgment of the administration for guidance.
15. A good teacher should put the interests of his/her school above everything else.
16. Teachers should not attempt to discuss any controversial issue (such as abolishing the House Un-American Activities Committee) which may jeopardize the school's public relations.
17. Schools should hire no one to teach unless he/she holds at least a 4-year bachelors degree.
18. Teachers of the same subject throughout the system should follow the same kind of lesson plan.
19. The ultimate authority over the major educational decisions should be exercised by professional teachers.
20. Teachers should take into account the opinions of their community in guiding what they say in class and in their choice of teaching materials.
21. It should be permissible to hire teachers trained at non-accredited colleges.
22. When a controversy arises about the interpretation of school rules, a teacher should not "stick her neck out" by taking a definite position.
23. The school should have a manual of rules and regulations which are actually followed.
24. Teachers should not allow themselves to be influenced by other teachers whose opinions and thinking are different than the administration's.

Scoring: SA = Strongly Agree; A = Agree; U = Undecided; D = Disagree; SD = Strongly Disagree
Items 1, 3, 5, 9, 11, 13, 17, 19, 21 are reversed scored.

Reprinted with permission of the author.

Principal Performance Rating Scale

Weiss, K. 1989. Evaluating principal performance. Ph.D. dissertation, New York University.

Comments: The instrument was developed to assess a principal's performance, as well as to be utilized by a principal in self-improvement. The assessment tool is based on basic administrative competencies such as organizational skills, leadership, decision making, staffing, staff evaluation, and the like. The instrument can be used to determine areas of strength and weakness in a principal's performance. The information obtained can be used as the basis of an administrative appraisal process in which goals and objectives can be cooperatively established by the superintendent, or some other supervisor, and the principal.

Scale Construction: The initial item pool consisted of 229 items. These were submitted to a panel of judges for clarification and content analysis. Seventy-nine items survived this process.

Sample: Thirty-seven principals (19 elementary, nine middle, and nine high school) from eight school districts in Nassau and Suffolk Counties in New York participated in the initial study. These districts were chosen because the principals had diversified characteristics in years of service as administrators, degrees earned, sex, and age.

Reliability: Alpha coefficients were obtained for the total instrument of 0.98 and for each subscale which ranged from 0.89 to 0.96.

Validity: Content, criterion-related, and construct validity are provided for the instrument, and five factors were produced from this process: educational, leadership, interpersonal , professional, and managerial.

Factor Analysis: A known-groups techniques was used for determining criterion and construct validity.

References:
Baehr, M. 1975. A national occupational analysis of the school principalship. Chicago, IL: Industrial Relations Center and Consortium for Educational Leadership. ERIC ED 116 340.

Human Synergistics. 1982. Educational Administrator Effectiveness Profile. Plymouth, MI: Author.

Principal Performance Rating Scale

Leadership

1. Encourages and emphasizes team work and staff participation.
2. Encourages staff to use their own.
3. Effectively shares decision making responsibilities with staff when appropriate.
4. Develops and disseminates goals and objectives of the school.
5. Seeks relevant input from staff in the planning process.
6. Shares responsibilities and authority with other staff members.
7. Is able to inspire and challenge staff.
8. Encourages staff initiative and innovation.
9. Delegates authority effectively.
10. Delegates tasks in order to assist staff in improving their skills.
11. Provides clear and consistent direction.
12. Utilizes committees in sharing responsibility for certain policy decisions.
13. Ensures that the authority and responsibility of each subordinate are clearly understood.
14. Uses appropriate support personnel effectively.

Educational

1. Works toward articulation between grades and school.
2. Observes and evaluates all members of the teaching staff on a regular basis.
3. Systematically evaluates the instructional program and uses the results for continuous program improvement.
4. Actively evaluates curriculum.
5. Supervises the instructional staff in the development and implementation of curriculum.
6. Seeks way to support and strengthen the teaching/learning process.
7. Initiates instructional improvement efforts based on educational research and proven methods.
8. Visits classrooms regularly to supervise and evaluate the instructional program.
9. Establishes and maintains expectations for student achievement.
10. Provides systematic and effective supervision to improve instruction.
11. Ensures that curriculum content is related to established goals and objectives.
12. Monitors effective use of classroom time.
13. Is actively involved in the development of curricula.
14. Provides for organizing, collecting and analyzing data to be used to identify curriculum needs.
15. Is continuously involved with the evaluation of the curriculum.

Interpersonal

1. Counsels teachers regarding their personal problems.
2. Works with the community to determine its expectations for the school.
3. Establishes good working relationships with members of the school board.
4. Establishes good working relationships with local news media.
5. Encourages members of the community to participate in school activities.
6. Effectively gives and receives cues to/from the staff and school community.
7. Effectively counsels and advises students and parents.
8. Works supportively with the board of education in recommending and implementing policy.
9. Uses effective techniques in establishing and maintaining good relations with the students.
10. Uses effective techniques in establishing and maintaining good relations with the community.
11. Demonstrates concerns and openness in the consideration of teacher and/or student problems.
12. Has the ability to listen, understand and appreciate others.

Professional

1. Views keeping up with new techniques and developments as important.
2. Attends professional meetings and seminars outside of the school district.
3. Behaves in an appropriate manner.
4. Keeps abreast of current and innovative trends in education.
5. Keeps informed and up-to-date regarding new developments in curriculum and instruction.
6. Participates in activities to improve personal knowledge and skills.
7. Maintains a regular program of reading and study in the professional field.
8. Achieves success and honors in the areas of scholarship or other areas relevant to the job.
9. Belongs to and participates in professional organizations directly related to job tasks.
10. Pursues a planned program of professional growth.
11. Creates a favorable impression by dressing and grooming appropriately.
12. Sets personal professional goals on a yearly basis.
13. Is punctual to work, meetings and appointments.
14. Participates actively in workshops and conferences.

Managerial

1. Efficiently prepares, monitors and implements budget requests.
2. Demonstrates knowledge of finance and budget.
3. Schedules instructional space to provide for maximum utilization and minimum disruption.
4. Accounts for budget expenditures.
5. Effectively plans and implements transportation procedures and resolves related problems.
6. Establishes procedures for maintenance and accountability of facilities, equipment and inventory.
7. Plans for beautification of building and grounds.
8. Maintains and monitors records required by law.
9. Provides for availability of supplies and equipment.
10. Supervises cafeteria programs.
11. Inspects physical plant on a regular basis.
12. Ensures that student records are systematically and accurately maintained.
13. Allocates funds based upon fair, predetermined and well understood criteria.
14. Effectively schedules and utilizes school facilities.
15. Establishes a system of control for the inventory of materials and supplies.
16. Identifies, proposes and plans construction needs.
17. Develops and implements fiscal procedures with input from staff members.
18. Develops master schedule to optimize utilization of personnel and facilities.
19. Ensures the safety of the physical plant and of the personnel.

Scoring: Unsatisfactory Performance = 1; Marginal Performance = 2; Satisfactory Performance = 3; Above Average = 4; and Outstanding = 5.

Reprinted with permission of the author.

Role

Role Conflict/Role Ambiguity Questionnaire

Rizzo, R.J. et al. 1970. Role conflict and ambiguity in complex organizations. *Administrative Science Quarterly* 15:150-163.

Comments: The role conflict scale was designed to measure the role ambiguity and role conflict of individuals within an organization. Role ambiguity is defined as the extent to which an individual is unclear about the role expectations of others, as well as the degree of uncertainty associated with one's role performance. It is often noted in the literature that role ambiguity leads to role conflict. Role Conflict is the degree to which expectations of a role are incompatible, or incongruent, with the reality of the role. This incompatibility may be due to conflicts between organizational demands and one's own values, problems of personal resource allocation, or conflicts between obligations to several different people.

Scale Construction: The questionnaire originally consisted of 30 items, 15 dealt with role ambiguity and 15 with role conflict. Of the role conflict items, 10 were stress worded and five were comfort worded. The role ambiguity items consisted of six that were stress worded and nine were comfort worded.

Reliability: The six items of the role ambiguity scale had an alpha coefficient of 0.73, and the eight items on the role conflict scale was 0.88.

Factor Analysis: The 30 items were factor analyzed using an image covariance method with a varimax rotation. Only 14 items were retained on two factors which accounted for 56% of the common variance. A high score on role ambiguity indicates feelings of comfort with a role; however, scoring on these items is usually done in the reverse to indicate ambiguity or discomfort with the role. Items 1, 3, 5, 8, 10, 13 provide a measure of role ambiguity (RA), while the remaining items are used to score role conflict (RC).

References:
Lane, T. and T.W. Johnson. 1981. What do role conflict and role ambiguity scales measure? *Journal of Applied Psychology* 66:464-469.

Wilson, S.M. 1979. Role conflict, role ambiguity, and job satisfaction among full-time principals and teaching principals in Maine. Ed.D. dissertation . George Peabody College.

Role Conflict/Role Ambiguity

1. I have clear, planned goals and objectives for my job.
2. I have to do things that should be done differently.
3. I know I have divided my time properly.
4. I receive an assignment without the assistance to complete it.
5. I know what my responsibilities are.
6. I have to buck a rule or policy in order to carry out an assignment.
7. I work with two or more groups who operate quite differently.
8. I know exactly what is expected of me.
9. I receive incompatible requests from two or more people.
10. I feel certain about how much authority I have.
11. I do things that are apt to be accepted by one person and not by others.
12. I receive an assignment without adequate resources and materials to complete it.
13. Explanation is clear of what has to be done.
14. I work on unnecessary things.

Scoring: A Likert-type scale was used ranging from Definitely not true of my job = 1 to Extremely true of my job = 7.

Reprinted with permission from R.J. House.

Parent-School Communities Questionnaire

Wiener, W.K. 1975. Measuring school boundary permeability. Paper presented at the New England Educational Research Association. ERIC ED 125 052.

Comments: The 50-item PSCQ was designed to measure the permeability of school boundaries. The concept of permeability assumes that any social system, such as a school, is surrounded by a psychological boundary that insulates it from its environment. The degree to which this boundary is permeable to input from outside the system is directly proportional to the openness of the system.

Scale Construction: Originally, the PSCQ consisted of 50 descriptive statements that respondents were asked to rate on a five-point Likert scale. The original factor analysis yielded dimensions dealing with the process parents used to contact school personnel; attempts by school personnel to contact parents; parental perceptions of the character of the school organization; and a dimension relevant to the quality and nature of parent-teacher interactions.

Sample: The first analysis was based on a sample of 500 parents taken from three elementary schools. The feedback from this study prompted a second factor analysis with 278 parent responses.

Validity: Interviews were conducted with a known-group of parents to determine the degree of correspondence between the parents interview comments and those items coded on the questionnaire.

Factor Analysis: The result of the second factor analysis--a principal axis analysis with a varimax rotation--produced three interpretable factors. The criterion for acceptance of items on a given factor was 0.500.

Definition of Factors: The three factors are: *Teacher-parent* interactions which deals with the quality of interactions between parent and teacher; *Parent-principal interactions* which is concerned with the quality of interactions between the parent and the school administration; and *Accessibility* which refers to parents perceptions of the mechanics involved in making contact with the school.

Reference:
Wiener, W.K. and A. Blumberg. 1973. The Parent School Communications Questionnaire: A measure of school boundary permeability. Paper presented at American Educational Research Association. ERIC ED 075 916.

The Parent School Communications Questionnaire:
A Measure of School Boundary Permeability

Factor I: Mechanical:

1. If my youngster is having a problem in school, the best way to contact the teacher is in writing rather than by phone.
2. Before talking with a teacher, I feel that I must first contact the principal.
3. It is difficult to get in touch with a teacher on the phone.
4. It is difficult to get in touch with the principal on the phone.
5. In order for me to see my youngster's teacher, I need only stop in at the school office without prior contact and ask.
6. In order for me to see the principal, I need only stop in at the school office without prior contact and ask.
7. The school secretary will forward my message to the principal or the teacher.

Factor II: Outreach:

8. My youngster's teacher contacts me personally when something goes wrong with his work.
9. My youngster's teacher contacts me personally when his work has been progressing particularly well.
10. The principal takes initiative in contacting parents about school matters.
11. The principal encourages parents to contact teachers about their children's school activities.
12. Teachers resist attending parent-teacher functions.
13. Teachers cooperate willingly with the parent group in discussing school issues.
14. Parent nights at school are events which I feel are useful and instructive.
15. Parents have a standing invitation to visit their youngster's classes with a few days notice.
16. After I have met with my youngster's teacher concerning a problem, the teacher contacts me with the follow-up information about the situation.
17. Ample notice is given by the school to inform me about parent organizational functions.
18. Most communications from the school are impersonal in tone.

Factor III: Organizational Climate:

19. Teachers see parents as a nuisance.
20. Teachers seem threatened by parents who ask questions.
21. Teachers are friendly and warm in their communications with parents.
22. When I walk into my youngster's classroom, I feel uncomfortable.
23. When I walk into the school, I sense a friendly warm atmosphere.
24. Teachers in the school like parents to contact them about their child.
25. Teachers do not think highly of the parent organization of the school.
26. The atmosphere at parent-teacher gatherings is strained and tense.
27. Teachers in the school are willing to listen to negative things I have to say about what is going on in school.
28. The principal is a limiting force on parent organization activities.
29. The principal actively supports the parent organization.

Factor IV: Interpersonal Climate:

30. I like to talk about my youngster's work with his teacher.
31. My youngster likes me to see his teacher on his behalf.
32. The principal sees parents as being a nuisance.
33. When I get a notice from a teacher that he wants to see me about my youngster, I feel tense.

34. When I talk with my youngster's teacher, I feel he is holding back information I would like to have.
35. When I talk to the principal, I feel that he is evasive.
36. I have no hesitancy at all about contacting a teacher about my youngster's work in school.
37. The principal is willing to listen to negative things I have to say about what's going on in the school.
38. If I complain to a teacher about my youngster's negative reaction to his teaching, I am afraid that teacher will act negatively toward my youngster.
39. The principal sees parents as a source to help him.
40. I feel free to stop and chat with teachers in the school.
41. The school secretary is helpful to me when I visit the school.

Factor V: Influences
42. Parent groups have no real influence on the school.
43. I feel that when I talk with the principal, I make an impact on him.
44. I feel that when I talk with my youngster's teacher, it makes an impression on him.
45. I trust the principal to communicate parental concerns to the teachers.
46. The principal only responds to pressure from a group of parents, not individuals.
47. Teachers seem to pay attention to parents.
48. The principal pays attention to parents.
49. The principal actively uses the parent organization to help in solving school problems.
50. I am made to feel that I as a parent, and not the school, must make all the changes to solve a problem.

Scoring: A five-point Likert scale ranging from "this is always true" = 5, to "this is never true" = 1.

Reprinted with permission of the author.

Self-Actualization

Index of Self-Actualization

Jones, A. and R. Crandall. 1986. Validation of a short Index of Self-Actualization. *Personality and Social Psychology Bulletin* 12:63-73.

Comments: The 15-item ISA discriminates between self-actualizing and non-self-actualizing individuals. Evidence of its reliability and validity are provided in the research.

Scale Development: The basis for this index was the Personal Orientation Inventory (Shostrom, 1964). Half of each of the 150 two-choice POI items were rewritten using an agree-disagree format. These new items as well as the POI were given to 73 college students. The 10 items that had the highest item-total correlation with the total score (one from each of the 10 subscales) on the POI were selected. Four additional items from the POI were selected (highest correlation without regard to subscale) as well as five items (highest factor loadings on various subscales) from the Personal Orientation Dimensions (Shostrom, 1975). The original 19-item index was reduced to 15 items based on Cronbach's alpha.

Sample: Approximately 500 people took part in validating the index. In general, classes of students in psychology, sociology, and business programs in two senior and three junior colleges in Texas participated. In addition, 73 college students from Illinois and 22 people from North Carolina participated.

Reliability: Test-retest reliability for a 12-day interval (67 students) was 0.69 using the original four-point scale. Test-retest reliability for a two-week interval (67 students) was 0.81 using a six-point scale. The correlation between the original four-point scale and the six-point scale was 0.91 (84 students). The coefficient alpha for the index with a four-point scale was 0.65. The new alpha was 0.72 (274 students).

Validity: The index was correlated with Eysenck's Personality Inventory (Eysenck & Eysenck, 1968); the Rational Behavior Inventory (Whiteman & Shorkey, 1978); Rosenberg's Self-Esteem Scale (Rosenberg, 1965); Budner's Tolerance of Ambiguity Scale (Budner, 1962); Slivken and Crandall's Leisure Ethic Scale (Crandall & Slivken, 1980); and the Personal Orientation Inventory (Shostrom, 1964).

Factor Analysis: A principal components factor analysis with a varimax rotation yielded five factors. The five factors are five items on autonomy or self-direction (2, 5, 9, 10, and 11); three items on self-acceptance and self-esteem (6, 8, and 14); two items on acceptance of emotions and freedom of expression of emotions (1 and 4); three items on trust and responsibility in interpersonal relations (3, 13, and 15); and two items on the ability to deal with undesirable aspects of like rather than avoiding them (7 and 12).

References:

Flett, G.L. et al. Factor structure of the Short Index of Self-Actualization. In A. Jones and R. Crandall, eds. 1991. Handbook of self-actualization. *Journal of Social Behavior and Personality* 6:321-329.

Richard, R.L. and S.M. Jex. Further evidence for the validity of the Short Index of Self-Actualization. In A. Jones and R. Crandall, eds. 1991. Handbook of self-actualization. *Journal of Social Behavior and Personality* 6:331-338.

Shostrom, E.L. 1975. *Personal Orientation Dimensions*. San Diego, CA: Educational and Industrial Testing Service.

Tucker, R.K. and D.R. Weber. 1988. Factorial validity of Jones and Crandall's Short Index of Self-Actualization. *Psychological Reports* 63:39-45.

Weiss, A.S. The measurement of self-actualization: The quest for the test may be as challenging as the search for the self. In A. Jones and R. Crandall, eds. 1991. Handbook of self-actualization. *Journal of Social Behavior and Personality* 6:265-290.

Short Index of Self-Actualization

1. I do not feel ashamed of any of my emotions.
2. I feel I must do what others expect of me.
3. I believe that people are essentially good and can be trusted.
4. I feel free to be angry at those I love.
5. It is always necessary that others approve what I do.
6. I don't accept my own weaknesses.
7. I can like people without having to approve of them.
8. I fear failure.
9. I avoid attempts to analyze and simplify complex domains.
10. It is better to be yourself than to be popular.
11. I have no mission in life to which I feel especially dedicated.
12. I can express my feelings even when they may result in undesirable consequences.
13. I do not feel responsible to help anybody.
14. I am bothered by fears of being inadequate.
15. I am loved because I give love.

Scoring: Strongly Agree = 6; Agree = 5; Somewhat Agree = 4; Somewhat Disagree = 3; Disagree = 2; and Strongly Disagree = 1. For items 2, 5, 6, 8, 9, 11, 13, and 14 the scoring is reversed. Self-actualizing responses receive a score of 6, while non-self-actualizing responses receive a score of 1.

Reprinted with permission of the author.

Personal Orientation Inventory

Shostrom, E.L. 1966. *Manual for the Personal Orientation Inventory*. San Diego, CA: Educational and Industrial Testing Service.

Comments: The 150-item POI discriminates among self-actualized, normal, and non-self-actualized individuals.

Scale Construction: Although the POI is based on Maslow's theory of self-actualization, items were also taken from the following humanistic, existential, or gestalt therapy writers: Perls, May, Angel, Ellenberger, Fromm, Horney, Rogers, Riesman, Watts, and Ellis. Items were also chosen from observed value judgments of clinically healthy and troubled patients. Scores of relative time competence and relative inner- and other-directedness.

Sample: One validation study was conducted using 650 freshmen at Los Angeles State College, 150 patients in therapy, 75 members on the Sensitivity Training Program at UCLA, and 15 school psychologists.

Reliability: Test-retest reliability coefficients of 0.91 and 0.93 were reported. Coefficients of reliability ranged from 0.55 (acceptance of aggression) to 0.85 (existentiality), with a median of 0.74.

Validity: The POI and the MMPI were correlated in one validation study. Significant relationships (0.01 level) between two groups were found on four of the MMPI scales (D, Pd, Pt, and Sc) and all 12 POI scales. The POI and the Eysenck Personality Inventory were correlated in another study. Significant relationships were found. The POI possesses predictive validity because it is able to differentiate between healthy and unhealthy groups. The POI is also able to differentiate between self-actualized, normal, and non-self-actualized groups.

Scales: The POI contains 10 subscales: 26 items on self-actualizing values, 32 items on existentiality, 23 items on feeling reactivity, 17 items on spontaneity, 26 items on self-acceptance, 16 items on nature of man, 16 items on self-regard, nine items on synergy, 25 items on acceptance of aggression, and 28 items on capacity for intimate contact.

Definitions of Subscales: *Self-actualizing values* refer to values held by self-actualizing people. *Existentiality* refers to the ability to react to situations without rigid adherence to principles. *Feeling reactivity* refers to the sensitivity of responsiveness to one's own needs and feelings. *Spontaneity* refers to the ability to be oneself or react spontaneously. *Self-acceptance* refers to acceptance of oneself in spite of weaknesses. *Nature of man* refers to the view of man, masculinity and femininity. *Self-regard* refers to self-worth. *Synergy* refers to the ability to surpass dichotomies. *Acceptance of aggression* refers to the ability to tolerate aggression. *Capacity for intimate contact* refers to the ability to cultivate intimate relationships.

References:

Doyle, J.A. 1976. Self-actualization, neuroticism, and extraversion revisited. *Psychological Reports* 39:1081-1082.

Margulies, N. 1969. Organizational culture and psychological growth. *Journal of Applied Behavioral Science* 5:491-508.

Scoring: A forced-choice format is used so that each item is written twice (items represent both ends of the continuum).

Sample Items:
39.   a. I trust my ability to size up a situation.
     b. I do not trust my ability to size up a situation.
60.   a. It is important that others accept my point of view.
     b. It is not necessary for others to accept my point of view.
80.   a. For me, work and play are the same.
     b. For me, work and play are opposites.
127. a. I like to participate actively in intense discussions.
     b. I do not like to participate actively in intense discussions.
150. a. I can overcome any obstacles as long as I believe in myself.
     b. I cannot overcome every obstacle even if I believe in myself.

Personal Orientation Dimensions

Shostrom, E.L. 1977. *Manual for the Personal Orientation Dimensions*. San Diego, CA: Educational and Industrial Testing Service.

Comments: The 260-item POD is a refinement and extension of the Personal Orientation Inventory. It contains 13 scales with 20 items in each scale that represent an aspect in the actualizing individual.

Scale Construction: The POD is based on item analyses and construct validation studies that were conducted on the POI. Items were written based on the development of the POI and the theoretical model of the actualizing individual. An item pool of 370 items was created and several samples participated in the development of the POD. Items are stated both in the positive and in the negative. Scales from the POI that had predictive and factorial validity were utilized by either adding new items or rewriting old items.

Sample: The original sample consisted of 402 college freshmen.

Reliability: Test-retest reliability coefficients over a one-week period ranged from 0.53 (weakness) to 0.79 (potentiation), and over a three-month period ranged from 0.55 (strength) to 0.72 (weakness).

Validity: In order to establish the predictive validity of the POD, it was administered to a group of actualizing individuals and a group of non-actualizing individuals. Significant differences were found for all scales. Concurrent validity was established by correlating the POD with the Eysenck Personality Questionnaire and the Clinical Analysis Questionnaire.

Factor Analysis: First order and second order analyses were performed. The POI scale of Time Competence became the POD scale of Time Orientation; Self-Regard became Strength; Self-Acceptance became Weakness; Existentiality became Potentiation; Nature of Man-Constructive became Trust in Humanity; Synergy became Synergistic Integration; and Acceptance of Aggression became Anger. The POD scales of Creative Living, Mission, and Manipulation Awareness are new scales.

Definition of Scales: *Time Orientation* refers to living in the present instead of blaming the past or relying on the future. *Core Centeredness* refers to believing in one's feelings. *Strength* refers to power, security, worth, adequacy, or competence. *Weakness* refers to humanness, vulnerability, hurt or helplessness. *Anger* refers to feelings and experiences of anger. *Love* refers to feelings and experiences of warmth, tenderness or affection. *Synergistic Integration* demonstrates that opposites or polarities are not necessarily opposites. *Potentiation* views life as a gestalt. *Being* refers to expressing feelings or thoughts. *Trust in Humanity* refers to viewing human nature as basically good. *Creative Living* refers to effectiveness and innovation. *Mission* refers to commitment to a life task. *Manipulation Awareness* refers to manipulative or controlling actions.

Data Analysis: Intercorrelations among the POD scales are reported as well as intercorrelations between the POD and the POI, and between the POD, the Eysenck Personality Questionnaire, and the Myer Briggs Type Indicator. Scale means, standard deviations, and reliabilities are presented. In addition, significant relationships between the POD and the Clinical Analysis Questionnaire are documented.

References:

Knapp, R.R. and L. Knapp. 1978. Conceptual and statistical refinement and extension of the measurement of actualizing: Concurrent validity of the Personal Orientation Dimensions (POD). *Educational and Psychological Measurement* 38:523-26.

Lerner, D.L. 1977. Self-actualizing profiles of scientists and actors as described by the Personal Orientation Dimensions. Ph.D. dissertation, United States International University.

Maslow, A.H. 1971. *The further reaches of human nature.* New York: Viking.

Rofsky, M. et al. 1977. Assessing the level of actualizing of psychiatric in-patients: Validity of the Personal Orientation Dimensions. *Educational and Psychological Measurement* 37:1075-79.

Shostrom, E.L. et al. 1976. Validation of the Personal Orientation Dimensions: An inventory for the dimensions of actualizing. *Educational and Psychological Measurement* 36:391-494.

Scoring: A forced-choice format is used so that each item is written twice (items represent both ends of the continuum). Machine scoring is available.

Sample Items: (not actual item numbers)
1. a. I feel that I have a right to expect others to do what I want of them.
    b. I do not feel that I have a right to expect others to do what I want of them.
2. a. I fear failure.
    b. I don't fear failure.
3. a. I follow diligently the motto, "Don't waste your time."
    b. I do not feel bound by the motto, "Don't waste your time."
4. a. I feel that people are more basically good than bad.
    b. I feel that people are more basically bad than good.
5. a. I feel dedicated to my work.
    b. I do not feel dedicated to my work.

Self-Concept

Tennessee Self-Concept Scale

Fitts, W.H. 1965. *Manual: Tennessee Self-Concept Scale.* Los Angeles, CA: Western Psychological Services.

Comment: The 100-item TSCS examines self-concept as a multidimensional construct that measures internal and external aspects of self-concept. Western Psychological Services provides a detailed Test Report for the TSCS. A revised manual (1988) includes information on administration, scoring, norms, psychometric properties, and a review of the literature which includes references to studies using the TSCS. Although questions have been raised about the factor structure of the TSCS, it is the most frequently cited instrument to measure self-concept.

Scale Construction: A large pool of items from other self-concept instruments and self-descriptions was the basis for the internal/external categories of the TSCS. Seven clinical psychologists matched items into each of 15 areas. When all the psychologists agreed on an item, it was included in the appropriate category. There were six items selected for each of the 15 areas. Ten items were selected from the L-Scale of the MMPI.

Sample: The original sample consisted of 626 individuals ranging in age from 12 to 68 and from diverse economic, social, and educational levels.

Reliability: The split-half reliability for the total score on the TSCS was 0.91. The results of additional reliability studies are presented in the manual. Test-retest reliabilities ranged from 0.60 (row variability) to 0.92 (total score and psychosis) over a two-week interval with a sample of 60 university students. Test-retest reliability of the major TSCS scores are provided.

Factor Analysis: Numerous factor analytic studies have been conducted on the TSCS. A detailed description and summary is presented. Overall, factor analysis yielded eight factors: three internal self (row) subscales (identity, behavior, and self-satisfaction) and five external self (column) subscales (moral-ethical, social, personal, physical, and family). Factor loadings from the confirmatory rotation of internal (row) and external (column) factors are reported.

Validity: Content validity was established by the representativeness of the TSCS items and the use of facet-design. In order to establish its convergent and discriminant validity, the TSCS has been correlated with the MMPI, the Edwards Personal Preference Schedule, and other personality scales. The results of the correlations are reported in the manual. Statistically significant correlations are highlighted. Although factor analytic studies support the internal and external aspects of self-concept, the 15 facets of self-concept are not supported. Several studies examined the relationship between the TSCS and various outcome variables to establish criterion validity.

Definition of Scales: *Physical Self* refers to body, health, physical appearance, skills, and sexuality. *Moral-Ethical Self* refers to moral worth, relationship to God, satisfaction with religion, and feelings of being a good or bad individual. *Personal Self* refers to personal worth, feelings of adequacy, and self-evaluation of the personality. *Family Self* refers to worth and value as a member of a family. *Social Self* refers to adequacy and worth with others in social interactions. In addition to these five external aspects of self-concept, the TSCS also provides scores on six empirical scales: *Defensive Positive* (29 items); *General Maladjustment* (24 items); *Psychosis* (23 items); *Personality Disorder* (27 items); *Neurosis* (27 items); and *Personality Integration* (25 items). In addition, scores are obtained for *Total Conflict*, and *Number of Deviant Signs*. The *Total Score* is considered to be the most important score because it represents overall self-esteem.

Data Analysis: Means, standard deviations, and internal consistency reliability for the WPS Test Report Sample are provided.

References:

Amundson, M.E. 1993. A study of the professional characteristics of juvenile court school educators in California and the self concept of juvenile court school educators in Southern California. Ed.D. dissertation, University of LaVerne.

Greenan, J.P. and others. 1994. Relationship between self-concept and self-ratings of students in vocational programs. *Journal of Industrial Teacher Education* 31:94-110.

Meyer, M.M. 1991. The effects of assertion training on assertive behaviors, self-acceptance, self-concept, and locus of control. Ph.D. dissertation, University of Missouri, Kansas City.

Myers, L.C. 1992. Self-concepts of career level II and III teachers and career ladder eligible teachers in the public schools of Tennessee. Ed.D. dissertation, East Tennessee State University.

Scoring: Completely False = 1; Mostly False = 2; Partly False and Partly True = 3; Mostly True = 4; and Completely True = 5. The TSCS has two scoring modes: the Counseling mode which includes 14 scores and the Clinical Research mode which includes 20 scores. Computer scoring is available as well as profiles.

Sample Items:

8.   I am a calm and easygoing person.
24. I have a lot of self-control.
48. I try to please others, but I don't overdo it.
60. I wish I didn't give up as easily as I do.
64. I am satisfied with the way I treat other people.
66. I ought to get along better with other people.
73. I try to change when I know I'm doing things that are wrong.
76. I take the blame for things without getting mad.
81. I try to understand the other fellow's point of view.
89. I sometimes use unfair means to get ahead.

Items from the *Tennessee Self-Concept Scale* copyright © 1983 by Western Psychological Services, copyright © 1964 by William H. Fitts. Reprinted with permission of the publisher, Western Psychological Services, 12031 Wilshire Boulevard, Los Angeles, California 90025. No additional reproduction may be made without the expressed, written consent of Western Psychological Services. All rights reserved.

Wallace Self-Concept Scale

Wallace, G.R. 1980. *WSCS technical manual.* St. Louis, MO: University of Missouri, St. Louis, Dept. of Behavioral Studies.

Comments: The WSCS is a 15-item bipolar adjective scale that measures an individual's perception of "Myself As A Person." It is a global measure of the self. There are two forms (A and B) in English and one form (A) in Spanish.

Scale Development: Based upon a review of the literature, an initial item pool consisting of 75 bipolar adjectives was developed. A panel of three judges rated the adjectives using a three point scale. Thirty-four items were retained and administered to the original sample. The 15 items that were included in the final version of the WSCS met the following criteria: the item scores correlated equal to or greater than 0.40 with the total WSCS and the item scores correlated equal to or less than 0.23 with the Marlowe-Crowne Social Desirability Scale. Form B was constructed by making the top half of Form A the bottom of Form B and vice versa. All the bi-polar items were also reversed. Forms A and B are considered alternate forms.

Sample: The original sample consisted of 100 people (teachers, college students, and businessmen). Descriptive statistics are provided for four groups: adults (1,257), adolescents (771), college students (287), and a total sample (2,301). Normative data (raw scores, frequencies, cumulative frequencies, NCEs, standardized T scores, and the normalized Z scores) are included for each of the four groups.

Validity: . Two types of validity are reported for Form A. Convergent validity is reported between the WSCS and the Tennessee Self-Concept Scale (0.45), the Rosenberg Self-Esteem Scale (0.60), the Personal Orientation Inventory (0.51), and the Piers-Harris Self-Esteem Concept Scale (0.64). Discriminant validity with the Marlowe-Crowne Social Desirability Scale is 0.23.

Reliability: Three types of reliability estimates are reported for Form A. Coefficient alpha for Form A was 0.81. Test-retest reliabilities ranged from 0.72 to 0.81 over a two-week period. Alternate form reliabilities between Form A and B ranged from 0.71 to 0.80 over a three-week period.

References:
Wallace, G.R. and S.P. Walker. 1990. Self-concept, vocational interests, and choice of academic major in college students. *College Student Journal* 23:361-367.

Wallace, G.R. et al. 1984. Factorial comparison of the Wallace Self-Concept Scale between special education teachers and regular classroom teachers. *Educational and Psychological Measurement* 44:199-207.

Wallace Self-Concept Scale (Form A)

1.	Eager	Indifferent
2.	Passive	Active
3.	Rigid	Flexible
4.	Participating	Avoiding
5.	Lethargic	Energetic
6.	Powerful	Powerless
7.	Negative	Positive
8.	Hardworking	Lazy
9.	Repulsive	Attractive
10.	Sharp	Dull
11.	Unpleasant	Pleasant
12.	Useless	Useful
13.	Happy	Sad
14.	Pessimistic	Optimistic
15.	Ugly	Beautiful

Scoring: Each bipolar adjective item is scored on a scale from 1 to 7. The six reverse scored adjectives are: eager, participating, powerful, hardworking, sharp, and happy.

Reprinted with permission of Gaylen R. Wallace, Ed.D. Department of Behavioral Studies, University of Missouri at St. Louis, St. Louis, MO 63121.

Self-Efficacy

Teacher Efficacy Scale

Gibson, S. 1984. Teacher Efficacy Scale. *Journal of Educational Psychology* 76:569-582.

Comments: The 30-item rating scale is designed to allow teachers to evaluate their degree of personal efficacy or their conviction that they can successfully execute behavior necessary to produce desired outcomes. Self efficacy beliefs would indicate that teachers' evaluations of their abilities can bring about positive student change.

Sample: The sample consisted of 208 teachers from 13 elementary schools within two neighboring school districts in California.

Validity: A multitrait-multimethod technique was employed to establish both convergent and discriminant validity on three traits--teacher efficacy, verbal ability, and flexibility.

Factor Analysis: A principal factoring solution was used with both orthogonal and oblique rotations. Two factors were produced suggesting that the two factors were relatively independent. One factor was named personal teaching efficacy; the second was teaching efficacy.

Data Analysis: Classroom observations related to academic focus and teacher feedback behaviors indicated differences between high- and low-efficacy teachers in time spent in whole class versus small group instruction, teacher use of criticism, and teacher lack of persistence in failure situations.

References:
Bandura, A. 1977. Self -efficacy: Toward a unifying theory of behavioral change. *Psychological Review* 84:191-215.

Bandura, A. 1978. Reflections on self-efficacy. *Advances in Behavioral Research and Therapy* 1:237-269.

Gibson, S. and R. Brown 1982. The development of a teacher's personal responsibility/self-efficacy scale. Paper presented at American Educational Research Association.

Teacher Efficacy Scale

1. When a student does better than usual, many times it is because I exerted a little extra effort.
2. The hours in my class have little influence on students compared to the influence of their home environment.
3. If parents comment to me that their child behaves much better at school than he/she does at home, it would probably be because I have some specific techniques of managing his/her behavior which they may lack.
4. The amount that a student can learn is primarily related to family background.
5. If a teacher has adequate skills and motivation, he/she can get through to the most difficult students.
6. If students aren't disciplined at home, they aren't likely to accept any discipline.
7. I have enough training to deal with almost any learning problem.
8. My teacher training program and/or experience has given me the necessary skills to be an effective teacher.
9. Many teachers are stymied in their attempts to help students by lack of support from the community.
10. Some students need to be placed in slower groups so they are not subjected to unrealistic expectations.
11. Individual differences among teachers account for the wide variations in student achievement.
12. When a student is having difficulty with an assignment, I am usually able to adjust it to his/her level.
13. If one of my new students cannot remain on task for a particular assignment, there is little that I could do to increase his/her attention until he/she is ready.
14. When a student gets a better grade than he usually gets, it is usually because I found better ways of teaching that student.
15. When I really try, I can get through to most difficult students.
16. A teacher is very limited in what he/she can achieve because a student's home environment is a large influence on his/her achievement.
17. Teachers are not a very powerful influence on student achievement when all factors are considered.
18. If students are particularly disruptive one day, I ask myself what I have been doing differently.
19. When the grades of my students improve, it is usually because I found more effective teaching approaches.
20. If my principal suggested that I change some of my class curriculum,, I would feel confident that I have the necessary skills to implement the unfamiliar curriculum.
21. If a student masters a new math concept quickly, this might be because I knew the necessary steps in teaching that concept.
22. Parent conferences can help a teacher judge how much to expect from a student by giving the teacher an idea of the parents' values toward education, discipline, etc.
23. If parents would do more with their children, I could do more.
24. If a student did not remember information I gave in a previous lesson, I would know how to increase his/her retention in the next lesson.
25. If a student in my class becomes disruptive and noisy, I feel assured that I know some techniques to redirect him quickly.
26. School rules and policies hinder my doing the job I was hired to do.
27. The influences of a student's home experiences can be overcome by good teaching.
28. When a child progresses after being placed in a slower group, it is usually because the teacher has had a chance to give him/her extra attention.

29. If one of my students couldn't do a class assignment, I would be able to accurately assess whether the assignment was at the correct level of difficulty.

30. Even a teacher with good teaching abilities may not reach many students.

Scoring: 1 = Strongly Disagree to 6 = Strongly Agree

Reprinted with permission of the author.

Principal Self-Efficacy Scale
Teacher Self-Efficacy Scale

Hillman, S.J. 1986. Measuring self-efficacy: Preliminary steps in the development of a multi-dimensional instrument. Paper presented at American Educational Research Association. ERIC ED 271 505.

Comments: Two parallel 16-item questionnaires were designed to measure either teachers or principals self-efficacy, that is, the extent to which they feel positive or negative concerning their achievement and productivity in the classroom or in the school. Both instruments are the same except principal items relate to the achievement of the school, while teacher items have a focus on the classroom.

Scale Construction: Half of the items presented positive situations that might occur in the classroom or school. Each item has four possible responses: (1) the first attributed the situation to either the teacher's ability or inability to teach; (2) this attributed the situation to either their effort of lack of effort; (3) placed responsibility on materials--test or subject content not the teacher; (4) this assigned responsibility to either luck or lack of luck.

Sample: As part of a larger study, 758 fourth-grade students, 35 teachers, and 19 principals completed their respective version of the self-efficacy instruments. They were taken from 20 public schools--ten from high achieving schools and 10 from low achieving schools with the state of Michigan.

Reliability: Each instrument has alpha coefficients that ranged from 0.81 to 0.93 on each of the four subscales.

Validity: Only content validity is discussed. Because of the relatively high alpha estimates for the total instrument and for each subscale, it was assumed that sufficient homogeneity existed among the items and scales to assume that a measure of construct validity was provided.

Factor Analysis: Apparently correlations were used to form the four subscales. There is no evidence of any other (i.e., factor analysis) procedures being used to form the subscales. The four subscales were labeled: positive and negative internal and positive and negative external.

References:
Bandura, A. 1981. Self-referent thought: A developmental analysis of self-efficacy. In J.H. Flavell and L. Ross (Eds.), *Social cognitive development.* Cambridge: Cambridge University Press.

Fuller, B. et al. 1982. The organizational context of individual efficacy. *Review of Educational Research* 52:7-30.

Stipek, D.J. and J.R. Weisz. 1981. Perceived personal control and academic achievement. *Review of Educational Research* 51:101-137.

Principal Self-Efficacy Instrument

1. If the achievement level of your school is high, it would be because
   A. you possess a natural ability to be an effective instructional leader.
   B. as a principal, you put a great deal of effort into emphasizing academic achievement.
   C. the achievement test used to measure the achievement level of your students was too easy.
   D. you were lucky to get a good school.

2. If your school appeared to be strong in a particular skill such as "Language-Spelling Skills", it would be because
   A. you possess a natural ability to be an effective instructional leader.
   B. as a principal, you emphasize the importance of students acquiring this skill.
   C. the materials used in the classroom covering this skill area were too much like the items on the achievement test.
   D. you were lucky to get a good school.

3. If very few of the students in your school by the end of the year are able to master the basic statewide objectives established for their grade level it would be because
   A. you do not possess a natural ability to be an instructional leader.
   B. you lack of effort in emphasizing the importance of all students mastering the basic objectives.
   C. the statewide objectives are unrealistic and too difficult to attain.
   D. you were not lucky enough to get assigned to one of the better schools.

4. If your school, which has a history of being a low-achieving school, increases its achievement level this year to above the norm, this would be because of
   A. your natural ability to be an instructional leader.
   B. your effort in supporting and emphasizing the importance of students' achievement.
   C. a change in the achievement testing, making it easier for your students to succeed.
   D. your being lucky. Recent redistricting brought brighter students to your school.

5. If the achievement level of your school is below the norm, it would be because
   A. you do not possess a natural ability to be an instructional leader.
   B. you did not put in the effort needed to emphasize high achievement.
   C. the materials used in the classroom did not emphasize the areas tested by the achievement measure.
   D. you were not lucky enough to get a school of high achievers.

6. If you received a negative evaluation from your superintendent in the area of instructional leadership, this would be because
   A. you do not possess a natural ability to be an instructional leader.
   B. you do not feel this is an important part of your job; therefore, you do not emphasize it.
   C. the evaluation was not fair with the standards by which you were measured being too difficult for anyone to attain.
   D. your superintendent just happened to be in a critical mood the day he/she wrote the evaluation.

7. If a new science program is initiated in you school and the students' achievement in this area increases significantly, this would be due to

A. your natural ability to be an effective instructional leader.

B. the effort you put into promoting the program and assisting teachers in working with it.

C. a good match between the objectives emphasized in the new science program and the achievement test.

D. your being lucky. Recent redistricting brought brighter students to your school, particularly those having a high aptitude for science.

8. Twenty-five percent (25%) of the students in grades 1-3 were retained and not promoted to the next grade. This rate is higher than any other school in the area. This would be due to:

A. your lacking natural ability in being an effective instructional leader.

B. your lack of effort in emphasizing the need for all students to achieve.

C. your school's standards for retention are more rigid than other schools'.

D. your not being lucky enough to get assigned to one of the better schools.

9. If students do well in your classes, it would be because

A. you have the natural ability to be an instructional leader.

B. you put a great deal of effort into emphasizing the importance of academic achievement.

C. the basic material covered is designed so that even the slowest of students can get some right.

D. you were lucky to get a bunch of kid this year who are smart and self-motivated.

10. Suppose your superintendent commended you on doing a fine job as evidenced by the high level of achievement demonstrated by your students. This would mean

A. a great deal, because you feel you have a natural ability as an instructional leader in your school.

B. a great deal, because you have put in a lot of effort and time into promoting and insuring a high level of achievement for all students.

C. very little, because you suspect the test used to measure the academic achievement of your students was very easy and most should pass it anyway.

D. very little, because you were simply lucky to be in a school where the majority of your students have a high enough IQ which enables them to achieve independently of anything you really do.

11. If your school scores very low in a particular subject area such as math on an achievement test, it would be because

A. you do not possess a natural ability to be an instructional leader, particularly in the area.

B. you did not emphasize the importance of achieving in this subject area as much as the other subjects.

C. the math section of the achievement test did not test what was taught.

D. you happened to get a school whose students don't have the ability to achieve in this area.

12. If 95% of the students in your school are mastering the basic objectives established for their grade level, this would be because

A. you possess a natural ability to be an instructional leader.

B. you have emphasized the importance of all students achieving at least the basic objectives before the end of the school year.

C. the basic objectives were established at such minimum level as to enable even the slowest of students to succeed in mastering them.

D. you were lucky to get a school whose student body tends to be very academically able.

Scoring: Strongly Agree = 5; Agree = 4; Unsure = 3; Disagree = 2; and Strongly Disagree = 1

Teacher Self-Efficacy Instrument

1. If a student does well in your class, it is probably because
    A. of your natural ability to teach.
    B. of the effort you put into teaching.
    C. the assignments are easy.
    D. you were lucky to get at least a few good students.

2. When your class is having trouble understanding something you have taught, it is usually because
    A. you do not possess a natural ability to teach.
    B. you did not put in enough effort.
    C. the material you are teaching is difficult to comprehend.
    D. you were unlucky in getting a particularly slow class this year.

3. When most of your students do well on a test, it is more likely to be because
    A. of your natural ability to teach.
    B. of the effort you put into teaching.
    C. the test was easy.
    D. you were lucky to get a class composed of generally good students.

4. When students in your class forget something that you had already explained, it is usually because
    A. you do not possess a natural ability to teach.
    B. you did not put in enough effort in explaining the topic.
    C. the topic area is particularly difficult.
    D. you were unlucky in getting a particularly slow class this year.

5. Suppose your principal says you're doing a fine job. This is likely to happen because
    A. of your natural ability to teach.
    B. of the effort you put into teaching.
    C. the material you are teaching is quite basic and easy to learn.
    D. you were lucky to get a good academically able class this year.

6. If most of the students in your class are doing very well, it is probably because
    A. of your natural ability to teach.
    B. of the effort you put into teaching.

C. the material you are teaching is quite basic and easy to learn.

D. you were lucky to get a good class academically to begin with.

7. If you are working with a student who can't understand a concept and he suddenly "gets it", it is likely to happen because

A. of your natural ability to teach.

B. of the effort you put into teaching.

C. the material takes a while to understand anyway.

D. you were lucky at that moment.

8. If few of your students by the end of the year are able to master the basic objectives established for their grade level, it is most likely because

A. you do not possess a natural ability to teach.

B. you did not put in enough effort.

C. the objectives were established unrealistically high.

D. you were unlucky in being assigned a particularly slow class this year.

9. When a large percent of the students in your class are doing poorly, it usually happens because

A. you do not possess a natural ability to teach.

B. you did not put in enough effort.

C. the topic area is particularly difficult.

D. you were unlucky in being assigned a particularly slow class this year in understanding and learning.

10. Suppose you present some new material to your students and most of them remember it. This is likely to be because

A. of your natural ability to teach.

B. of the effort you put into teaching.

C. the material is quite basic and easy to learn.

D. you were lucky to have a good class academically to begin with.

11. When your students do poorly on a test, it is because

A. you do not possess a natural ability to teach.

B. you did not put in enough effort in teaching the material covered on the test.

C. the test was too difficult.

D. you were unlucky in being assigned a particularly slow class this year.

12. If a child does not do well in your class it is probably because

A. you do not possess a natural ability to teach.

B. you did not put in enough effort in helping this child.

C. the material is particularly difficult.

D. you happened to get some poor students this year who started off way below the others.

13. When you are having a hard time getting your students interested in a lesson, it is usually because

A. you do not possess a natural ability to teach.

B. you are not putting in enough effort.

C. the lesson is particularly boring.

D. you were unlucky in getting a group of students who generally are difficult to motivate.

14. If all of your students by the end of the school year are mastering the basic objectives established for their grade level, it is most likely because
    A. of your natural ability to teach.
    B. of the effort you put into teaching.
    C. the objectives are a minimum and easy for all to obtain.
    D. you were lucky to get students who, on the whole, are particularly bright.

15. When your students seem interested in your lesson right from the beginning, it is because
    A. of your natural ability to teach.
    B. of the effort you put into teaching the lesson.
    C. the topic is one which students generally find interesting.
    D. you were lucky to get students who are generally highly motivated to learn.

16. On those days when you are depressed and feel you are not doing as good a job as you would like, it is because
    A. you do not possess a natural ability to teach.
    B. you do not put in enough effort.
    C. the material you are covering is very difficult to teach.
    D. it is one of those unlucky days when everything goes wrong.

Scoring: See above.

Self-Esteem

Texas Social Behavior Inventory

Helmreich, R. and J. Stapp. 1974. Short forms of the Texas Social Behavior Inventory (TSBI), an objective measure of self-esteem. *Bulletin of the Psychonomic Society* 4:473-475.

Comments: The 32-item long form of the TSBI measures self-esteem or social competence. Based on the results of factor and item analyses with over 1,000 people, two short forms each with 16 items were developed.

Sample: Over 8,000 students at the University of Texas at Austin have completed the TSBI.

Reliability: Based on a sample of 238 male and 262 female undergraduate students at the University of Texas at Austin the following Alpha coefficients were reported. On Form A, they ranged from 0.85 (men) to 0.86 (women) and from 0.85 (men) to 0.88 (women) on Form B. The alpha coefficients on the original 32-item TSBI ranged from 0.92 (men) to 0.93 (women). Form A and B are highly correlated with the original scale. The criteria for the two 16-item short forms were: equivalence of part-whole correlations, equivalence of means between forms and between sexes, equivalence of score distributions, and parallel factor structures.

Validity: Factor analysis and part-whole correlations confirmed the similarity of the two forms. The TSBI has been correlated with the Personal Attributes Questionnaire. Correlations of 0.81 and 0.83 are reported with the masculinity subscale for men and women, and correlations of 0.42 and 0.44 are reported with the femininity subscale for men and women.

Factor Analysis: Principal axis rotation produced only one factor, whereas, an oblique rotation yielded four factors: confidence, dominance, social competence, and social withdrawal (male) or relations to authority figures (female).

References:
Helmreich, R. et al. 1974. The Texas Social Behavior Inventory (TSBI): An objective measure of self-esteem or social competence. *Journal Supplement Abstract Service. Catalog of Selected Documents in Psychology* 4:79.

Spence, J.T. et al. 1974. The Personal Attributes Questionnaire: A measure of sex-role stereotypes and masculinity-femininity *Journal Supplement Abstract Service. Catalog of Selected Documents in Psychology* 4:43.

Spence, J.T. et al. 1975. Ratings of self and peers on sex-role attributes and their relations to self-esteem and conceptions of masculinity and femininity. *Journal of Personality and Social Psychology* 32:29-39.

Texas Social Behavior Inventory (Form A)

1. I am not likely to speak to people until they speak to me.
2. I would describe myself as self-confident.
3. I feel confident of my appearance.
4. I am a good mixer.
5. When in a group of people, I have trouble thinking of the right things to say.
6. When in a group of people, I usually do what the others want rather than make suggestions.
7. When I am in disagreement with other people, my opinion usually prevails.
8. I would describe myself as one who attempts to master situations.
9. Other people look up to me.
10. I enjoy social gatherings just to be with people.
11. I make a point of looking other people in the eye.
12. I cannot seem to get others to notice me.
13. I would rather not have very much responsibility for other people.
14. I feel comfortable being approached by someone in a position of authority.
15. I would describe myself as indecisive.
16. I have no doubts about my social competence.

Scoring: (a) Not at all characteristic of me; (b) Not Very; (c) Slightly; (d) Fairly; (e) very much characteristic of me. The lower self-esteem response receives a score of 0, while the higher self-esteem response receives a score of 4. The following items on Form A receive a 0: (1e, 2a, 3a, 4a, 5e, 6e, 7a, 8a, 9a, 10a, 11a, 12e, 13e, 14a, 15e, 16a). The following items on Form B receive a 0: (1e, 2e, 3a, 4a, 5a, 6a, 7a, 8a, 9a, 10a, 11a, 12e, 13e, 14a, 15a, 16a).

Reprinted with permission of the author.

Sex-Role (Gender Identification)

Women as Managers Scale

Peters, L.H. et al. 1974. Women as Managers Scale (WAMS): A measure of attitudes toward women in management positions. *JSAS Catalog of Selected Documents in Psychology*, Ms. No. 585.

Comments: The authors suggest using the WAMS in field settings. It might be interesting to adapt the WAMS to an educational setting.

Scale Construction: The original 55-item WAMS included general descriptive traits of managers and female-specific stereotypic traits that could impede their obtaining managerial positions. Based on the results of item analysis and a principal components analysis, the new scale contained 21 items (11 worded positively and 10 worded negatively).

Sample: The original sample consisted of 541 advanced undergraduates from four universities in the Midwest and South. The validation sample consisted of 180 men and 100 women who worked for an international distributing company.

Reliability: The corrected split-half (odd-even) reliability was 0.91.

Validity: To establish the validity of the WAMS, six predictions were tested. Four out of six predictions were supported at the 0.05 level. One prediction was supported at the 0.10 level, while one prediction was not supported (work history of female participants' mothers). In addition, part of the sample was used in a cross-validation study.

Factor Analysis: Although a principal components factor analysis yielded three factors, additional analysis suggested a single factor.

Data Analysis: Descriptive statistics for the sample are provided. One-way ANOVAs were used to test the six predictions. A step-wise regression of attitudes on personal data and organizational data are reported.

References:
Crino, M.D. et al. 1981. A comment on the dimensionality and reliability of the Women as Managers Scale (WAMS). *Academy of Management Journal* 24:866-876.

Garland, H. and K.H. Price 1977. Attitudes toward women in management and attributions for their success and failure in a managerial position. *Journal of Applied Psychology* 62:29-33.

Terborg, J.R. et al. 1977. Organizational and personal correlates of attitudes toward women as managers. *Academy of Management Journal* 20:89-100.

Women as Managers Scale

1. It is less desirable for women than men to have a job that requires responsibility.
2. Women have the objectivity required to evaluate business situations properly.
3. Challenging work is more important to men than it is to women.
4. Men and women should be given equal opportunity for participation in management training programs.
5. Women have the capability to acquire the necessary skills to be successful managers.
6. On the average, women managers are less capable of contributing to an organization's overall goals than are men.
7. It is not acceptable for women to assume leadership roles as often as men.
8. The business community should someday accept women in key managerial positions.
9. Society should regard work by female managers as valuable as work by male managers.
10. It is acceptable for women to compete with men for top executive positions.
11. The possibility of pregnancy does not make women less desirable employees than men.
12. Women would no more allow their emotions to influence their managerial behavior than would men.
13. Problems associated with menstruation should not make women less desirable than men as employees.
14. To be a successful executive, a women does not have to sacrifice some of her femininity.
15. On the average, a women who stays at home all the time with her children is a better mother than a woman who works outside the home at least half time.
16. Women are less capable of learning mathematical and mechanical skills than are men.
17. Women are not ambitious enough to be successful in the business world.
18. Women cannot be assertive in business situations that demand it.
19. Women possess the self-confidence required of a good leader.
20. Women are not competitive enough to be successful in the business world.
21. Women cannot be aggressive in business situations that demand it.

Scoring: Strongly Disagree = 1; Disagree = 2; Slightly Disagree = 3; Neither Disagree nor Agree = 4; Slightly Agree = 5; Agree = 6; and Strongly Agree = 7. The scoring is reversed for the following items: 1, 3, 6, 7, 15, 16, 17, 18, 20, and 21.

Personal Attributes Questionnaire

Spence, J.T. et al. 1974. The Personal Attributes Questionnaire: A measure of sex-role stereotypes and masculinity-femininity. *JSAS Catalog of Selected Documents in Psychology* 4:42.

Comments: The 24-item PAQ measures attributes that differentiate between the sexes. In addition, Spence et al. developed the 55-item Attitudes toward Women Scale (the short form has 15 items) which has items that describe the privileges, rights, and roles that women should have or be allowed to have.

Scale Construction: The original 55-item PAQ contains three scales: a masculine scale (M) with 23 items, a feminine scale (F) with 18 items, and a masculine-feminine scale (M-F) with 13 items. One item could not be classified. The PAQ is based on over 130 items generated by students as characteristics that differentiated between males and females. The 55 items not only describe characteristics that differentiate between males and females, but also represent the actual ratings of university males and females. The current 24-item PAQ contains the same three scales with eight items in each scale.

Sample: One set of normative data is available based on the rounded mean of the medians of the men and women in the high school sample. Another set of normative data derived by using the same procedure (rounded mean of the medians of the men and women) is available based on 715 university students.

Reliability: Cronbach alpha reliabilities were 0.78 (M-F scale), 0.82 (F scale), and 0.85 (M scale). Correlations between the short form and the original scale were 0.91 (M-F scale) and 0.93 (M and F scales).

Validity: Factor analytic procedures confirmed the unidimensionality of the M and F scales. Information about concurrent and predictive validity is reported.

Definition of Scales: The *Masculinity Scale* consists of items that are socially desirable for both sexes, although men possess these characteristics more than women. The *Femininity Scale* consists of items that are socially desirable for both sexes, although women possess these characteristics more than men. The *Masculinity-Femininity Scale* consists of items whose social desirability varies between the sexes.

Data Analysis: Two samples of university students yielded significant differences between the means of men and women on every item of the PAQ. Males scored higher on the M and M-F items, and scored lower on the F items. In addition, part-whole correlations were computed between each of the item scores and each of the three scales.

References:
Jones, B.J.W. 1993. Career socialization, locus-of-control and perceptions of sex role stereotypes among female administrators in Georgia's technical institutes. Ph.D. dissertation, Georgia State University.

Waelde, L.C. and others. 1994. Stressful life events: Moderators of the relationships of gender and gender roles to self-reported depression and suicidality among college students. *Sex Roles: A Journal of Research* 30:1-22.

Personal Attributes Questionnaire

1. Not at all aggressive .... Very aggressive
2. Very whiny .... Not at all whiny
3. Not at all independent .... Very independent
4. Not at all arrogant .... Very arrogant
5. Not at all emotional .... Very emotional
6. Very submissive .... Very dominant
7. Very boastful .... Not at all boastful
8. Not at all excitable in a major crisis .... Very excitable in a major crisis
9. Very passive .... Very active
10. Not at all egotistical .... Very egotistical
11. Not at all able to devote self completely to others .... Able to devote self completely to others
12. Not at all spineless .... Very spineless
13. Very rough .... Very gentle
14. Not at all complaining .... Very complaining
15. Not at all helpful to others .... Very helpful to others
16. Not at all competitive .... Very competitive
17. Subordinates oneself to others .... Never subordinates oneself to others
18. Very home oriented .... Very worldly
19. Very greedy .... Not at all greedy
20. Not at all kind .... Very kind
21. Indifferent to others' approval .... Highly needful of others' approval
22. Very dictatorial .... Not at all dictatorial
23. Feelings not easily hurt .... Feelings easily hurt
24. Doesn't nag .... Nags a lot
25. Not at all aware of feelings of others .... Very aware of feelings of others
26. Can make decisions easily .... Has difficulty making decisions
27. Very fussy .... Not at all fussy
28. Gives up very easily .... Never gives up easily
29. Very cynical .... Not at all cynical
30. Never cries .... Cries very easily
31. Not at all self-confident .... Very self-confident
32. Does not look out only for self; principled .... Looks out only for self; unprincipled
33. Feels very inferior .... Feels very superior
34. Not at all hostile .... Very hostile
35. Not at all understanding of others .... Very understanding of others
36. Very cold in relations with others .... Very warm in relations with others
37. Very servile .... Not at all servile
38. Very little need for security .... Very strong need for security
39. Not at all gullible .... Very gullible
40. Goes to pieces under pressure .... Stands up well under pressure

Scoring: A bipolar scale is used. Each item receives a score of 0 to 4.

Reprinted with permission of the author.

Stress/Burnout

Teacher Stress Inventory

Fimian, M.J. and P.S. Fastenau. 1990. The validity and reliability of the Teacher Stress Inventory: A re-analysis of aggregate data. *Journal of Organizational Behavior* 11:151-157.

Comments: The 49-item TSI assesses occupational stress in teachers. It contains ten factors; the first five represent sources of stress whereas the remaining five represent manifestations of teacher stress. The TSI presents evidence of validity and reliability. A Media Specialist Stress Inventory is also available.

Scale Construction: After reviewing the literature on teacher stress, a list of 135 items was written. Content analyses and editing reduced the number to 63 items. Additional content validation procedures, factor analyses, and tests of internal consistency were conducted, thereby reducing the number to 30 items. Twelve items were added, and then the TSI was administered to four samples. The TSI contained two dimensions: frequency and strength. The revised 41-item TSI was factor analyzed. An oblique six-factor solution was accepted. The number of items remaining was reduced to 38. Alpha coefficients ranged from 0.70 to 0.90.

Sample: The total sample consisted of 3,401 teachers from seven states in the eastern United States. These teachers represent 21 different samples. Overall, there were 962 regular education teachers and 2,352 special education teachers. Eighty-seven teachers did not identify themselves as either regular or special education teachers.

Reliability: Alpha coefficients (Cronbach) for the ten factors were: 0.75 (professional investment); 0.82 (behavioral manifestations); 0.83 (time management); 0.86 (discipline and motivation); 0.87 (emotional manifestations); 0.80 (work-related stressors); 0.88 (gastronomical manifestations); 0.78 (cardiovascular manifestations); 0.82 (fatigue manifestations); and 0.82 (professional distress). All alpha coefficients were greater than 0.75, and the alpha for the entire inventory was 0.93. Means and standard deviations are presented.

Validity: This study re-examined the factor structure and internal consistency of the TSI. Content validity was accomplished by having 92 experts in the field examine the TSI. Factor analyses were conducted to further refine the TSI.

Factor Analysis: Principal components factor analyses were conducted as well as oblique and varimax rotations. The results of these analyses yielded ten factors. The factors are: four items on professional investment (11, 13, 14, and 15); four items on behavioral manifestations (29, 28, 31, and 27); eight items on time management (47, 45, 44, 46, 48, 49, 43, and 42); six items on discipline and motivation (17, 16, 19, 18, 20, and 21); five items on emotional manifestations (22, 24, 23, 25, and 26); six items on work-related stressors (1, 3, 5, 4, 2, and 6); three items on gastronomical manifestations (35, 34, and 39); three items on cardiovascular manifestations (32, 33, and 30); five items on fatigue manifestations (40, 41, 38, 36, and 37); and five items on professional distress (7, 8, 9, 12, and 10). Factor loadings, communalities, alpha reliabilities, means and standard deviations are presented.

Definition of Factors: *Professional investment* refers to the feeling of distance that teachers feel on their jobs; it refers to a minimum investment in teaching careers for a variety of reasons. *Behavioral manifestations* refer to the variety of inappropriate ways that teachers deal with their stress. *Time management* refers to the "balancing act" features related to teaching. *Discipline and motivation* refer to two aspects of the teacher student relationship. *Emotional manifestations* refer to the different ways that teachers respond emotionally to stress. *Work-related stressors* refer to a variety of environment-specific events that are sources of teacher stress. *Gastronomical manifestations* refer to a variety of stomach ailments related to teacher stress. *Cardiovascular manifestations* refer to different cardiovascular problems associated with stress. *Fatigue manifestations* refer to a variety of fatigue problems associated with stress. *Professional distress* refers to the ways that teachers see themselves as professionals; it is like a "professional self-concept" scale.

References:

Fimian, M.J. 1984. The development of an instrument to measure occupational stress in teachers: The Teacher Stress Inventory. *Journal of Occupational Psychology* 57:277-293.

Fimian, M.J. 1988. *The Teacher Stress Inventory and test manual.* Brandon, VT: Clinical Psychology Publishing Company.

Teacher Stress Inventory

1. There is little time to prepare for my lessons/responsibilities.
2. My personal priorities are being shortchanged due to time demands.
3. I have too much work to do.
4. My caseload/class is too big.
5. The pace of the school day is too fast.
6. There is too much administrative paperwork in my job.
7. I lack promotion and/or advancement opportunities.
8. I am not progressing in my job as rapidly as I would like.
9. I need more status and respect on my job.
10. I lack recognition for the extra work and/or good teaching I do.
11. My personal opinions are not sufficiently aired.
12. I receive an inadequate salary for the work I do.
13. I lack control over decisions made about classroom/school matters.
14. I am not emotionally/intellectually stimulated on the job.
15. I lack opportunities for professional improvement.
16. **I feel frustrated**...having to monitor pupil behavior.
17. ...because of discipline problems in my classroom.
18. ...attempting to teach students who are poorly motivated.
19. ...because some students would do better if they tried harder.
20. ...because of inadequate/poorly defined discipline policies.
21. ...when my authority is rejected by pupils/ administration.
22. **I respond to stress**...by feeling insecure.
23. ...by feeling unable to cope.
24. ...by feeling vulnerable.
25. ...by feeling depressed.
26. ...by feeling anxious.
27. ...by calling in sick.
28. ...by using prescription drugs.

29. ...by using over-the-counter drugs.
30. ...with rapid and/or shallow breath.
31. ...by using alcohol.
32. ...with feeling increased blood pressure.
33. ...with feelings of heart pounding or racing.
34. ...with stomach pain of extended duration.
35. ...with stomach cramps.
36. ...with physical exhaustion.
37. ...with physical weakness.
38. ...by becoming fatigued in a very short time.
39. ...with stomach acid.
40. ...by sleeping more than usual.
41. ...by procrastinating.
42. I rush in my speech.
43. There isn't enough time to get things done.
44. I have to try doing more than one thing at a time.
45. I become impatient if others do things too slowly.
46. I have little time to relax and enjoy the time of day.
47. I easily over commit myself.
48. I think about unrelated matters during conversations.
49. I feel uncomfortable wasting time.

Scoring: No Strength; not noticeable; not applicable = 1; Mild Strength; barely noticeable = 2; Medium Strength; moderately noticeable = 3; Great Strength; very noticeable = 4; and Major Strength; extremely noticeable = 5.

Reprinted with permission of the publisher. Fimian, M.J. and P.S. Fastenau. 1990. The validity and reliability of the Teacher Stress Inventory: A re-analysis of aggregate data. *Journal of Organizational Behavior* 11:151-157. Reprinted by permission of John Wiley & Sons, Ltd.

Student Stress Inventory

Fimian, M.J. et al. 1989. The measure of classroom stress and burnout among gifted and talented students. *Psychology in the Schools* 26:139-153.

Comments: Over 90 percent of the experts concluded that the items on the SSI were related to student stress. Interrater reliability was high. Factor analysis yielded five interpretable factors. The factors found in the SSI are similar to those found in the Teacher Stress Inventory. The authors suggest further work on content validation and adding items to two of the scales to increase their reliability.

Scale Construction: Based on a review of the literature, a pilot form of the SSI was created and completed by 311 gifted students. At the same time, a group of 14 experts assessed the content validity of the SSI by determining the relevancy between each item and student stress. Items with 60 percent agreement were retained. Relevancy mean scores were studied. Nineteen items were deleted because they had factor loadings of less than 0.35. Additional factor and reliability analyses were conducted to further refine the SSI. The final version contains 41 items.

Sample: The sample consisted of 311 gifted students from Florida, North and South Carolina, and Virginia who attended summer camp at Appalachian State University in North Carolina.

Reliability: Alpha coefficients (Cronbach) were 0.85 (student distress); 0.63 (social/academic problems); 0.83 (emotional manifestations; 0.76 (behavioral manifestations); and 0.80 (physiological manifestations). The total scale alpha was 0.80.

Validity: Items were written after a review of the observational and conceptual literature thereby establishing face validity. Fourteen experts assessed the content validity of the SSI by comparing the items to the construct of student stress. A relevancy mean score for each subscale was computed. Expert ratings, means, percentages, and interrater reliabilities are reported. The concurrent validity of the SSI was determined by correlating student stress with student burnout (Maslach Burnout Inventory), student stress with tedium (the Tedium Measure), and student stress with Quality of School Life (Epstein and McPortland, 1978).

Factor Analysis: Principal components factor analyses were conducted with oblique and varimax rotations. The results of the oblique rotation yielded five factors. The five factors are: 14 items on student distress (27, 22, 28, 23, 3, 16, 13, 11, 4, 25, 15, 7, 1, and 10); six items on social/academic problems (20, 24, 26, 31, 18, and 21); ten items on emotional manifestations (37, 43, 36, 52, 55, 41, 47, 32, 49, and 35); six items on behavioral manifestations (56, 59, 53, 42, 48, and 60); and six items on physiological manifestations (45, 44, 57, 34, 50, and 54). Component loadings, means, and standard deviations are reported.

Definition of Factors: *Student distress* refers to negative feelings about school including not having enough time to relax and enjoy the day and feeling unimportant in school. *Social/academic problems* refer to various social and academic problems in school that contribute to stress such as having to do the same things in school week after week. *Emotional manifestations* refer to the emotional ways students react to stress such as feeling cranky. *Behavioral manifestations* refer to the techniques that students use to respond to stress such as acting defensively with others. *Physiological manifestations* refer to reactions such as eating more or less than usual and breaking out in a cold sweat.

References:

D'Aurora, D.L. and M. J. Fimian. 1988. Dimensions of life and school stress experienced by young people. *Psychology in the Schools* 25:44-52.

Epstein, J.L. and J.M. McPortland. 1978. *Administration and technical manual: The Quality of School Life Scale.* Boston: Houghton-Mifflin.

Fimian, M.J. and A.H. Cross. 1986. Stress and burnout among preadolescent and early adolescent gifted students: A preliminary investigation. *Journal of Early Adolescence* 6:247-267.

Pines, A.M. et al. 1981. *Burnout: From tedium to personal growth.* New York: The Free Press.

Student Stress Inventory

1. I have enough time to relax and enjoy the school day.
2. I have to deal with too many people each day.
3. I am important in school.
4. I am excited about the things I learn in school.
5. There are too many interruptions in my daily classroom routine.
6. I am all alone when I am at school.
7. I know exactly what is expected of me in school.
8. The school day seems to go either too fast or too slow for me.
9. My teacher(s) doesn't have enough time for me.
10. How well I did before in school really matters to my teacher(s) today.
11. It is easy for me to talk to my teachers.
12. Every one else in my class gets the "lucky breaks."
13. I feel physically comfortable in my classroom or school.
14. My grades are good enough.
15. I feel comfortable with the different ways in which my teachers teach.
16. My teacher(s) likes me.
17. I am helpless or hopeless.
18. We seem to do the same things in my classes week after week.
19. I feel no pressure to get my school work done.
20. I don't remember everything that I learn in school.
21. Some of my classmates get better treatment than I do.
22. I easily make friends and follow up interests out of school.
23. The information my teacher(s) gives me helps me do better in school.
24. Some of my teachers have too much power over me.
25. I am learning a lot in school.
26. My parents expect too much of me in school.
27. I am accepted by the other students.
28. My classmates really care about what I think and feel.
29. Tests and quizzes make me nervous.
30. I am not progressing in my studies rapidly enough.
31. I have too much information to deal with on a daily basis.

I RESPOND TO STRESS AT SCHOOL BY/WITH...

32. feeling insecure.
33. not being able to sit still.
34. rapid breathing.
35. putting things off to another day.
36. feeling scared.

37. feeling worried.
38. crying.
39. feeling dizzy.
40. becoming tired in a very short time.
41. feeling anxious.
42. acting defensively with others.
43. feeling pressured.
44. stomach pain of extended duration.
45. stomach acid.
46. sleeping more than usual.
47. feeling unable to cope with school.
48. allowing my friendships to fall apart.
49. feeling vulnerable.
50. feeling of increased blood pressure.
51. feeling physically exhausted.
52. feeling depressed.
53. "bad mouthing" certain classmates, teachers, or school staff.
54. feeling my heart pounding or racing.
55. feeling angry.
56. picking on someone else.
57. getting stomach cramps.
58. not talking to anybody.
59. talking back to teachers.
60. calling in sick.

Scoring: No Strength; not noticeable = 1; Of Mild Strength; barely noticeable = 2; Of Medium Strength; moderately noticeable = 3; Of Great Strength; very noticeable = 4; and Of Major Strength; extremely noticeable = 5.

Reprinted with permission of the Clinical Psychology Publishing Company, Inc. Brandon, VT.

Administrative Stress Index

Gmelch, W.H. and B. Swent. 1982. Management team stressors and their impact on administrators' health. Paper presented at American Educational Research Association. ERIC ED 218 761.

Comments: The 35-item ASI identifies major sources of administrators' stress by establishing clear categories of occupational stressors (stress-inducing situations). Comparisons were made among sources of stress and various administrative positions. In addition, the relationship between sources of stress and administrator physical health was examined.

Sample: All 1,211 participants in the study were members of the Confederation of Oregon School Administrators. Three hundred and fifty-four were elementary administrators, 397 were junior high and high school administrators, 151 were superintendents or superintendents/principals, 254 were assistant superintendents and central office staff, and 89 were curriculum directors, transportation supervisors, and athletic directors.

Validity: The ASI is comprised of the 15 items from the Job-Related Index (Indik, Seashore, and Slesinger, 1964) and 23 items developed from stress logs and a review of the literature that examined sources of administrator stress. The items were then placed in one of the five stress categories. The index was piloted using 25 school administrators. After the initial pilot study, the index was revised and piloted on another group of 20 administrators. The development of the ASI provides evidence for its content validity.

Factor Analysis: Each of the five factors contains seven items. The items have been rank ordered from 1 (highest) to 35 (lowest). For convenience, the rank order has been used as the item number. Administrative constraints consists of items 1, 2, 3, 8, 10, 17, and 23; administrative responsibilities 4, 6, 16, 18, 19, 22, and 29; interpersonal relations 5, 12, 14, 15, 20, 26, and 31; intrapersonal conflict 7, 9, 13, 24, 28, 31, and 34; and role expectations 11, 21, 24, 27, 30, 33, and 35.

Definition of Factors: *Administrative constraints* refers to inadequate time, meetings, and rules. *Administrative responsibilities* refers to the managerial tasks of evaluation, negotiation, and supervision. *Interpersonal relations* refers to resolving differences among and between colleagues and supervisors. *Intrapersonal conflict* refers to conflicts between one's performance and one's internal beliefs and expectations. *Role expectations* refers to the difference in expectations of self and the various publics served.

Data Analysis: Mean scores for each of the 35 items and the five factors are provided. In addition, analysis of variance tests for significant differences between the factors and administrative position as well as mean scores and analysis of variance for the top seven stressors by administrative position are reported.

References:
Gmelch, W.H. 1982. *Beyond Stress to Effective Management*. New York: John Wiley and Sons.

Gmelch, W.H. and J.S. Burns. 1991. Sources of stress for academic department chairs: A national study. Paper presented at the Association for the Study of Higher Education.

Ogden, D.L. 1992. Administrative stress and burnout among public school administrators in Georgia. Ph.D. dissertation, Georgia State University.

Administrative Stress Index

1. Complying with state, federal, and organizational rules and policies
2. Feeling that meetings take up too much time
3. Trying to complete reports and other paperwork on time
4. Trying to gain public approval and/or financial support for school programs
5. Trying to resolve parent/school conflicts
6. Evaluating staff members' performance
7. Having to make decisions that affect the lives of individual people that I know (colleagues, staff members, students, etc.)
8. Feeling that I have too heavy a work load, one that I cannot possibly finish during the normal work day
9. Imposing excessively high expectations on myself
10. Being interrupted frequently by telephone calls
11. Feeling I have to participate in school activities outside of the normal working hours at the expense of my personal time
12. Handling student discipline problems
13. Feeling that the progress on my job is not what it should or could be
14. Feeling staff members don't understand my goals and expectations
15. Trying to resolve differences between/among staff members
16. Being involved in the collective bargaining process
17. Writing memos, letters and other communications
18. Administering the negotiated contract (grievances, interpretation, etc.)
19. Supervising and coordinating the tasks of many people
20. Trying to resolve differences between/among students
21. Thinking that I will not be able to satisfy the conflicting demands of those who have authority over me
22. Preparing and allocating budget resources
23. Having my work frequently interrupted by staff members who want to talk
24. Knowing I can't get information needed to carry out my job properly
25. Feeling pressure for better job performance over and above what I think is reasonable
26. Trying to influence my immediate supervisor's actions and decisions that affect me
27. Not knowing what my supervisor thinks of me, or how he/she evaluates my performance
28. Feeling that I have too little authority to carry out responsibilities assigned to me
29. Speaking in front of groups
30. Being unclear on just what the scope and responsibilities of my job are
31. Attempting to meet social expectations (housing, clubs, friends, etc.)
32. Trying to resolve differences with my superiors
33. Feeling that I have too much responsibility delegated to me by my superiors
34. Feeling that I am not fully qualified to handle my job
35. Feeling not enough is expected of me by my superiors

Scoring: A five-point Likert-type is used.

Reprinted with permission of the author.

Teacher Burnout Scale

Seidman, S.A. and J. Zager. 1986-87. The Teacher Burnout Scale. *Educational Research Quarterly* 11:26-33.

Comments: The 21-item TBS was designed specifically to measure teacher burnout.

Scale Construction: A 65-item scale was administered to 217 elementary and secondary school teachers from southern Indiana. The results were factor analyzed using a varimax rotation. Five factors emerged. The revised 23-item scale was administered to a sample of 365 teachers from northern Texas. The results were factor analyzed using a varimax rotation. Four factors emerged. The final version of the TBS contains 21 items.

Sample: The TBS was administered to 490 public school teachers from Fort Worth, Texas.

Reliability: Coefficients of internal consistency (Cronbach's alpha) were 0.89 for career satisfaction, 0.84 for perceived administrative support, 0.80 for coping with job-related stress, and 0.72 for attitudes towards students. Test-retest reliability coefficients over a six to eight week interval (89 public school teachers) were 0.82 for career satisfaction, 0.78 for perceived administrative support, 0.56 for coping with job-related stress, and 0.76 for attitudes towards students. All reliability coefficients were significant at the 0.001 level.

Validity: The factor analysis on the 490 teachers from Fort Worth established the existence of four orthogonal factors which are consistent with the literature. In addition, teachers who scored high on the four scales reported that they were more burned out than teachers who scored lower. The scores on the TBS were also correlated with the Maslach Burnout Inventory (frequency dimension). The correlations were low to moderately high (construct validity). The predictive validity of the TBS was determined by using an ANOVA to test whether or not the burnout scores of teachers in low-stress/burnout schools would be lower than the teachers in high-stress/burnout schools. Significant main effects were found on all four scales. A Tukey HSD was then performed indicating that all four comparisons were statistically significant at the 0.05 level.

Factor Analysis: A four factor orthogonal varimax solution was accepted using criterion of eigenvalues greater than 1.0 and factor loading above 0.40. The four factors are: five items on career satisfaction (1, 5, 10, 12, and 19); six items on perceived administrative support (3, 8, 11, 15, 18, and 20); six items on coping with job-related stress (2, 4, 7, 9, 13, and 14); and four items on attitudes toward students (6, 16, 17, and 21).

Definition of Factors: *Career satisfaction* refers to the selection of teaching as a career. *Perceived administrative support* refers to whether or not teachers believe they receive adequate encouragement and assistance from their supervisors. *Coping with job-related stress* refers to feelings of lethargy, depression, and other negative manifestations of stress. *Attitudes towards students* refer to positive and negative teacher attitudes.

Reference:
Zager, J. 1982. The relationship of personality, situational stress and anxiety factors to teacher burnout. Ph.D. dissertation. Indiana University.

Teacher Burnout Scale

1. I look forward to teaching in the future.
2. I feel depressed because of my teaching experiences.
3. I get adequate praise from my supervisors for a job well done.
4. The teaching day seems to drag on and on.
5. I am glad that I selected teaching as a career.
6. The students act like a bunch of animals.
7. My physical illnesses may be related to my stress in this job.
8. I feel that the administrators are willing to help me with classroom problems, should they arise.
9. I find it difficult to calm down after a day of teaching.
10. Teaching is more fulfilling than I had expected.
11. I believe that my efforts in the classroom are unappreciated by the administrators.
12. If I had to do it all over again, I would not become a schoolteacher.
13. I feel that I could do a much better job of teaching if only the problems confronting me were not so great.
14. The stresses in this job are more than I can bear.
15. My supervisors give me more criticism than praise.
16. Most of my students are decent people.
17. Most students come to school ready to learn.
18. I feel that the administrators will not help me with classroom difficulties.
19. I look forward to each teaching day.
20. The administration blames me for classroom problems.
21. Students come to school with bad attitudes.

Scoring: Strongly Agree, Moderately Agree, Slightly Agree, Slightly Disagree, Moderately Disagree, and Strongly Disagree.

Reprinted with permission of Joanne Zager and Steven A. Seidman.

Supervisory Behavior

Principal Instructional Management Rating Scale

Hallinger, P. and J. Murphy. Assessing the instructional management behavior of principals. *The Elementary School Journal* 86:217-247.

Comments: The 71-item PIMRS measures the instructional leader behavior of elementary and secondary school principals. Each item focuses on a specific job-related behavior of the principal, and according to the authors, is useful for school evaluation, staff development, research, and district policy analysis. Thus, the instrument may indirectly become a useful tool for the evaluation of a school's effectiveness. The design of the instrument attempted to remedy earlier measurement shortcomings by isolating the curriculum and instructional management functions from other managerial duties.

Sample: Teachers, principals, and central office supervisors from one school district with ten elementary schools in California responded to the initial development of the instrument.

Reliability: The lowest alpha coefficient for the 11 subscales was 0.75.

Validity: Content, discriminant, and construct validation of the instrument are provided and ample evidence of each procedure provided.

Factor Analysis: A factor analysis of the 71-item instrument yielded 11 interpretable factors, or subscales. The principal's behavior/performance can be evaluated separately on each of the following 11 subscales which were named as follows: framing goals, communicating goals, monitoring student progress, supervising/evaluating instruction, coordinating the curriculum, protecting instructional time, maintaining high visibility, providing incentives for teachers, promoting professional development, enforcing academic standards, and providing incentives for learning.

Data Analysis: The data analysis indicated that individual principal profiles were obtained which discriminated substantially among principals as to their instructional management behavior. Principal and supervisory ratings generally supported those ratings provided by teachers.

References:
Hallinger, P. 1983. Assessing the instructional management behavior of principals. Ed.D. dissertation, Stanford University.

Hallinger, P. and C. Hausman. 1993. From Attila the Hun to Mary had a little lamb: Redefining roles in restructured schools. Paper presented at American Educational Research Association. ERIC ED 359 647.

Principal Instructional Management Rating Scale

To what extent does your principal...?

FRAMING THE SCHOOL GOALS

1. Develop goals that seek improvement over current levels of academic performance.
2. Frame academic goals with target dates.
3. Frame the school's academic goals in terms of staff responsibilities for meeting them.
4. Use needs assessment or other questionnaires to secure staff input on goal development.
5. Use data on student academic performance when developing the school's academic goals.
6. Develop goals that are easily translated into classroom objectives by teachers.

COMMUNICATING THE SCHOOL GOALS

7. Communicate the school's academic goals to people at school.
8. Refer to the school's academic goals in informal settings with teachers.
9. Discuss the school's academic goals with teachers at faculty meetings.
10. Refer to the school's academic goals when making curricular decisions with teachers.
11. Ensure that the school's goals are reflected in highly visible displays in the school (e.g., posters or bulletin boards indicating the importance of reading or math).
12. Refer to the school's goals in student assemblies.

SUPERVISING AND EVALUATING INSTRUCTION

13. Conduct informal observations in classrooms on a regular basis (informal observations are unscheduled, last at least 5 minutes, and may or may not involve written feedback or a formal conference).
14. Ensure that the classroom objectives of teachers are consistent with the stated goals of the school.
15. Meet with teachers and aides to ensure that they are working toward the same objectives.
16. Review student work products when evaluating classroom instruction.
17. Evaluate teachers on academic objectives directly related to those of the school.
18. Point out specific strengths in teacher instructional practices in postobservation conferences.
19. Point out specific weaknesses in teacher instructional practices in post observation conferences.
20. Note specific strengths of the teacher's instructional practices in written evaluations.
21. Note specific weaknesses of the teacher's instructional practices in written evaluations.
22. Note student time on-task in feedback to teachers after classroom observations.
23. Note specific instructional practices related to the stated classroom objectives in written evaluations.

COORDINATING THE CURRICULUM

24. Make clear who is responsible for coordinating the curriculum across grade levels (e.g., the principal, vice principal, or a teacher).
25. Ensure that the school's academic goals are translated into common curricular objectives.
26. Draw on the results of schoolwide testing when making curricular decisions.
27. Ensure that the objectives of special programs are coordinated with those of the regular classroom.
28. Monitor the classroom curriculum to see that it covers the school's curricular objectives.
29. Assess the overlap between the school's curricular objectives and the achievement test(s) used for program evaluation.

30. Participate actively in the review and/or selection of curricular materials.

MONITORING STUDENT PROGRESS
31. Meet individually with teachers to discuss student academic progress.
32. Discuss the item analysis of tests with the faculty to identify strengths and weaknesses in the instructional program.
33. Use test results to assess progress toward school goals.
34. Distribute test results in a timely fashion.
35. Inform teachers of the school's performance results in written form (e.g., in a memo or news-letter).
36. Inform students of the school's performance results.
37. Identify students whose test results indicate a need for special instruction such as remediation or enrichment.
38. Develop or find the appropriate instructional program(s) for students whose test results indi-cate a need.

PROTECTING INSTRUCTIONAL TIME
39. Ensure that instructional time is not interrupted by public-address announcements.
40. Ensure that students are not called to the office during instructional time.
41. Ensure that truant students suffer specified consequences for missing instructional time.
42. Ensure that tardy or truant students make up lost instructional time.
43. Visit classrooms to see that instructional time is used for learning and practicing new skills and concepts.

MAINTAINING HIGH VISIBILITY
44. Take time to talk with students and teachers during recess and breaks.
45. Visit classrooms to discuss school issues with teachers and students.
46. Attend or participate in cocurricular or extracurricular activities.
47. Cover classes for teachers until a late or substitute teacher arrives.
48. Tutor or provide direct instruction to students.

PROVIDING INCENTIVES FOR TEACHERS
49. Reinforce superior performance by teachers in staff meetings, newsletters, or memos.
50. Compliment teachers privately for their efforts or performance.
51. Acknowledge special effort or performance by teachers in memos for their personal files.
52. Reward special efforts by teachers with opportunities for professional development (e.g., new roles or in-service training).

PROMOTING PROFESSIONAL DEVELOPMENT
53. Inform teachers of opportunities for professional development.
54. Select in-service activities that are consistent with the school's academic goals.
55. Support teacher requests for in-service that is directly related to the school's academic goals.
56. Distribute journal articles to teachers on a regular basis.
57. Actively support the use of skills acquired during in-service training in the classroom.
58. Ensure that instructional aides receive appropriate training to help students meet instructional objectives.
59. Arrange for outside speakers to make presentations on instruction at faculty meetings.
60. Provide time to meet individually with teachers to discuss instructional issues.
61. Sit in on teacher in-service activities concerned with instruction.

62. Set aside time at faculty meetings for teachers to share ideas on instruction or information from in-service activities.

DEVELOPING AND ENFORCING ACADEMIC STANDARDS

63. Set high standards for the percentage of students who are expected to master important instructional objectives.
64. Encourage teachers to start class on time and to teach to the end of the period.
65. Make known what is expected of students at different grade levels.
66. Enforce a promotion standard requiring mastery of grade-level expectations.
67. Support teachers when they enforce academic policies (e.g., on grading, homework, promotion, or discipline).

PROVIDING INCENTIVES FOR LEARNING

68. Recognize students who do superior academic work with formal rewards such as the honor roll or mention in the principal's newsletter.
69. Use assemblies to honor students for their academic work and/or behavior in class.
70. Recognize superior student achievement or improvement by seeing students in the office with their work products.
71. Contact parents to communicate improved student performance in school.

Scoring: 5 = Almost Always; 4 = Frequently; 3 = Sometimes; 2 = Seldom; and 1 = Almost Never.

Reprinted with permission of the author. Developed and published by Philip Hallinger, 1983.

Supervising Teacher Behavior Description Questionnaire

Sistrunk, W.E. and others. 1983. Investigations of supervisory behavior: A symposium. Paper presented at Mid-South Education Research Association. ERIC ED 238 203.

Comments: The 54-item STBDQ was modified from the Supervisory Behavior Description Questionnaire. Both instruments are useful in evaluating behaviors of supervisory educational personnel in terms of whether respondents prefer supervisors to behave in a directive, collaborative, or nondirective manner in relation to specific supervisory tasks. The STBDQ was designed specifically for supervising teachers in order to obtain feedback in the process of supervising student teachers.

Scale Construction: The instrument provides three broad dimension scores: Directive, Collaborative, and Nondirective; three subscale scores: Planning and organizing, Instructional management, and Instructional evaluation as well as a total score.

Sample: The total sample of 227 was composed of 132 student teachers and 95 supervising teachers.

Reliability: Alpha coefficients for the dimensions were as follows: total score 0.97, directive 0.95, collaborative 0.95, and nondirective 0.96; and for the subscales 0.88, 0.94, and 0.93 respectively.

Validity: Attempts to obtain construct, content, and criterion related validity were provided.

Factor Analysis: Factor analysis in order to produce the dimensions and subscales was performed; however, details concerning this analysis were not provided.

Reference:
Sistrunk, W.E. 1982. The Supervisory Behavior Description Questionnaire (SBDQ) Forms 1 and 2 as research instruments. Paper presented at the Mid-South Educational Research Association.

Supervising Teacher Behavior Description Questionnaire
Form 2

1. The supervising teacher should write and plan units and lessons for the student teaching experience.
2. The supervising teacher should collaborate with the student teacher in writing and planning units and lessons.
3. The supervising teacher should permit the student teacher to plan and write his/her own units and lessons.
4. The supervising teacher should determine the educational objectives and how they are to be achieved.
5. The supervising teacher should collaborate with the student teacher in determining the educational objectives and how they are to be achieved.
6. The supervising teacher should permit the student teacher to determine the educational objectives and how they are to be achieved.
7. The supervising teacher should group students within the classroom for instructional purposes.
8. The supervising teacher should collaborate with the student teacher in grouping students within the classroom for instructional purposes.
9. The supervising teacher should permit the student teacher to group students within the classroom for instructional purposes.
10. The supervising teacher should tell and/or show the student teacher how to improve students' study and work habits.
11. The supervising teacher should collaborate with the student teacher in telling and/or showing the students how to improve their study and work habits.
12. The supervising teacher should permit the student teacher to tell and/or show the students how to improve their study and work habits.
13. The supervising teacher should require standard procedures and format of unit and lesson plans.
14. The supervising teacher should collaborate with the student teacher in developing standard unit and lesson plans.
15. The supervising teacher should permit student teachers to develop standard unit and lesson plans.
16. The supervising teacher should show the student teacher how to use machines and materials.
17. The supervising teacher should collaborate with the student teacher in learning how to use machines and materials.
18. The supervising teacher should permit the student teacher to learn how to use machines and materials.
19. The supervising teacher should assign specific instructional tasks to the student teacher.
20. The supervising teacher should collaborate with the student teacher in the choice of instructional tasks.
21. The supervising teacher should permit the student teacher to select his/her own instructional tasks.
22. The supervising teacher should preview and select curricular materials prior to their use by the student teacher.
23. The supervising teacher should collaborate with the student teacher in previewing and selecting curricular materials prior to their use by the student teacher.
24. The supervising teacher should permit the student teacher to preview and select his/her own curricular material.

25. The supervising teacher should decide if curricular materials are contributing to the desired educational objectives.

26. The supervising teacher and the student teacher should collaborate in deciding if curricular materials are contributing to the desired educational objectives.

27. The supervising teacher should permit the student teacher to decide if curricular materials are contributing to the desired educational objectives.

28. The supervising teacher should determine the areas of improvement needed by the student teacher and tell/show him/her how to improve.

29. The supervising teacher and the student teacher should collaborate in determining the areas of improvement needed by the student teacher and the means of improving.

30. The supervising teacher should permit the student teacher to determine the areas of improvement needed by the student teacher and how to improve.

31. The supervising teacher should provide a framework for implementation of educational innovations by the student teacher.

32. The supervising teacher and the student teacher should collaborate in providing frameworks for the implementation of educational innovations by the student teacher.

33. The supervising teacher should permit the student teacher to devise frameworks for implementing educational innovations in his/her classes.

34. The supervising teacher should identify instructional problems encountered by the student teacher.

35. The supervising teacher should collaborate with the student teacher in identifying instructional problems encountered by the student teachers.

36. The supervising teacher should permit the student teacher to identify his/her instructional problems.

37. The supervising teacher should require the student teacher to develop written long range instructional plans.

38. The supervising teacher and the student teacher should collaborate in the development of long range written instructional plans.

39. The supervising teacher should permit the student teacher to develop long range written instructional plans.

40. The supervising teacher should establish objectives and procedures for evaluating the student teacher's instruction.

41. The supervising teacher and the student teacher should collaborate in establishing objectives and procedures for evaluating the student teacher's instruction.

42. The supervising teacher should permit the student teacher to establish objectives and procedures for evaluating his/her instruction.

43. The supervising teacher should base the evaluation of the student teacher's progress on research.

44. The supervising teacher and the student teacher should collaborate in developing research-based criteria for evaluating the student teacher's progress.

45. The supervising teacher should permit the student teacher to develop research-based criteria for evaluating student teacher progress.

46. The supervising teacher should tell/show the student teacher how to teach more effectively.

47. The supervising teacher and the student teacher should collaborate in determining how the student teacher can teach more effectively.

48. The supervising teacher should permit the student teacher to determine how he/she can teach more effectively.

49. The supervising teacher should select instruments for evaluating student teacher progress.

50. The supervising teacher and the student teacher should collaborate in selecting instruments for evaluating student teacher progress.

51. The supervising teacher should permit the student teacher to select instruments for evaluating student teacher progress.
52. The supervising teacher should conduct action research about teaching on a regular basis.
53. The supervising teacher and the student teacher should collaborate in conducting action research about teaching on a regular basis.
54. The supervising teacher should permit the student teacher to conduct action research about teaching on a regular basis.

Scoring: It is a semantic differential scale that ranges from Satisfying/Dissatisfying; and/or Motivating/Nonmotivating.

Reprinted with permission of the author, Walter E. Sistrunk, Professor of Education Emeritus, Mississippi State University, P.O. Box JG, Mississippi State, MS 39762.

Audit of Principal Effectiveness

Valentine, J.W. and M.L. Bowman. 1988. The Audit of Principal Effectiveness: Instrumentation for principalship research. ERIC ED 311 554.

Comments: The instrument was designed to provide useful feedback to principals about their administrative skills. The development of the various scales was based on the effective school literature which indicates that principals of more effective schools possess the following characteristics: (1) are assertive instructional leaders, (2) are goal and task oriented, (3) are well organized, (4) convey high expectations for students and staff, (5) define and communicate policies effectively, (6) visit classrooms frequently, (7) are visible and available to students and staff, (8) provide strong support to teachers, and (9) are adept at parent and community relations. Thus, the literature and research of principal effectiveness is used as a foundation for the instrument.

Scale Construction: Operating with the guidelines above, 162 items describing effective principal behavior were identified. These were categorized under 12 theoretical constructs. Because of the length of the instrument, it was divided into two forms--Form A and B with 81 items each.

Sample: The two forms of the instrument were mailed to 3,660 teachers across the United States. The teachers were randomly selected based on seven geographic regions and by elementary, middle and high school.

Validity: Studies dealing with congruent and discriminant validity were provided.

Factor Analysis: The sample of 3,660 teacher responses was submitted to factor analysis with a varimax rotation. A factor loading of 0.40 or higher was used to retain an item on the factor. An 110 item instruments survived this procedure--55 items on each of Form A and B. Form A extracted five factors and Form B four factors. The five factors on Form A are: instructional management, teacher relations, directional leadership, affective involvement, and affective congruence. Form B produced student orientation, organizational development, organizational linkage, and adaptive leadership.

References:
Edmonds, R.R. 1982. Programs of school improvement: An overview. *Educational Leadership* 40:4-11.

Sweeney, J. 1982. Research synthesis on effective school leadership. *Educational Leadership* 39:346-352.

Audit of Principal Effectiveness

Sample Items:

1. The principal has high professional expectations and standards for self, faculty and school.
2. The principal encourages changes in the school program that lead to a better school for the students.
3. The principal utilizes resources from outside the school to assist in the study, development, implementation and/or evaluation of the school.
4. The principal informs staff of new developments and ideas in education.
5. The principal is able to anticipate the effects of decisions.
6. The principal utilizes a systematic process for change which is known and understood by the faculty.
7. When deserving, teachers are complimented by the principal in a sincere and honest manner.
8. The principal takes the time to listen to teachers.
9. The principal finds the time to interact with students.
10. The principal positively reinforces students.
11. The principal keeps teachers informed about those aspects of the school program of which they should be aware.
12. The principal communicates to teachers the reasons for administrative practices used in the school.
13. The principal works with other leaders of the school in the implementation of a team approach to managing the school.
14. The principal encourages faculty to be sensitive to the needs and values of other faculty in the school.
15. The principal is knowledgeable of the varied teaching strategies teachers might appropriately utilize during instruction.
16. The principal maintains an awareness and knowledge of recent research about the learning process.
17. The principal promotes the diagnosis of individual and group learning needs of students and application of appropriate instruction to meet those needs.
18. The principal uses objective data such as test scores to make changes in curriculum and staffing.

Scoring: Respondents are asked to indicate the degree to which each item is descriptive of the skill of an effective principal.

Reprinted with permission of the author. © Jerry W. Valentine and Michael L. Bowman.

Teacher Attitudes/Beliefs

Affective Work Competencies Inventory

Brauchle, P.E. et al. 1983. The factorial validity of the Affective Work Competencies Inventory. *Educational and Psychological Measurement* 43:603-609.

Comments: The 45-item AWCI measures five work attitudes and habits that represent intrinsic value components. According to the authors, it is possible that the most effective method of teaching affective work competencies for job success is through student emulation of teacher behavior.

Sample: The AWCI was administered to 798 industrial workers, 567 industrial supervisors, and 120 vocational educators. The responses of 1,485 people were examined to study their perceptions of affective work competencies.

Reliability: Kuder-Richardson formula 20 estimates for the five factors were: 0.64 (ambition), 0.80 (self-control), 0.76 (organization), 0.89 (enthusiasm), and 0.79 (conscientiousness). They ranged from a high of 0.89 (enthusiasm) to a low of 0.64 (ambition).

Validity: Content validity was established through the development of the AWCI. The original instrument contained 95 items in 15 competency clusters. Factor analysis was undertaken as a way of establishing the construct validity of the instrument.

Factor Analysis: A principal components factor analysis with a varimax orthogonal rotation yielded five factors with loadings above 0.35. The five factors accounted for 76.3 percent of the variance. The five factors are: four items on ambition (31, 46, 1, and 32); eight items on self-control (65, 82, 55, 10, 69, 40, 36, and 94); four items on organization (57, 80, 92, and 83); 16 items on enthusiasm (86, 75, 89, 77, 70, 95, 93, 64, 78, 66, 48, 79, 88, 71, 67, and 76); and 13 items on conscientiousness (30, 39, 19, 16, 58, 68, 60, 81, 24, 72, 90, 45, and 74).

References:
Brauchle, P.E. 1979. Self and supervisor perceptions of affective work competencies in CETA trainees: A comparative study. Ph.D. dissertation. University of Missouri, Columbia.

Morgan, K.R. 1980. The relative effect of two different methods of instruction upon the affective work competencies of trade and industrial students. Ph.D. dissertation, University of Missouri, Columbia.

Petty, G.C. 1978. Affective work competencies of workers, supervisors, and vocational educators. Ph.D. dissertation, University of Missouri, Columbia.

Affective Work Competencies Inventory

1. Setting personal work/job goals
2. Setting goals for self-improvement
3. Acquiring new skills to advance in job
4. Participating in group activities
5. Becoming angry at others
6. Blowing my stack
7. Getting angry
8. Controlling temper
9. Staying angry or upset all day
10. Maintaining even temperament
11. Complaining
12. Complaining about job tasks
13. Keeping work area clear
14. Keeping work area clean and organized
15. Keeping supplies neatly arranged
16. Keeping records and files in order
17. Working hard to accomplish new goals
18. Accepting challenging assignments
19. Putting forth extra effort
20. Adjusting to change
21. Completing difficult tasks
22. Performing work eagerly
23. Speaking favorably of future work assignments
24. Completing work without constant supervision
25. Responding to greetings from co-workers
26. Listening to instructions
27. Adjusting to various work situations
28. Reading directions
29. Organizing work activities
30. Returning material and equipment to places
31. Practicing safe work habits
32. Volunteering suggestions
33. Avoiding work
34. Disturbing others who try to work
35. Reminded by others to begin work
36. Pushing work onto other workers
37. Saying one will do something and not doing it
38. Talking out of turn at group meetings
39. Gazing out the window or at the clock
40. Annoying other people
41. Interrupting others
42. Being late for work or meetings
43. Working hard only when someone is watching
44. Losing interest in work
45. Arguing about job assignments

Scoring: A Likert scale is used to measure work attitudes, values, and habits.

Reprinted with permission of Gregory Petty.

Minnesota Teacher Attitude Inventory

Cook, W.W. et al. 1951. Minnesota Teacher Attitude Inventory. Psychological Corporation, 555 Academic Court, San Antonio, TX 78204-2498.

Comments: The 150-item MTAI is used to assess attitudes that determine how well a teacher will get along with students. MTAI scores have been reported as unstable during the time between pre-service and regular classroom teaching. The scores can be used to identify attitudes along a continuum that ranges from traditional to progressive.

Scale Construction: Leeds wrote 378 items in both positive and negative statements based on a review of the literature on teacher-pupil interaction. Two groups of 100 teachers (identified as superior or inferior) responded to the statements. One hundred sixty-four items differentiated between these two teacher groups. Another sample of 100 teachers participated. The final form of the MTAI contains 129 items that were developed by Leeds and 21 items developed by Callis.

Sample: The original sample consisted of one hundred teachers who were identified as superior teachers and one hundred teachers who were identified as inferior teachers. Another sample of 100 teachers in grades 4 through 6 responded to the inventory.

Factor Analysis: Yee and Fruchter factor analyzed the MTAI. Orthogonal varimax rotations yielded five factors. Only items with factor loading above 0.42 are reported. Sixty items met this criterion. Children's irresponsible tendencies and lack of self-control, contains 20 items (19, 21, 23, 24, 35, 36, 52, 54, 63, 65, 75, 76, 80, 92, 109, 110, 114, 116, 126, and 128); conflict between teachers' and pupils' interests, contains 15 items (20, 34, 99, 119, 121, 124, 131, 132, 133, 134, 136, 137, 141, 144, and 149); rigidity and severity in handling pupils, contains 12 items (13, 27, 47, 72, 81, 85, 86, 88, 103, 115, 118, and 129); pupils' independence in learning, contains seven items (15, 16, 53, 64, 71, 77, and 93); and pupils' acquiescence to the teacher, contains six items (1, 90, 101, 107, 113, and 146). The first three factors are related to traditionalism, while the last two factors are related to progressivism.

Validity: Based upon Leed's study, correlations with principals' ratings were 0.46, 0.59 with observers' ratings, and 0.31 with students' ratings. Based upon Callis' study, correlations were 0.19 with principals' ratings, 0.40 with observers' ratings, and 0.49 with students' ratings.

Reliability: Corrected split-half reliability was 0.93.

References:
Johnson, W.A. 1983. Personality correlates of preferences for preprofessional training by special education and regular class trainees. *Education* 103:360-368.

Yee, A.H. 1970. Do principals' interpersonal attitudes agree with those of teachers and pupils? *Educational Administration Quarterly* 6:1-13.

Yee, A.H. and B. Fruchter. 1971. Factor content of the Minnesota Teacher Attitude Inventory. *American Educational Research Journal* 8:119-133.

Scoring: Strongly Agree; Agree; Undecided or Uncertain; Disagree; and Strongly Disagree. Responses are scored +1, 0, or -1. Therefore, scores range from -150 to +150. Yee and Kriewall scored items +2, +1, 0, -1, and -2.

Sample Items:

5.   Teaching never gets monotonous.

106.   A teacher should not be expected to do more work than he is paid for.

144.   Teachers can be in the wrong as well as pupils.

Teachers' Beliefs About Administrators Scale

Feldman, D. and L.H. Gerstein. 1988. A factor analytic study of three teacher belief scales. *Measurement and Evaluation in Counseling and Development* 21:72-80.

Comments: The 12-item TBA scale can be used to determine how teachers feel about their administrative support systems. In addition to the TBA scale, the authors also developed the Teachers' Beliefs About Parents Scale and the Perceptions of Parental Beliefs Concerning Teachers. Psychometric information for all three scales is included in the article. All three scales could be used to determine the content and quality of the relationships between teachers, parents, and administrators.

Scale Construction: A review of the literature on administrative responsibilities and previous studies on teacher attitudes towards administrators were studied in order to identify concepts. Five education professors and six doctoral students sorted concepts (100% interrater agreement).

Sample: The sample consisted of 462 teachers who were taking graduate courses at three state universities in Arizona, Indiana, and Texas.

Reliability: The scale had an alpha (Cronbach) coefficient of 0.92.

Validity: Content validity was established by scale construction. Construct validity was established by factor analytic procedures.

Factor Analysis: Principal components factor analysis with a varimax rotation yielded one factor with 12 items. The final factor solution was cross validated. These beliefs centered on administrative leadership, administrative partnership, and administrative support.

Data Analysis: Factor analysis was undertaken to establish a meaningful factor structure and to eliminate items. Tests for reliability were run to determine the internal consistency of the scale. Factor loadings, means, and standard deviations were reported.

References:
Hoy, W.K. and J.E. Henderson. 1983. Principal authenticity, school climate, and pupil-control orientation. *Alberta Journal of Educational Research* 29:123-130.

Robson, D.L. 1981. Administering educational services for the handicapped: Role expectations and perceptions. *Exceptional Children* 47:377-378.

Teachers' Beliefs About Administrators

I believe that ADMINISTRATORS

1. Know that beginning teachers need time to become master teachers.
2. Realize that teacher training in classroom discipline does not imply that teacher's sovereign territory of total management of problem behavior.
3. Support both parents and teachers, seeking to develop common ground with mutual regard and respect.
4. Seek to discover on a firsthand basis, in the environment of noted conflict, possible solutions.
5. Resolve problems between parents and teachers that maintain the "face" or "egos" of both parties.
6. Serve as an equivalent partner in behavior management responsibility.
7. Display academic leadership.
8. Display school discipline leadership.
9. Develop positive school climate.
10. Want to improve their interactions with parents.
11. Want to improve their interactions with teachers.
12. Are partners in the educational process.

Scoring: A percentage likelihood scaling format (0%-100%) with 10-point intervals is used.

Reprinted with permission of Feldman, D. & Gerstein, L.H. 1988. Teachers' beliefs about administrators scale. Yorktown, IN: Educational Technology Resources.

Teaching Behaviors Questionnaire

Marchant, G.J. and N.D. Bowers. 1990. An attitude inventory for research-based effective teaching behaviors. *Educational and Psychological Measurement* 50:167-174.

Comments: The 36-item TBQ could be used for pre-service and post-service teacher training. In addition, it could also be used to select and screen teachers and principals. Teacher education programs might use the results to identify areas for training.

Scale Construction: The research on effective teaching was reviewed and the following six categories related to teaching generated the items for the TBQ: instructional design and structure; active teaching; giving information; questioning the student; reacting to student responses; and handling seatwork and homework assignments. A pilot test was conducted on four graduate classes of 60 teachers.

Sample: Three hundred teachers, 100 principals, 50 college education faculty, and 50 undergraduate education students from Illinois, Indiana, and Wisconsin participated in the study.

Reliability: The alpha coefficient for the TBQ was 0.76. Reliabilities for each group are provided. They ranged from a high of 0.78 (college education faculty) to a low of 0.62 (undergraduate education students).

Data Analysis: Means and standard deviations are presented for each group in the sample. Item-total correlations were computed. The distribution of the data was studied to prove normality. Significant differences among the various groups have been identified.

References:
Marchant, G.J. 1988a. Attitudes toward research-based effective teaching behaviors. Ph.D. dissertation. Northwestern University.

Marchant, G.J. 1988b. Attitudes toward research-based effective teaching behaviors from teachers, principals, and college faculties and students. Paper presented at Mid-Western Educational Research Association. ERIC ED 303 449.

Marchant, G.J. and N.D. Bowers. 1988. Teacher agreement with research-based effective teaching behaviors. Paper presented at American Educational Research Association. ERIC ED 302 503.

Teaching Behaviors Questionnaire

1. The teacher should allow the students to figure out the main idea of a lesson on their own.
2. The teacher should provide drill and practice after each skill or section taught.
3. The teacher should explain assignments and go over practice examples with the students before they are allowed to work independently.
4. The teacher should monitor the progress of each student daily.
5. The teacher should spend most of the class time teaching the student as one whole group.
6. The teacher should sit at the teacher's desk while the students are doing seat work, and have students come up to the desk when they need help.
7. The teacher should call on both volunteering and non-volunteering students after asking a question in class.
8. The teacher should redirect relevant student questions to the class and incorporate comments into the lesson.
9. The teacher should expect all of the students to master the course content.
10. The teacher should quickly ask the class another question when a student gives an incorrect answer to a question asked in class.
11. The teacher should not let the students know which assignments are for a grade and which are for practice.
12. The teacher should introduce classroom rules and procedures one-at-a-time as they become necessary throughout the year.
13. The teacher should make class presentations of less than 20 minutes.
14. The teacher should wait at least 3 seconds after asking a question in class before calling on a student.
15. The teacher should convey a strong sense of enthusiasm to the students.
16. The teacher should receive 60 to 80 percent correct by most of the students on assignments that the students are expected to work on independently.
17. The teacher should rephrase the question to the student when an incorrect answer is given in class.
18. The teacher should continue to work on problem material when performance on assignments is poor.
19. The teacher should only call on volunteering students after asking a question in class.
20. The teacher should move around the classroom during the time that the students are working independently at their seats.
21. The teacher should stick to the lesson regardless of student comments.
22. The teacher should primarily emphasize academic instruction in the classroom.
23. The teacher should expect about half of the students to master the curriculum.
24. The teacher should not use praise excessively in the classroom.
25. The teacher should save drill and practice until the students have a number of skills to practice.
26. The teacher should often use unfamiliar and abstract words in classroom lessons and presentations.
27. The teacher should inform the students exactly what determines the grade on an assignment.
28. The teacher should overtly acknowledge correct answers that a student gives to a question asked in class.
29. The teacher should expect the students to figure out instructions as part of an assignment.
30. The teacher should identify the main ideas of a lesson during the lesson and at the end of the lesson.
31. The teacher should continue to the next scheduled unit when performance is poor, and in the future the teacher should avoid material similar to that which the students had problems.
32. The teacher should receive 90 to 100 percent correct by most of the students on assignments that students are expected to work on independently.
33. The teacher should spend time at the beginning of the school year teaching classroom rules and procedures.
34. The teacher should monitor the progress of each individual student every two to four weeks.

35. The teacher should begin lessons and presentations to the class with a review or an overview of the material.
36. The teacher should immediately call on a student after asking a question in class.

Scoring: Strongly Disagree = 4; Disagree = 3; Agree = 2; and Strongly Agree = 1. The scoring is reversed for the following items: 2, 3, 4, 5, 7, 8, 9, 13, 14, 15, 17, 18, 20, 22, 24, 27, 28, 30, 32, 33, and 35.

Reprinted with permission of Gregory J. Marchant, Educational Psychology, Ball State University, Muncie, IN 47306-0595.

Occupational Work Ethic Inventory

Petty, G.C. 1995. A new look at selected employability skills: A factor analysis of the occupational work ethic. *Journal of Vocational Education Research* 20.

Comments: The 50-item OEWI (Petty, 1991) assesses the intrinsic aspect of the workplace. The work ethic factors provide a research base for educators who are preparing students for the transition from school to work. It has been validated with over 2,279 workers.

Sample: The sample for the most recent study consisted of 1,151 employees in private and public organizations in the Southeast. In a previous study (1994), over 2,220 employees from six occupational groups were surveyed.

Reliability: In a pilot study, the alpha correlation was 0.95. In additional studies, the alpha coefficients ranged from 0.90 (Hatcher) to 0.95 (Hill).

Validity: Content validity was established by choosing items from a review of the literature on work attitudes, work values, and work habits. The items were reviewed by a panel of experts. Another panel of experts sorted the original items into categories. This process was repeated until consensus was reached. The four categories were: dependable, ambitious, considerate, and cooperative. Several factor analytic studies were conducted to establish the construct validity of the OWEI.

Factor Analysis: A principal components factor analysis with a varimax orthogonal rotation yielded four factors. The four factors are: 15 items on interpersonal skills (17, 22, 28, 29, 31, 32, 33, 37, 41, 42, 43, 46, 47, 48, and 50); 16 items on initiative (5, 6, 7, 10, 11, 14, 15, 18, 20, 27, 35, 36, 38, 40, 45, and 49); seven items on being dependable (1, 3, 4, 8, 12, 16, and 23); 10 items on reversed items (9, 13, 21, 24, 25, 26, 30, 34, 39, and 44.).

Data Analysis: Factor loadings, item means, and standard deviations are reported.

References:

Hatcher, T. 1993. The work ethic of apprentices and instructors in a trade union apprenticeship training program. Ph.D. dissertation. University of Tennessee, Knoxville.

Hill, R.B. 1992/1993. The work ethic as determined by occupation, education, age, gender, work experience, and empowerment. Ph.D. dissertation. University of Tennessee, Knoxville.

Petty, G.C. and R.B. Hill. 1994. Are men and women different? A study of the occupational work ethic. *Journal of Vocational Education Research* 19.

Petty, G.C. 1995. Adults in the work force and the occupational work ethic. *Journal of Studies in Technical Careers* 15:133-140.

Petty, G.C. 1995. Vocational-technical education and the occupational work ethic. *Journal of Industrial and Teacher Education* 32:45-58.

Occupational Work Ethic Inventory

At work I can describe myself as:

1.	dependable	26.	negligent
2.	stubborn	27.	persevering
3.	following regulations	28.	likable
4.	following directions	29.	helpful
5.	independent	30.	apathetic
6.	ambitious	31.	pleasant
7.	effective	32.	cooperative
8.	reliable	33.	hardworking
9	tardy	34.	rude
10.	initiating	35.	orderly
11.	perceptive	36.	enthusiastic
12.	honest	37.	cheerful
13.	irresponsible	38.	persistent
14.	efficient	39.	hostile
15.	adaptable	40.	dedicated
16.	careful	41.	devoted
17.	appreciative	42.	courteous
18.	accurate	43.	considerate
19.	emotionally stable	44.	careless
20.	conscientious	45.	productive
21.	depressed	46.	well groomed
22.	patient	47.	friendly
23.	punctual	48.	loyal
24.	devious	49.	resourceful
25.	selfish	50.	modest

Scoring: 1 = Never; 2 = Almost Never; 3 = Seldom; 4 = Sometimes; 5 = Usually, 6 = Almost Always; and 7 = Always.

Reprinted with permission of the author. For additional information contact George C. Petty, Department of Human Resource Development, University of Tennessee at Knoxville, Knoxville, TN 37996-2755.

Educational Beliefs Questionnaire

Silvernail, D.L. 1992. The development and factor structure of the Educational Beliefs Questionnaire. *Educational and Psychological Measurement* 52:663-667.

Comments: The 20-item EBQ measures beliefs about five educational concepts by using five educational philosophies. Additional research will determine whether the three-factor solution is viable. The author suggests using a structured interview in addition to the EBQ to see if the verbal beliefs and written beliefs of participants are congruent. This would provide an alternate way of determining the validity of the EBQ.

Scale Construction: This 67-item pilot instrument was built upon the work of Kerlinger and Kaya. A 5x5 item grid was developed using five educational philosophies (essentialism, traditionalism, progressivism, reconstructivism, and existentialism) and five educational concepts (the purpose of schools, curriculum content, methods of instruction, the role of the teacher, and the role of the student). After a panel of three educational theorists reviewed the items, the 25-item EBQ was administered to a group of volunteers.

Sample: The sample consisted of 610 volunteer teachers K-12 from 11 schools in a state in northern New England.

Reliability: Alpha coefficients were 0.71 (perennialism orientation), 0.72 (romanticism orientation), and 0.64 (progressivism) with a total scale coefficient of 0.73.

Validity: Face validity was established by the panel of judges who reviewed the items for clarity and accuracy. Construct validity was determined through various factor analytic procedures.

Factor Analysis: Factor analysis with a varimax rotation yielded a final three factor solution. The three factors are: seven items on perennialism orientation (1-7); nine items on romanticism orientation (8-16); and four items on progressivism (17-20). Factor loadings are reported.

Definition of Factors: *Perennialism orientation* refers to the philosophies of essentialism and traditionalism; it contains items that relate to the importance of schools in transmitting cultural heritage and strong authority roles for teachers. *Romanticism orientation* refers to the philosophies of reconstructivism and existentialism; it contains items that relate to the importance of schools as sources of new social ideas and individual self-awareness and the role of teachers as facilitators in the natural development of youngsters. *Progressivism* refers to the progressive philosophy found in the instruments developed by Kerlinger and Kaya; it contains items that relate to the role of schools in developing socially conscious adults and the importance of acquiring problem-solving skills and knowledge.

References:
Kerlinger, F. and E. Kaya. 1959. The construction and factor analytic validation of scales to measure attitudes toward education. *Educational and Psychological Measurement* 19:13-29.

Silvernail, D.L. and L. Goldsberry. 1992. The development and validation of an Educational Philosophy Beliefs Questionnaire: Work in Progress. Paper presented at American Educational Research Association.

Educational Beliefs Questionnaire

The following are not complete statements. In the total instrument, a appropriate cue is provided for each of the item stems listed below.

1. Students need more supervision
2. Drill/factual knowledge important
3. Demonstration/recitation essential
4. Teacher strong authority
5. Student receiver of knowledge
6. Need highly structured environment
7. Subjects should represent heritage
8. Curriculum focus on social problems
9. Schools should promote self-awareness
10. Students should have more freedom
11. Students should design program
12. Students should learn from peers
13. Schools sources of new ideas
14. Personality of students important
15. Learning should be experimental
16. Schools should preserve values
17. Students should learn essential skills
18. Students should learn essential knowledge
19. Teachers should be facilitators
20. Schools should foster intellectual

Scoring: A six-point Likert scale is used.

Reprinted with permission of the author.

Attitudes About Merit Pay

Weber. L. 1988. An instrument for assessing attitudes about merit pay. *Educational Research Quarterly* 12:2-7.

Comments: This 16-item instrument addresses two problems associated with merit pay: definitions and criteria. In addition, it provides information about reliability and validity.

Sample: The original instrument was administered to 237 teachers and 86 administrators in northern Virginia. Two months later, 193 teachers, 107 administrators, and 135 parents participated in a replication study in Virginia.

Reliability: In the replication study, the total group alpha for the 16 items was 0.92; 0.93 for the teachers, 0.87 for the administrators, and 0.91 for the parents.

Validity: Five aspects of merit pay were identified through a review of the literature. These aspects were examined by 12 public school educators and a 34-item instrument was developed to assess merit pay; its effect on morale and instruction; methods for deciding on merit; and monetary issues (content validity).

Factor Analysis: Linkage and factor analyses were performed and yielded similar results: one factor emerged that assessed a general attitude toward merit pay.

Reference:
Carter, E.L. 1983. Merit pay programs for teachers: Perceptions of school board members in Virginia. Ed.D. dissertation, Virginia Polytechnic Institute and State University.

Attitudes About Merit Pay

1. A merit pay program will attract better qualified people to the teaching profession.
2. Merit pay would not enhance the positive relationship among teachers and administrators.
3. A merit pay system will have a negative impact on the morale of teachers in the system.
4. Nominees for a merit pay increase can be objectively identified.
5. Merit pay will positively affect teacher morale.
6. Competition for merit pay will inhibit spontaneity and innovation by teachers within classrooms.
7. A merit pay plan has no place in the public school setting.
8. Teachers working under merit pay will be less cooperative with their peers.
9. A merit pay system should be included in the salary schedule.
10. Students' standardized test scores results should be a factor used when evaluating teachers for merit purposes.
11. Standardized test scores in the school system would improve if a merit system of pay were adopted.
12. Accord between administrative and instructional staff will be negatively affected if a merit system is adopted.
13. Merit pay should not be implemented in the public schools.
14. A merit pay program will improve the quality of instruction for gifted students.
15. A merit pay program will result in a higher retention rate of better teachers.
16. Tenured teachers receiving unsatisfactory evaluations should be denied automatic salary increases so that funds will be available for merit pay.

Scoring: Agree = 1; Tend to Agree = 2; Tend to Disagree = 3; Disagree = 4. Scoring is reversed for negative items (2, 3, 6, 7, 8, 12, and 13). Low mean values (equal to or less than 2.5) represent a favorable attitude.

Reprinted with permission of Educational Research Quarterly.

Pupil Control Ideology Form

Willower, D.J. et al. 1967. *The school and pupil control ideology.* University Park, PA: Penn State Studies Monograph No. 24.

Comments: The 20-item PCI provides an operational measure for pupil control orientation. Control ideology ranges on a continuum from custodial to humanistic. The authors state that as a result of the item analysis, only two items out of twenty were representative of the humanistic orientation. Another instrument, the Pupil Control Behavior Form was developed by Helsel and Willower. The PCB measures educators pupil control behavior on the same continuum as the PCI. The PCB is usually completed by students.

Scale Construction: Based upon a review of the literature, the author's experience in the public schools, the operational definition of pupil control ideology, and field notes from a prior study, fifty-seven items were written. This original form of the PCI was administered to a sample of 58 people. Through item analysis, a 38-item form was developed. As a result of the pilot studies, the number of items that were positive to the humanistic orientation were eliminated. Based on the item analysis, 20 out of 38 items were retained because they had biserial correlation coefficients greater than 0.325.

Sample: The original sample consisted of a combination of 58 graduate students in education and in-service teachers. The revised form was then administered in seven schools in New York and Pennsylvania. Five elementary and two secondary schools participated from urban, suburban, and rural areas. One elementary and one secondary school were selected because of their reputation as "humanistic" schools. Overall, 170 teachers responded.

Reliability: A split-half reliability coefficient of 0.91 was obtained by correlating even-item subscores with odd-item subscores. The corrected reliability coefficient was 0.95. An additional reliability test was done using only one elementary school and one secondary school (55). This yielded a coefficient of 0.83 and a corrected coefficient of 0.91.

Validity: Principals identified approximately 15 per cent of their faculties as having either a custodial ideology or a humanistic ideology. Then, the mean scores of these teachers on the PCI was compared. T-tests were performed to see if teachers considered to have a custodial ideology differed from those teachers considered to have a humanistic ideology. The results were significant at the 0.01 level. In addition, a cross-validation study using the seven schools was conducted. The results were significant at the 0.001 level.

Definition of Dimensions: *The custodial orientation* is similar to the traditional school which is characterized by a highly controlled setting; the maintenance of order; students are considered to be irresponsible and undisciplined; relationships with students are impersonal; pessimism and mistrust prevail; the school is viewed as an autocratic organization; and power and communication flow downward. The *humanistic orientation* views the school as an educational community in which interaction and experience guide its members; learning is viewed as a worthwhile activity in and of itself; relationships with students are personal; teachers are optimistic; teachers want to make the classroom climate democratic; and there are open channels of communication.

Data Analysis: Means, standard errors squared, and the results of t-tests for each major hypothesis tested are presented.

References:

Appleberry, J.B. and W.K. Hoy. 1969. The pupil control ideology of professional personnel in "open" and "closed" elementary schools. *Educational Administration Quarterly.* 5:74-85.

Helsel, R.R. and D.J. Willower. 1974. Toward definition and measurement of pupil control behavior. *Journal of Educational Administration* 12:114-123.

Schilling, K.J. 1988. The relationship among the conflict management styles utilized by the elementary school administrators, the organizational climate of an elementary school, and the pupil control orientation of the elementary teachers. Ed.D. dissertation, Loyola University, Chicago.

Vitagliano, J.A. 1985. Pupil control ideology and pluralistic ignorance in a residential facility for the hearing impaired: Hearing and non-hearing teacher perspectives. Ph.D. dissertation, Louisiana State University and Agricultural and Mechanical College.

Woolfolk, A.E. et al. 1990. Teachers' sense of efficacy and their beliefs about managing students. *Teaching and Teacher Education* 6:137-148.

Pupil Control Ideology Form

1. It is desirable to require pupils to sit in assigned seats during assemblies.
2. Pupils are usually not capable of solving their problems through logical reasoning.
3. Directing sarcastic remarks toward a defiant pupil is a good disciplinary technique.
4. Beginning teachers are not likely to maintain strict enough control over their pupils.
5. Teachers should consider revision of their teaching methods if these are criticized by their pupils.
6. The best principals give unquestioning support to teachers in disciplining pupils.
7. Pupils should not be permitted to contradict the statements of a teacher in class.
8. It is justifiable to have pupils learn many facts about a subject even if they have no immediate application.
9. Too much pupil time is spent on guidance and activities and too little on academic preparation.
10. Being friendly with pupils often leads them to become too familiar.
11. It is more important for pupils to learn to obey rules than that they make their own decisions.
12. Student governments are a good safety valve, but should not have much influence on school policy.
13. Pupils can be trusted to work together without supervision.
14. If a pupil uses obscene or profane language in school, it must be considered a moral offense.
15. If pupils are allowed to use the lavatory without getting permission, this privilege will be abused.
16. A few pupils are just young hoodlums and should be treated accordingly.
17. It is often necessary to remind pupils that their status in school differs from that of teachers.
18. A pupil who destroys school material or property should be severely punished.
19. Pupils cannot perceive the difference between democracy and anarchy in the classroom.
20. Pupils often misbehave in order to make the teacher look bad.

Scoring: A five-point Likert-type scale is used. Strongly Agree = 5; Agree = 4; Undecided = 3; Disagree = 2; and Strongly Disagree = 1. The scoring is reversed for the two positive items representing the humanistic ideology (5 and 13). The higher the score, the more custodial the orientation. The lower the score, the more humanistic the orientation.

Reprinted with permission of Willower, D.J. et al. 1967. *The school and pupil control ideology.* University Park, PA: Penn State Studies Monograph No. 24.

Author Index

Instrument Index